The Jewish Image

Citadel Press

in American Film

By Lester D. Friedman

Secaucus, New Jersey

Acknowledgments

Many people had a hand in this project. To all those listed below, I express my thanks for their kindness and good humor. My wife, Carolyn, provided both emotional support and practical suggestions. Valuable discussions came from Richard Corliss, Alan Berger, Bruce Dearing, Owen Shapiro, and Delia Temes. Denise Stevens helped a great deal at Syracuse University's E.S. Bird Library. Much-needed funds came from Donald Goodman, Dean of the College of Health Related Professions, a United University Professions Experienced Faculty Development Award, and a Research Foundation for the State University of New York grant. Anne Starowicz deserves praise for her excellent typing, as does Jennifer Jones for her proofreading efforts. Allan Wilson, at Citadel Press, gave me valuable editorial assistance and guidance. Charles Silver (Museum of Modern Art), Emily Sieger (Library of Congress), Sharon Rivo/Mimi Krant (National Center for Jewish Film), and John Kuiper (Eastman House) all allowed me to screen films at their institutions.

A number of people helped me secure stills for this book: Sharon Rivo/Mimi Krant (National Center for Jewish Film), Nat Tobin (Crescent Advertising), Jan-Christopher Horak/Elizabeth Tape (Eastman House), Pat Erens, Mary Corliss (Museum of Modern Art), Jerry Ohlinger (Jerry Ohlinger's Movie Material Store), Paula Klaw (Movie Star News), Michael Berman (Paramount), Sheri Natcow (Columbia), Larry Steinfeld (Orion), Lois Marks (MGM), Maureen McKiernan (20th Century-Fox), Bruce Stern (Warner Brothers), Nancy Morrisrace (Touchstone), Neal Peters Collection. Without these people, this book would never have been completed.

Copyright © 1987 by Lester D. Friedman

Portions of this book appeared in *Hollywood's Image of the Jew,* by Lester D. Friedman, copyright © 1982 by Frederick Ungar Publishing Co., Inc.

Published by Citadel Press
A division of Lyle Stuart Inc.
120 Enterprise Ave., Secaucus, N.J. 07094
In Canada: Musson Book Company
a division of General Publishing Co. Limited
Don Mills, Ontario

Queries regarding rights and permissions should be addressed to: Lyle Stuart, 120 Enterprise Avenue, Secaucus, N.J. 07094

Manufactured in the United States of America

DESIGNED BY LESTER GLASSNER

Library of Congress Cataloging-in-Publication Data

Friedman, Lester D.
  The Jewish image in America film.

  Bibliography: p.
  Includes index.
  1. Jews in motion pictures. 2. Moving-pictures—
United States. I. Title.
PN1995.9.J46F72 1987   791.43′09′0935203924   86-32698
ISBN 0-8065-1019-6

Dedication

For my parents, Eva and Eugene Friedman, who have always given me their encouragement, support, and love.

Hollywood—the American Dream—is a Jewish idea. In a sense, it's a Jewish revenge on America. It combines the Puritan ethic ... with baroque magnificence. The happy ending was the invention of Russian Jews, designed to drive Americans crazy.

—Jill Robinson in Studs Terkel's
American Dreams: Lost and Found

CONTENTS

Izzy Goldberg (George Jessel) wonders who broke his window in PRIVATE IZZY MURPHY *(1926).*

Chapter 1

A Short History of the
Jewish-American Cinema

America became conscious of its films and its Jews almost simultaneously. From primitive, flickering one-reelers, through Hollywood's golden age, and up to contemporary films, moviegoers who may never have met or even seen Jews in daily life encountered them on local movie screens.[1] Celluloid Jews appear in a variety of shapes and sizes— sinister shysters, pathetic victims, baffled buffoons, sympathetic workers, struggling students, gallant warriors, star-crossed lovers, and sadistic gangsters being just a few. But ironically, and in spite of their numbers, Jewish film characters have received scant attention from scholars and historians, while the screen sagas of other minorities, notably Blacks and American Indians, have been studied in some depth. This critical silence regarding Jewish-American films (movies centering on Jewish issues rather than directed or produced by Jews) and Jewish-American screen characters (figures defined as Jewish within the films rather than roles played by Jewish performers) is even more surprising considering that men like Samuel Goldwyn, Nicholas Schenck, David O. Selznick, Louis B. Mayer, Irving Thalberg, Harry Cohn, Carl Laemmle, Jesse Lasky, William Fox, B.P. Schulberg, and Jack Warner long dominated the movie community. Films featuring Jewish characters have, from story idea to final cut, historically faced a gauntlet of highly placed Jewish executives.

Unlike films about other American minorities, movies with Jews were often scrutinized by one segment of that minority group with the power to decide how the entire group would be presented to society as a whole. The resulting images of Jews in films constitute a rich and varied tapestry woven by several generations of moviemakers responding to the world around them. Their works dynamically depict both the Jews' profound impact on American society and that society's perception of the Jews within its midst. Some films are lamps that help extinguish the darkness of ignorance. Others simply mirror long-held prejudices. But whether they explain or exploit their Jewish characters, all these films either implicitly or explicitly show how Jews affect American life and how American life influences Jews; it is a two-way process inherent in the first Jewish-American movie as well as in the latest.

As part of a mass-media art form that must take into account a predominantly non-Jewish audience, these films reveal, reflect, and redefine the ever-changing role of Jews in American society by shaping—some would say distorting—the group's historical movements into a series of powerful and evocative images that freeze the spirit of an age and allow us to examine it. This is not to say the movies are factual. Clearly they distort life, but it is often these very distortions that make them so significant: they testify to the anxieties and strengths of a particular historical period. The messages we receive from a given movie may not be at all what its creators intended, or for that matter, not what the person sitting next to us in the theater receives. As with any art form, good movies allow for a variety of interpretations, ones that change over the years as surely as do the seasons. Films never tell the total story of any one incident or historical period. They present aspects of a situation, subjective views that select and highlight certain parts of the whole.

A discussion of Jewish-American films and characters, therefore, necessarily becomes an exploration of Jewish historical and cultural problems in America, as well as of the ways in which the movies attempt to explain and, ultimately, to solve them. But it is more. The assimilation process of America's Jews is valuable for anyone interested in American culture. Those Jews who strive to keep their own ethnic identity while they demand to be recognized as full-fledged Americans test the very premise of our democratic ideals. They help mark the boundaries of what a state can ask of its citizens and what a citizen owes his country. The once-cherished notion of the great "melting pot" has gone the way of the horse and buggy. It has been replaced by an understanding that, while we are all Americans, we are something more as well. We are all hyphenated citizens. The story of America's celluloid Jews, therefore, remains important not only for what it tells us about one of the country's most prominent minorities, but also for what it reveals about the American Dream, and ultimately, about America itself.

In 1881 a series of programs and anti-Jewish decrees in Russia forced waves of East-European Jews to emigrate to the United States. Though small groups of East-European Jews inhabited America as early as 1852, millions more streamed to her shores from 1881 to 1924, when a series of restrictive immigration laws stemmed the flood of refugees. By 1926 there were 3,111 congregations, 1,782 synagogues and 4,100,000 Jews here, and modern historians estimate that eighty-five percent of all Jews living in America today trace their roots back to these East-European immigrants. This extraordinary period of immense immigration forced a growing American awareness of the entity called "The Jews," much to the embarrassment of the 250,000 well-established German and Spanish Jews already here who had slipped into American life with little fanfare. So the quiet and orderly process of assimilation going on since 1644 ended in the confusion of Ellis Island and the noisy din of city streets. America's Jews were about to become more conspicuous then ever before, and both they and their adopted country would be profoundly changed by the experience.

These brash newcomers were far different from their German and Spanish predecessors. Though the earlier settlers emigrated from different sections of their respective homelands, they were largely a cosmopolitan group well accustomed to minority status in a predominantly Gentile population. The East-European Jews, however, came mostly from small Jewish towns, villages, and *shtetls,* self-sufficient little enclaves as isolated as possible from surrounding Christians. But despite their seeming unpreparedness to adapt to the well-established social, economic, and cultural values of American life, these East-European "green-horns" leaped from alienation to assimilation in a remarkably short time. Unlike some groups, they had emigrated not simply to improve their lot financially: they came to save their lives, and they came to stay. There was no safe place to which they might return as could other minority groups, so they brought with them, whenever possible, their entire families. After time had dimmed bad memories, some looked nostalgically backward, but very few wanted to return to those harsh lands whose peoples had hounded and murdered their kin for centuries.

The particular talents of these East-European

heirs to a long tradition of wandering and accommodation aided them in their resettlement. The unique characteristics of a rapidly urbanizing, democratic society allowed Jewish immigrants relatively easy access to the American dream. The Jews, as Milton Konvitz notes, traditionally valued scholarship, emphasized thrift and industry, possessed an intense desire to become "respectable," readily deferred immediate satisfactions for long-term goals, and tended to settle in urban rather than rural locations.[2] Thus, the elements of specific racial traits cultivated over years of a common religious heritage, a democratic country ready to accommodate industrious newcomers, a psychology already adjusted to minority status, a need to make America a home rather than just a place to await return to a homeland, and an intense desire to succeed in this new land all combined to facilitate the rapid rise of the East-European immigrants from ghetto to country club.

But there was a catch. These immigrants to the *goldene medine,* the golden land, quickly discovered that any commitment to the tenets and traditions of Judaism received its stiffest challenge not from brutal pogroms or cruel inquisitions, but from the seductive and intoxicating receptiveness of America. Since America offered new beginnings for everyone and presented only limited social and economic obstacles, the Jew's potential field of success was no longer confined to a small community of his brethren or measured by his mastery of an arcane Talmudic law. American success depended on commercial prosperity, on how one could support himself and his family. Thus the increasingly strong dichotomy between America as a place of economic salvation and one of spiritual peril played an important role in the subsequent history of the East-European immigrants.

Ironically, all the traits that helped make the newcomers successful simultaneously drove them further from traditional Jewish religious beliefs and practices. Economic freedom made commerce an obsession. The need to make America a permanent home motivated a hasty embrace of its values. Educational opportunities created a generation openly critical of traditional Judaism. Quickly recognized by its leaders, the major problem for the American Jewish community became not how to survive in the face of overt hostility but how to retain a Jewish identity within the fluid American class and economic structure that threatened to dissolve group ties and totally absorb Jews into American culture. For many Jews, the entry price into American life required a casting off of "foreignisms": their religious observances, their names, and their traditions. The Promised Land of economic salvation was also a Sodom of spiritual peril.

The eagerness of the immigrant Jews to fit into American life is understandable given the contemporary social and intellectual trends, particularly those embodied in the uniquely American concept of "the melting pot." This idea first appears in J. Hector St. John de Crèvecoeur's *Letters from an American Farmer* (1782), wherein he describes America as a place where "individuals of all nations are melted into a new race of men." In Israel Zangwill's play *The Melting Pot* (1908), David, an immigrant Jewish composer in love with a Gentile girl (Vera), speaks of his vision for his new land: "America is God's Crucible, the great Melting where all races of Europe are melting and re-forming...God is making the American...The real American has not arrived. He is only in the Crucible, I tell you—he will be the fusion of all races, perhaps the coming superman."[3]

Nowhere is Zangwill's message more evident than in the lives of those immigrants who harnessed the immense power of the visual image and guided the movie industry's evolution from seedy infancy as vaudeville chaser to the most popular art form of the twentieth century. It now seems inevitable that these ambitious newcomers would be drawn to the risky film business, since their low status and lack of capital forced them to search for economic opportunities requiring a minimum initial investment, operating on a cash basis, and not containing a management structure of potentially hostile Gentiles.

Coming from diverse backgrounds, men like Samuel Goldwyn, Marcus Loew, William Fox, and Adolph Zukor began renting cheap storefronts in immigrant neighborhoods and charging a nickel admission to the movies. Forty-two of the 120 motion-picture house in Manhattan were located on the Lower East Side as of 1908, many of these not in residential areas but strung along the Bowery, a traditional center for popular entertainment. Other theaters, however, were situated in nearby "Jewish Harlem," and there were seven times more movie theaters in Jewish areas than in other largely ethnic settlements. By the mid-twenties, the once ramshackle companies of aggressive Jewish immigrants had evolved into vast entertainment empires that survived until the 1950s. So it came to pass that these barely literate businessmen with an innate insight into the dreams and nightmares of the American public, men who never completely lost their accents or forsook their religion, became rulers of opulent dream factories that spewed forth cans of American fantasies.

A quick way to index attitudes toward Jews presented in the silent films is to glance at their typical screen occupations. Jews mostly occupy lower-class positions, with several occupations recurring in the early films: pawnshop owners, clothing merchants, money brokers, sweatshop workers, peddlers, tailors, grocery store/delicatessen owners. One occupation that attracted Jews, however, is not represented in ethnic films of the period: moviemaking. There are some obvious exceptions to these low, socioeconomic occupations, screen evidence of the upwardly mobile Jew. In *The Song of Solomon* (1914) the title character is a "song plugger" who makes it to the big time, in *A Woodland Christmas in California* (1912) the Jewish father sells curios, in *The Missing Diamond* (1914) Jacob Levy is an absent-minded diamond merchant, and in *A Daughter of Israel* (1914) Israel Levy is an antique dealer.

In time the Jewish immigrants attained even greater material prosperity, and the silent films reflect their movement to economic respectability. By 1922 *A Tailor-Made Man* features Abraham Nathan as a wealthy shipping magnate. Three years later in 1925, *Abie's Imported Bride* focuses on the son of a well-to-do mill owner who collects money to relieve suffering and hunger in Russia. In less than twenty years, then, screen Jews move from being objects of charity to providers of it, a celluloid illustration and endorsement of the financial achievements of Jews in the offscreen world. Screen Jews in subsequent decades show even greater diversity in occupational roles, reflecting how American Jews became involved in more varied aspects of American economic life.

Other than three *Disraeli* films, silent era movies about historical Jewish personages appear rather infrequently. In 1914, however, Great Players brought our *Uriel Acosta,* a production about the famous seventeenth-century Jewish author who twice renounced his faith. Throughout the movie, Acosta emerges as a divided man who is never fully certain of his own identity and who eventually surrenders to the irreconcilable dualities in his nature by committing suicide in 1647. Another famous historical Jew, Mendel Beiliss, becomes the focus of a 1913 film (partially shot in Kiev) that traces his humble beginnings, his accusation and arrest for ritual murder, his long trials and intense suffering in jail at the hands of the anti-Semitic Russian authorities, and his eventual acquittal. *Accused by Darkest Russia* represents an early example of the Jew as victim safely distanced by the foreign setting. It is an image not altered very much in American cinema until the creation of Israel in 1948, after which Jews suddenly appear as fighters as well as martyrs.

Cohen Saves the Flag (1913) does not contain a "real" Jewish person but does place a Jew within a very specific historical setting as it spotlights the rivalry between Cohen and Levy, both Union army soldiers and both desperately in love with Rebecca. After Levy falsely accuses him of cowardice and orders him shot, Cohen is rescued by a general who recognizes him as the man who saved the American flag at Gettysburg. Though without specific historical analogues, the unique Ford Sterling one-reeler fits into this category because of its specific historical settings, its attempt at realistic portrayals, and its emphasis on Jews as participants in past events of American life. Coincidentally, the film presents one of the few mass-media mentions of the 10,000 Jews, including nine generals and dozens of officers, in opposing armies during the Civil War.

The silent films that incorporate historical Jewish personages appear quite limited in number, especially when compared to the other categories in this film era. The main reason for this is that few real Jewish-American role models existed as potential subjects upon which to base biographical films. Interested filmmakers, therefore, necessarily relied on non-American figures or anonymous prototypes in defined historical situations. Also, the Jew as flesh-and-blood citizen living in the contemporary world represented a far less comfortable subject for filmmakers than did nondescript Biblical Jews or fictional Jewish types inherited from a long vaudeville tradition. In future decades, biographical films with subjects including Fanny Brice, the Rothschilds, Al Jolson, Mickey Marcus, and Lenny Bruce appear in the American cinema, but the subject of historical Jewish personages remains basically small in comparison to films focusing on other concerns of Jewish-American life.

In addition to these moguls and their bankers, the streets of immigrant America spawned a veritable army of Jewish performers who invaded and conquered the entertainment worlds of vaudeville and film: Al Jolson, George Gershwin, George Jessel, the Marx Brothers, Eddie Cantor, Sophie Tucker, Irving Berlin, Fannie Brice, Ben Blue, Jack Benny, George Burns, George Sidney, Milton Berle, Ted Lewis, Bennie Fields, and so many more. The crowded ghetto streets of New York nurtured the comic and imitative talents of these entertainers, while the growing number of summer resorts in the Catskills' "Borscht Belt" provided a superb training ground for aspiring performers. The entertainment industry that valued talent above all else became wide-open territory for industrious and talented immigrants and their children. Further-

more, by the early 1890s a good portion of the theatrical booking business in New York City was in Jewish hands, thanks to the Klaw and Erlanger syndicate, the Shubert brothers, Marcus Loew and Adolph Zukor, the Schenck brothers, and a host of other agents and stage managers; there was, therefore, less racial prejudice here than in more established industries.

The rapid growth and immense popularity of the movie industry coincided with the influx of East-European Jews whose values, talents, and achievements permanently altered American society. Clearly, both Jews and film production existed in America before the early twentieth century, but nothing even hinted at the media revolution that was to result from the combination of Jews and films. Indeed, from the very beginnings of the industry until the present, it is impossible to ignore the influence of Jews on the movie business or to overlook the importance of a Jewish consciousness in American films. How could L. B. Mayer or Jack Warner not treat a movie that portrayed a significant aspect of his life or racial history differently from a picture about black sharecroppers or one about Indians on the Western plains? So while America did in a very real sense discover its Jews and its films together, it is perhaps even more correct to say Jews made America conscious of its films, and in turn, films made America more aware of its Jews.

Ramon Novarro plays a Jewish prince of the House of Hur in BEN HUR *(1927).*

The Silent Stereotypes

Most writers who discuss images of Jews in American silent films seem woefully unaware of the vast number of such movies actually made during this era. A typical example is Stuart Sammuels's essay that begins"...from the early 1900s till 1945, in an industry where Jews were the major source of directors, actors, studio executives, producers, lawyers, and scriptwriters, the image of the Jews was almost invisible on the screen."[4] Invisible? Between 1900 and 1929 alone, approximately 319 films featured clearly discernible Jewish characters—a figure far surpassing the number of films featuring other ethnic types and certainly enough to draw some general conclusions about how Jews were depicted in this one medium so heavily influenced by Jewish artists. For purposes of discussion, the most important silent films can be separated into several general areas: occupational; historical Jewish personages; Biblical Jews; classic Jewish characters adapted from literary sources; Jews as hapless victims of society; clever/sneaky Jews; Jewish-Gentile (excluding Irish) relationships; Jewish-Irish relationships; Jews as butts/creators of humor; ghetto life; and foreign Jews. Some of these categories overlap, since a film

about a clever/sneaky Jew may well also be about ghetto life, have humorous intentions, and entail Jewish-Gentile relationships. But, for the most part, these categories show the diversity of Jewish roles in the silent era and facilitate an understanding of the creators of our earliest national cinema.

Most silent Biblical films treat Jews simply as pre-Christians, so they represent one of the earliest yet least ethnically developed categories in this study. Their makers were not very interested in recording Jewish history accurately; the point was to cloak as much flashy spectacle and fleshy seduction as possible beneath the seven veils of sanctimoniousness, Jews, even when designated specifically as such in Biblical epics, appear as no different from anyone else, with scant attention paid to their faith or heritage. Even the films of Cecil B. DeMille—Hollywood's reigning Biblical scholar, whose Old Testament tabloid tales include *The Ten Commandments* (1923/1956), *King of Kings* (1927) and *Samson and Delilah* (1949)—remain much more valuable for their attention to decor and decolletage than for their historical or religious insights. His films emphasize sex and violence at the expense of anything else. For the

student of Jewish-American films, these Biblical epics prove a vast Sinai of tedium and mediocrity relieved only occasionally by some small oasis of cinematic interest.

Just as silent film directors turned naturally to modern and Biblical history for ready-made plots that perhaps incidentally contained Jewish characters, so they quickly cannibalized classic literary works that often featured Jewish figures. Not surprisingly, the two most popular works are Shakespeare's *The Merchant of Venice* and Dickens's *Oliver Twist.* These two works alone account for at least eleven adaptations during this period, not including films such as *A Female Fagin* (1913), which draws its inspiration from Dickens.

Early versions of *The Merchant of Venice* were filmed in 1908 and 1912. A 1913 film, *Shylock,* features Harry Baur in the title role, and another version was made in 1914. Because they are only a reel or two long, the first two films severely truncate Shakespeare's drama. Both the first, made by Vitagraph, and the second, by Thanhouser with William J. Bowman as Shylock, stress Shylock's villainy at the expense of the other characters and plot components. The 1914 Universal version directed by Phillips Smalley doubles the running time of the previous ones, and also centers on the role of the vengeful Jewish moneylender who demands his gruesome pound of flesh. With some minor variations, all these *Merchant of Venice*

Fagin (Tully Marshall) stirs up more mischief in OLIVER TWIST (1916).

Fagin (Alec Guinness) lectures his band of young thieves in OLIVER TWIST *(1948).*

adaptations show Shylock as a despicable and malevolent character possessing few, if any, redeeming qualities. Though he is not totally a caricature, his "Jewishness" remains clearly prominent in his physical appearance and his usurious profession. No real attempts to nuance his portrait or to deal with what today would be considered the more flagrantly offensive aspects of Shylock's characterization exist in the silent era; in fact, his physical features usually heighten stereotypcial "Jewishness": gaunt appearance, hooked nose, and strange hat.

The six direct adaptations (1909, 1910, 1912, 1912, 1916, 1922) and one modern variation (*Oliver Twist, Junior,* 1921) represent something of a different approach to the Jewish character taken from Dickens's classic novel. All, including the second 1912 version made in England but widely distributed in the United States by Kineto Film Traders of New York, concentrate mainly on the story from the time Bill Sykes and the Artful Dodger find Oliver and take him to join Fagin's band of young thieves. Thus, like the Shylock character in *The Merchant of Venice,* the Jewish character functions as a figure of corruption, as well as the most villainous character in the film; however, the 1910 film contains a strange forgiveness/redemption scene in which Oliver pardons Fagin.

Nat Goodwin's Fagin in the 1912 *Oliver Twist,* adapted from Comyns Carr's popular stage play, was a large success, reaping solid profits and many favorable critical reactions. Apparently, Goodwin consciously toned down the harsher aspects of Fagin and made him a more acceptable character for twentieth-century American audiences which would inevitably contain large numbers of Jews. Later, Tully Marshall (1916), Irving Pichel (1933), and Ron Moody (who won an Oscar nomination in 1968 as Fagin in the musical *Oliver!*) all drew on aspects of Goodwin's characterization, realizing Fagin would be more acceptable as a charming rogue than as a totally despicable villain. But by far the most popular retelling of the Dickens tale, at least until 1948 when English director David Lean's *Oliver Twist* (featuring Alec Guinness as Fagin) proved to be such a success, is the 1922 version with Jackie Coogan as Oliver and Lon Chaney as Fagin. Chaney was singled out for his "vivid" presentation of Fagin, and though the film does not dwell on Fagin's Jewishness, Chaney uses several stereotypical characterizations: he has an overly bulbous nose and rubs his hands together every time money is mentioned.

Other than *The Merchant of Venice* and the *Oliver Twist* films, at least two additional literary works with Jewish characters were filmed during the silent era. In 1914, Biograph made *Gwendolyn* based on George Eliot's novel *Daniel Deronda.* Its plot centers on Deronda's ignorance of his Jewish ancestry, his love for Mirah (a Jewish singer), her brother's refusal to let her marry a man he supposes to be a Gentile, and the lovers' eventual reconciliation and marriage after Deronda's mother reveals that he is really Jewish. Another work with a Jewish heroine, Walter Scott's *Ivanhoe,* appeared in 1913 after being made in England by Universal. Less involved with the Jewish subplot than the English-made *Rebecca the Jewess* (1914) or the 1952 remake with Elizabeth Taylor as Rebecca, the film includes a segment in which the heroic knight saves a Jewish merchant and his lovely daughter.

The silent-film adaptations of literary works featuring Jewish characters do little to alter any unsympathetic portraits found in their original sources. Even Oliver's pardon of Fagin fails to lessen that character's sinister qualities. Though Fagin may at times be presented as a charming rogue, or Shylock even less often as a man with some justification for his grisly demand, the predominant portrayal of Jews in such literary adaptations show them as usurers, villains, cheats, and crooks. Early filmmakers simply recycle literary presentations that include what today, however, we would label as racist stereotypes. To a degree, all silent film characters—heroes as well as villians—were stereotypes. Nor were the Jews the only minority group unflatteringly depicted: Blacks and Native Americans suffered the same celluloid fate.

At this point in history, most of the early pioneers of American cinema possessed neither the minority consciousness, nor the artistic sophistication, nor even the awareness of the medium's power necessary to create well-rounded ethnic portraits that provide more than a burlesque of minorities. They themselves may have shared some of the bigoted conceptions commonly held at the time. Even those who were Jewish seemed little concerned with negative impressions of Jews in the movies, putting their pocketbooks before

Nathan Cohen (George
Sidney) and Patrick Kelly
(Charles Murphy) toast their
partnership at the end of
THE COHENS AND THE KELLYS
(1926).

their pride. However, the early days of the industry found Jews more often as theater owners than as film producers.[5] Though it may seem unfair to condemn early filmmakers for such simplistic portrayals, the fact remains that they cared little for the subtleties of minority character development. They never seemed to have even contemplated the potential, and in some cases the very real, injury such distorted caricatures did to contemporary Jews struggling to make their way in America.

Though in silent film drawn from literary sources Jews often appear as the creators of evil, there exists a small group of films that show Jews singled out as victims because of their religion. The Jew as victim occurs less regularly and usually as a minor character in most films set in America; however, in films set in foreign lands, Jews are featured almost exclusively as innocent victims of ignorant anti-Semitic officials, biased government leaders, and blindly prejudiced leaders. A quick look at some of the films with American settings, however, clearly establishes the basic pattern.

Two films entitled *The Yiddisher Cowboy* (1909, 1911) appear during the silent years; both feature Jewish central characters, but the second more obviously than the first shows the structure common in many films. Ikey Rosenthal, a hapless peddler, finally lands a job at the Bar-X Ranch in Wyoming. Outfitted as he is in chaps, spurs, and cowboy hat, he at first feels like a real cowboy. But after being taunted and finally forced at gunpoint to do a "Yiddisher dance," the angry Ikey refuses to join the other hands who head into town on a payday spree. Instead, he uses his money to set up a small pawnshop and when the penniless cowboys return forces them to hock their guns as security for their loans. Now, he possesses the power to revenge himself and starts shooting at those who previously tormented him. Thus, the pattern emerges: Jew is taken advantage of, Jew turns the tables (usually by wit rather than force), Jew gains potential for revenge if he wishes. It is a structure prevalent in many films.

Silent-screen Jews often turn adverse situations to their advantage and emerge as winners because of their inherent cleverness, as in the *Yiddisher Cowboy*. Only rarely do they manage to triumph because of physical prowess, fate, or even Gentile kindness. Yet the silent film directors who depict

Nathan Cohen (George Sidney) shrinks from an angry Patrick Kelly (Charles Murphy) after accidentally crushing his hat in THE COHENS AND THE KELLYS *(1926).*

this cleverness frequently present it as unethical, morally dishonest, or illegal. Even when the tactics Jewish businessmen employ are not obviously dishonest, their actions appear suspicious if not downright immoral. In fact, some silent films obsessively deny that Jewish prosperity and success have anything to do with hard work, patience, self-sacrifice, or business acumen. In *Cohen's Advertising Scheme* (1904), for instance, Cohen's activities are not dishonest, but are certainly questionable. The film begins as the owner of a clothing store fails to attract new customers by announcing a phony fire sale. Even when he gives a destitute panhandler a new coat, seemingly an act of compassion and charity (though perhaps to atone for his lies), his gesture is immediately unmasked as a ruse; when the vagrant turns around, we see imprinted on the back of his coat: "Go to I. Cohen for Clothes." Jewish generosity is only an excuse for manipulations. More dishonesty appears in *Such a Business* (1914) when Ike Levy, a hatter, employs his son to knock hats off passersby

The intermarriage wedding (Charles "Buddy" Rogers and Nancy Carroll): ABIE'S IRISH ROSE *(1928).*

and thus generate new business, and in *A Female Fagin* (1913), where Rosy Rosalsky runs a crime school for young girls.

Several other films feature Jewish shop owners perfectly willing to burn down their stores for the insurance money. The chief examples of the "genre" are *Cohen's Fire Sale* (1907) and *The Firebug* (1913). In both films, however, fate foils the Jews' dishonest plots. A speedy fire department puts out the fire in the first, and rival firebugs extinguish each other's blazes in the second. Many films also display Jewish salesmen as charlatans who pass off worthless goods on innocent customers. In *Lucky Cohen* (1914) an unscrupulous Jew sells brass as gold, in *A Flurry in Diamonds* (1913) Izzy Bernstein merchandises glass as diamonds to unsuspecting farmers, in *The Magic Cup* (1921) Abe Timberg substitutes paste beads for pearls, in *Get Rich Quick Billington* (1913) Jack Cohen pedals phony certificates, and in *Guaranteed Rainproof* (1914) Sam Cohen sells cheap suits that shrink dramatically in the slightest drizzle.

Mention must be made, however, of one film that goes against these negative portraits of unsavory Jewish businessmen: *George Washington Cohen* (1928). Here G. W. Cohen (George Jessel) gets into one scrape after another because his parents teach him never to tell a lie. He loses his job in a cigar store when he refuses to push an inferior brand. Then, after finding and returning a lost wallet to a wealthy businessman, Mr. Gorman (Robert Edeson), Cohen is given a job in which he reveals that his boss's wife is having an affair with his partner. Eventually George learns that honesty, at least in the business world, is a perilous policy. For the sake of Gorman's ward (Florence Allen), he tells the judge he lied about Mrs. Gorman's affair; the judge then sentences him to five years for perjury. *George Washington Cohen* shows Jewish honesty as a natural outgrowth of a strong family life of love, understanding, and ethical training. However, if he wants to succeed in the new world of commerce, the Jew must learn to temper his honesty with practicality.

Scurrilous tactics attributed in these films to Jewish businessmen take on a darker meaning in other films where Jews defile four of the most sacred areas of American life: love, democracy, sports, and family relationships. *Levy's Seven Daughters* (1915) centers around a plot by which Levy tricks Strauss into marrying off his seven wealthy sons to seven poor shopgirls posing as Levy's daughters. The democratic election process flounders in *The New Fire Chief* (1912), where Abraham Guberman (Richard Lee) cheats to win election as the fire chief of a small town. Of course, the dry-goods store owner turned fire fighter brings about disaster when he refuses to allow his men to fight fires after 5 P.M. because they are a "union fire department," and when he has them draw cards to decide who will rescue a woman trapped in a burning building. The final title, "Abie proves himself a real fire fighter," is sarcastically juxtaposed with a shot of Guberman putting out a small leaf fire.

Not even sports are safe from the corruption of unethical Jewish behavior. When in *How Mosha Came Back* (1912) cowardly Mosha Sumtufsky decides that "fighting is no business" and unceremoniously crawls out of the boxing ring during his match with Spud Wilson, his girlfriend refuses to speak to him unless he avenges the humiliating defeat. During a subsequent rematch with Spud, "Mosha prays and is given an injection of false courage": his second drugs the champ so that Mosha can win. Later we discover this is all a fond dream of the skinny, bearded Mosha, but the point remains that Jews even dream sneaky, unscrupulous thoughts.

Perhaps most offensive of all are films such as *Levinsky's Holiday* (1913), which portray Jewish family relationships as determined by the marketplace. Clothing salesman Ike Levinsky takes his son, Jakey, to the circus, but unwilling to cough up the price of a ticket he disguises himself as the Bearded Lady. When this fails, he is hustled off to become the target in the "Hit the Nigger" booth. When Jakey discovers his father there, he begins selling rotten eggs for customers to throw at him. Instead of punishing the boy, Ike congratulates him on his business acumen. The film thus displays the father-son relationship at its basest. Instead of passing along moral values or ethical traditions, Ike impresses on his son the intense desirability of "making it" at any price—even at the expense of filial respect—a willingness to employ any means to get ahead in the business world.

These films suggesting that Jews can only achieve success through devious and dishonest means may have been intended as rationalizations that poured soothing balm on the ruffled egos of "native" Americans who were faced with increasingly strong Jewish competition in the marketplace. Since some of these Gentiles were in the movie business, it may also explain the bitterness which lurks just beneath the surface of many such films. Whatever the truth, many silent movies containing Jewish businessmen show them in the worst possible light. They suggest that even when the Jew is punished for his actions he fails to reform and goes on to swindle more poor and unsuspecting non-Jews. These are among the least sympathetic portraits of Jews in silent films, though their harshness is somewhat mitigated by their ostensible good humor. Even so, the category represents one clear area in which racial tensions surface between recent Jewish immigrants and Americans of an earlier immigration. Beneath the films' sprightly exteriors, light-hearted humor, and jovial antics runs a persistent racial tension.

Because it inevitably revolves around the Jew's interaction with his non-Jewish world, the clever/sneaky Jew category leads quite naturally to the large area of Jewish-Gentile relationships. Here more than in any other area the films most clearly spotlight the often bitter conflicts between old traditions and new societal demands; the immigrant's fierce drive for upward mobility puts pressure on ethical concerns, and the continual problem of how to maintain a unique ethnic identity in a melting pot culture that demands homogenous values becomes a central theme. These films fall into three general areas: love entanglements, family relationships, and interracial compassion. Once again, the divisions provide useful but somewhat artificial distinctions, for love entanglements usually include family conflicts between parents and children, and compassion, which often manifests itself in the adoption of a Gentile baby, usually matures into love entanglements.

As one might expect, love entanglements proved most popular with silent film directors. Films based on such themes appealed to the rapidly expanding audiences filling increasing numbers of movie theaters. They provided an area of easy access and immediate interest for immigrants who made up a significant part of this new audience. Almost all these films present some form of generational conflict arising from a Jewish child's desire to marry a non-Jew. In a few such films the elders persuade the wayward child to abandon the loved one and reunite with his/her parents. But this rejection of love almost always results in some form of tragedy. In *Faith of Her Fathers* (1915) the kindhearted Bertha (Cleo Madison) heeds the lessons of her father, Tamor (Murdock MacQuarre), a rabbi, and his young associate who forcefully recites the sufferings her ancestors endured in order to remain true to their faith. Because she fails to put love above religious prohibition, she finally dies of a "broken heart" on her tenement doorstep. Bertha's failure to grasp the new world's values via marriage to a young Christian missionary (Joe King), whom her father befriends and then rejects, becomes the film's central tragedy, as it is for many silent films in which the child capitulates to parental pressure.

A more realistic portrayal of the problems of intermarriage, however, occurs in *The Pawnbroker's Daughter* (1913), in which Manuel Dreyfus's college-educated daughter (Alice Joyce) falls in love with a handsome Gentile, Edward Marshall. But when the man's cruel and domineering mother insults her father and verbally abuses her, the girl rejects him only to discover that her former suitor, a Jew, has already married someone else. Thus she remains alone and dejected at the end of the film. In another film, *The Barrier of Faith* (1915), Rose Aarons (Norma Talmadge) is punished for her rash intermarriage when her insensitive and alcoholic Gentile husband dies in a barroom brawl. Penitently returning home on Passover, she seeks her family's forgiveness and is once again united with them.

Yet these films and the others like them that reaffirm religious hegemony are few in number compared to the many films that support and even encourage intermarriage. The basic pattern of these films remains fairly consistent: children of Jewish and Gentile couple fall in love, their parents (most often viewed from the Jewish perspective) refuse to give the match their blessing, the couple marries anyhow, the birth of their child (or possibly some type of calamity) reconciles the parents to the marriage and they finally acknowledge that love is stonger than any religious ties. *The Jew's Christmas* (1913) is a good example of this type of film. Rabbi Isaac's daughter, Leah (Lois Weber), marries a Gentile and is promptly disowned by her father. The old man's narrowmindedness further complicates matters when Sam, his son, returns home tipsy. He too is thrown out, and he vows never to return home until his father celebrates Christmas. Thus, the film posits the acceptance and celebration of Christmas as an admission of acculturation. Eventually, to please his granddaughter, the old rabbi sells one of his sacred books to purchase the child a fine Christmas tree, and the entire family is reconciled in the spirit of "peace on earth, good will towards men." Other films in this generational conflict-eventual reconciliation mode include: The *Romance of the Jewess* (1908, Griffith), *The Old Chess Players* (1912), *The Question* (1911), *Solomon's Son* (1912), *We Americans* (1928), *The Woman He Loved* (1927), *The Peddler's Find* (1912), *Unto the Third Generation* (1913), *The Oath* (1921) and *None So Blind* (1923).

As is obvious in the few films described above, early Jewish screen families often find themselves enmeshed in bitter conflicts between love and tradition. Inevitably, the younger generation's thorough indoctrination into democratic values of romance and marriage clash with the older generation's traditional beliefs in religious values and old world customs. Sometimes, as in some of the films just described, the younger generation teaches the older that America is a new land in which democratic freedom replaces old world dictates. But other times the shabbiness of their parents' occupations and surroundings causes acute embarrassment for young Jews trying "to pass" in a Gentile world. For example, Morris in Frank Capra's *The Younger Generation* (1928) refuses to acknowledge his parents and passes them off as peasant servants. Such children feel ashamed of their humble origins and go to any lengths to separate themselves from their parents and all they represent.

Such rejection is seen as cruel and heartless by some of the silent filmmakers who depict something of value in the attitudes of the rejected parents. In *A Passover Miracle* (1914) Sam Ratkowitz forsakes his family, which has suffered to put him through medical school, for the charms of a Gentile stenographer. When she inevitably leaves him, the repentant young man returns home during the Passover Seder. His father finds him standing at the door opened for the prophet Elijah. All is forgiven, and Sam enters his home once again. In *The Faith of Her Fathers* (1914), Ruth (Irene Hunt) is ashamed of her pawnbroker father's unsavory profession and refuses to tell her rich Gentile friends what he does for a living. To get as far away from her heritage as she can, Ruth rejects the gentle advances of Nathan, a Jew, and encourages those of Dick North, a Gentile. Yet when she must choose between seeing her father jailed as a thief or maintaining her deception, Ruth reveals her guilty secret, accepts her origins, rejects Dick, and decides to marry Nathan.

Millionaires (1926) and *Father and Son or the Curse of the Golden Land* (1913) present a somewhat different twist to this basic plot structure. In the first, a sudden lucky break turns Esther (Vera Gordon) and Meyer (George Sidney) Rubens, owners of a small ghetto cleaning and pressing shop, into overnight millionaires. But Esther finds herself embarrassed by Meyer's boorish old-world habits. He can neither play golf, nor ride horses, nor make satisfactory use of a full table-setting of silverware. Reba (Louise Fazenda), her sister, convinces Esther she will never get into the "charmed circle" she has set her heart on being accepted by as long as she remains handicapped by uncouth Meyer. Ironically, as Esther later discovers, the fancy set she so ardently cultivates much prefers the down-to-earth ways of Meyer to her own pretentious manners. Recognition of Meyer's worth allows Esther to re-evaluate the money that has occasioned so much grief. In the second film, Wolf Saltzman forsakes his old-world wife and son for the charms of a fully Americanized Jewish girl, only to realize the cruelty of his choice; by the film's end he vows to atone for his wrongs.

Finally, there is the entire area of Jewish compassion and charity. Though usually handled with touches of sarcasm in the clever/sneaky Jew films, several filmmakers make an honest effort to break out of racist stereotypes. The ads for *A Man Is a Man* (1908), for example, promise a central character unlike the Jew with his "long whiskers, derby hat pulled down to the ears, and hands moving like the fins of a fish." Instead, the film strives to present one whose "manhood, sentiments, and convictions are not burlesqued." Indeed, the film does depict a Jewish character whose compassion stretches far beyond that of his Gentile counterpart, a rich man who drives over the poor peddler's daughter and then asks the grief-stricken father to hide him from the angry mob. He does. The last shot shows both men bringing flowers to the little girl's grave, the final title reading, "A man is a man, be he Jew or Gentile." Other films, like *Cohen's Generosity* (1910) in which a pawnbroker raises an immigrant Irish boy, contrast Jewish compassion with Gentile indifference or hostility.

A number of films in this subcategory deal with Jews adopting babies. Sometimes, as in *The Peddler's Find* (1912), a conflict arises when the adopted Gentile child falls in love with the couple's biological (and therefore Jewish) offspring. At other times, such as in *A Daughter of Israel* (1914) and *Rose of the Tenements* (1926), problems created by adoptive Jewish parents are straightened out by revealing the orphan's Christian origins. In several of these movies, the Jew is just one part of a multi-ethnic triumvirate that adopts the child: Herman Schultz, Abie Ratz, Patrick O'Malley *(For the Love of Mike,* 1927); Sally Mack, Abraham Lapidowitz, Tony Garibaldi *(Sally in Our Alley,* 1927). These movies stress the harmony between the various ethnic minorities crowded together in New York's squalid ghettos and emphasize how loving understanding can eventually triumph over the old-world habits and ethnic mistrust learned through centuries of hostility.

Though they fall within the area of Jewish-Gentile relationships, films about Jews and Irishmen constituted their own category and must be treated separately. Specific areas of interaction such as friendship, politics, and inter-ethnic rivalry which appear sparingly in the "Jewish-Gentile Relationships" category are focused on quite frequently in the films about Jews and Irishmen. Though many of the films discussed in this book are categorized mainly by their major themes, the topics that emerge are often filtered through a uniquely Jewish-Irish perspective that accounts for their humor, pathos, and conflicts.

Bohn and Stromgren in *Light and Shadows* grossly overstate the issue by proclaiming the portrayal of Jews in silent films is virtually one long Jewish-Irish joke, but their exaggeration contains a splinter of truth. Why do the films deal so heavily with Jews and the Irish and not the Chinese or Italians? Most obviously, there are certain historical and cultural similarities that bind the two groups together, as well as clear differences that create conflicts. Like the Jews, although somewhat earlier, the Irish who immigrated to America in large numbers brought an "alien" religion to Protestant America. In addition, many Irish immigrants managed an almost equally swift economic rise, so that the socioeconomic split between the "shanty" and the "lace-curtain" Irish appears early, much like the division between the German and East-European Jews. American Jews have traditionally sensed that anti-Catholicism and anti-Semitism were somehow related, so they vigorously opposed the Know Nothing Party, fiercely supported Al Smith, and provided John F. Kennedy with more votes (88 percent) than did the Catholics themselves (81 percent). Irish and Jewish stereotypes commonly appeared in vaudeville theaters and burlesque houses, making the jump from stage to screen presentations relatively easy. Finally, the phenomenal success of Anne Nichols's play *Abie's Irish Rose* (1924), inspired a host of imitators. For whatever sociological or historical reasons that occasioned it, Hollywood from its earliest days happily paired the Jews and the Irish, sometimes with good humor and other times with only slightly masked hostility. The words from a title card in *Frisco Sally Levy* (1927) aptly sum up the attitudes of early filmmakers: "The sun cannot shine in Ireland when it's raining in Jerusalem."

The first film featuring Jewish-Irish interaction is *Levi and Cohen—The Irish Comedians* (1903), in which two vaudeville comics perform before an unappreciative audience that pelts them with various vegetables. Though critics like Josh Kanin see this as allowing audiences to vent their latent anti-Semitic feelings, the film really has little to do with anything except a silly vaudeville situation pictorialized. After all, the unseen crowd appears blissfully unaware of the performers' religions or even whether they are Irish comedians passing themselves off as Jews or Jewish comedians calling themselves Irish. Other silent films pair Jews and Irishmen together as compatible business partners: *Cohen and Murphy* (1910) has Jack Cohen and John Murphy as amiable co-owners of a hotel; *Old Clothes* (1925) and *The Rag Man* (1925) feature Tim Kelly (Jackie Coogan) and Max Ginzberg (Max Davidson) as cut-rate haberdashers; *Sweet Daddies* (1926) has Pat O'Brien (Charles Murphy) and Abie Finkelbaum (George Sidney) join forces to import molasses from the Bahamas; *Cohen's Luck* (1915) shows Abe Cohen and Mrs. McGee as co-holders of a winning lottery ticket.

These harmonious business partnerships, however, are balanced by fierce rivalries between grocers Cohen (Charles Bennet) and Flannigan (Major MacGuire) in *Shorty and Sandy Work Together* (1913), between clothing store owners Hyman Cohen (George Sidney) and Tim Clancy (Will Armstrong) in *Clancy's Kosher Wedding* (1927), and between irate husbands Cohen and Kelly in *Cohen's Outing* (1913). This hostile competition between two upwardly mobile immigrant groups sometimes spills over from the business to the political arena in films such as *Cohen's Luck* (1915) in which Abe Cohen (William Wadsworth) loses his job for not supporting O'Rourke as alderman, and *Levi and McGuiness Running for Office* (1913) which culminates in what one viewer called a "race riot between Irish and Jews." Actually only a few other films carry this rivalry out to its natural conclusion—fierce, large-scale brawls—including *Becky Gets a Husband* (1912), *For the Love of Mike and Rosie* (1916), and *The Riot* (1913).

Yet the films highlighting Jewish-Irish hostilities are far outnumbered by those emphasizing eventual friendship and understanding between members of the two groups. *Ireland and Israel* (1912), for example, shows enduring friendship between Abie Wedertsky and Pat Riley. The Irishman makes the Jew welcome in America, even teaching him to box so he can defeat a gang of hoodlums who harass him, and years later the now-prosperous Jew seeks out the downtrodden Irishman and rescues him from poverty. A much more bizarre story of Jewish-Irish cooperation appears in *Traffickers on Souls* (1914) where Inspector McGuiness and his Jewish emergency squad join forces with Inspector Levy and his Irish cops. Disguising themselves as widows, the two clever cops break up a vicious white slavery ring. In recognition of their bravery, McGuiness get a turkey and Levy a ham. In *Sailor Izzy Murphy* (1927), starring George Jessel, the title character pretends to be Irish to save his girlfriend.[6]

The Westerner had the wide open spaces; the Keystone Cops caromed across L.A.'s boulevards. For the silent-film Jew, the typical setting was the congested, cluttered Lower East Side world of New York City (though at least two—*A Citizen in the Making* (1912) and *Levi's Dilemma* (1910)—range as far west as Chicago). Within this screen environment, the curse of poverty, the healing power of love, and the problems of family life are the predominant, often overlapping, issues for the film's characters. For example, in *Little Miss Smiles* (1922), an early John Ford film about the poor Aaronson family, Mama Aaronson is going blind, son Davie wants to become a boxer, and daughter Ester loves a Gentile doctor. A similar series of Job-like ghetto misfortunes burden religious Reb Shmuel (Wilton Lackaye) in the film version of Israel Zangwill's *The Children of the Ghetto* (1915): his son dies in a barroom brawl, his daughter marries a Gentile, his wife dies unexpectedly. Finally, however, his daughter returns, and as the title puts it, "His simple and unwavering faith is rewarded in the sunset of his days."

More often than not, poverty causes ghetto inhabitants much unhappiness. In those films centering around monetary problems, the plots follow three basic patterns: 1) poverty destroys the characters; 2) the characters somehow manage to obtain money and escape the ghetto; 3) poverty brings out the character's finer qualities. Typical of the films that show the destruction poverty can cause is *Blood of the Poor* (1912), which focuses on the bitter life of a poor ghetto tailor. Unable to pay his rent, the tailor instead allows his beloved daughter to become a servant in his landlord's household. The landlord's son seduces and then callously abandons her. The tailor, crushed by this dishonor, dies, and the daughter proudly refuses her seducer's offer of money to make amends.

A far larger number of films, however, show

industrious—sometimes lucky—Jews escaping the deprivation of ghetto life: in Raoul A. Walsh's *Regeneration* (1915) the escape is by education; in *Cohen's Luck* (1915) by owning a winning lottery ticket; in *The Pawnbroker's Daughter* (1913) by returning a lost purse; in Griffith's *A Child of the Ghetto* (1910) by the power of country life; in *Breaking Home Ties* (1922) by becoming a lawyer; and in *Hungry Hearts* (1922) by a new son-in-law's generosity.

But the myriad problems poverty brings are often counter-balanced by the finer qualities adversity draws out of seemingly heartless ghetto inhabitants. In *Old Isaacs, the Pawnbroker* (1908) a young girl travels from one charitable agency to another desperately trying to obtain money for her critically ill mother. All refuse to help. Finally, as one last hope, she takes her only doll to a crusty Jewish pawnbroker. He is so moved that he not only gives her the money but buys food for the family, gets a doctor to treat the mother, and of course returns the girl's doll. *The Stone Heart* (1915) features Augustus Phillips, who the ads say "had to live a while in the East Side element to take the Shylock part," as Abraham Burnstein, a sweatshop owner who exploits poor waifs. When little Nan Cowles (Viola Dana) arrives late one morning because she has to tend her sick mother, Burnstein unceremoniously fires her, and the distraught girl steals five dollars from his desk to pay a doctor. Burnstein follows her with the law in tow, but when he arrives at Nan's squalid flat a miraculous change occurs: his stone heart softens and he nurses the mother through the night. Nevertheless, the filmmakers, as though unable to accept this sympathetic change of heart, show him taking the few stolen dollars back from Nan's clenched hands after the exhausted child finally falls into a fitful sleep. "Business is Business," declares Burnstein.

Finally, there are the many films revolving around love entanglements in the ghetto. Often the conflict involves a newcomer to America torn between a loved one from the old country and from the new: in *The Ghetto Seamstress* (1910) David must choose between Betty Muscova from Russia and Clara Greenfield from the United States; in *Cheated Love* (1913) Sonya must choose between David Dahlman (a settlement worker) and

Mischa (an Odessa doctor); in *The Heart of a Jewess* (1921) Jake must choose between Rebecca and a more Americanized woman with a $10,000 dowry. Other films, for example *A Citizen in the Making* (1912), show immigrant sweethearts sticking together, and some (*Love in the Ghetto*, 1913; *The Girl of the Ghetto*, 1910; *Just Around the Corner*, 1921; *Cupid Puts One Over on the Shadchen*, 1915) simply recycle typical romantic misadventures, add a dash of chicken soup, and set the action in the lower East Side.

The quintessential ghetto film remains director Frank Borzage's screen adaptation of Fannie Hurst's novel *Humoresque* (1920). While Marxist critic Harry A. Potamkin attacked the film as "an impertinent fable written by a sentimental woman, further sentimentalized by the director, and almost obscenely sentimentalized by the performance of Vera Gordon," and called it a "highly extravagant and incorrect study of Jewish society," the film won praise from *The New York Times* for its vivid atmosphere, genuine acting, and visual style. Hurst's tear-provoking tale tells of a young Jewish boy (Gaston Glass) pushed by his *Yiddishe mama* (Vera Gordon) to become a great violinist. His arm is injured in the war, but he is miraculously healed through love and goes on with his musical career. The conflict between the mother who wants her son to become an artist and the father (Dore Davidson) who wants him to learn a useful trade, the son's willingness to forego a $2,000 per night fee to "enter a Greater-World symphony" in uniform, the many shots of the Lower East Side ghetto life, the romance between the boy and the crippled then healed Minnie Ginsberg (Miriam Battista) who changes her name to Gina Berg and becomes a famous singer, and the romantic ending made possible by love's healing power all coalesce to make *Humoresque* a neat collage of ghetto life themes and conflicts. In *Humoresque* we are offered a vision of life as it might have been rather than as it was in the ghetto, as Borzage presents the Lower East Side less as a depressed neighborhood than as an exalted state of mind.

Of course, not all silent films about Jews are so serious in intent. Sig Altman in *The Comic Image of the Jew* even concludes that the "Jew is the comic figure par excellence in films," that "the very word

Mama Kantor (Vera Gordon) urges her son (Gaston Glass) to become a musician in the quintessential ghetto melodrama HUMORESQUE *(1920).*

'Jewish' has become laden with humorous overtones," and that "Jewish identity is itself a kind of automatic comic device projected at an audience 'programmed' to receive it."[7] Altman's book represents a notable attempt to trace the role of comedy throughout Jewish history and art and to place contemporary Jewish humor (and humorists) in a historical perspective. Several of his points, briefly summarized below, contribute to an understanding of the films under discussion. First, the role of the jester has for centuries been an important one in Jewish culture. The *badken* or *marshallik* was a sort of Lear's fool allowed the privilege of caustic humor and social criticism without fear of reprisal. Second, Jewish self-deprecating and self-ironic humor has been the constant companion of a people forced for so long to live under someone else's rules. This adaptation of the "Stepin Fetchit" demeanor to ward off possible aggression and to make Jews seem as inoffensive as possible was a necessary tactic in a hostile world. An "I'll-Say-It-About-Myself-Before-You-Do" attitude represents a defense mechanism strengthened by years of persecution, powerlessness, and paranoia. Third, Jewish humor has been a crucial part of Jewish writing from Sholem Aleichem, to I. B. Singer, to Philip Roth. An expression both of self-love and self-hatred, such humor in early films springs directly from a vaudeville ethos where ethnic stereotypes like the drunken Irishman and the dumb Swede were commonplaces that raised few eyebrows and even fewer consciousnesses. Finally, even though the comic images of Jews presented in silent films were often created, acted, and fostered by Jews themselves, the interpretation of such urges as hostile, demeaning outlets for latent anti-Semitic feelings cannot be totally dismissed.

Silent comedy was a genre of continuing characters—from Chaplin's tramp to Ben, the Mack Sennett mutt—and Jews had their share of comedy series. In addition to "The Cohens and The Kellys" series with Charlie Murphy and George Sidney (1926, 1928, 1929, 1930, 1932 1933), there were six 1914 "Izzy" films with Max Davidson (*How Izzy Stuck to His Post, How Izzy Was Saved, Izzy and His Rival, Izzy's Night Out, Izzy and the Diamond, Izzy the Detective*), five 1913 "Mike and Jake" films with Max Asher and Harry MacCoy (*Mike and Jake as Heroes, Mike and Jake as Pugilists, Mike and Jake in Mexico, Mike and Jake in Society, Mike and Jake in the Wild West*), and three Potash and Perlmutter films with Alexander Carr and George Sidney (*Potash and Perlmutter,* 1923; *Partners Again,* 1923; *In Hollywood with Potash and Perlmutter,* 1924). This last series predated the highly successful "Cohens and Kellys" series but focused on two Jews—Abe Potash and Morris Perlmutter—so no inter-ethnic rivalry existed.

Most of the films in this category feature gullible, silly Jews as butts of the comic action, and some cross over the thin line between robust humor and racism. For example, even the less racially sensitive reviewers of the silent age attacked *A Bad Day for Levinsky* (1909) for the "malicious feelings expressed in the fun that one cannot help but believe holds up a certain people to scorn." *Motion Picture World* barely restrained its anger at *Oh, Sammy* (1913), calling it "a farce of grotesque Jewish noses." Several other films can also be interpreted as poking less than comfortable fun at commonly accepted Jewish stereotypes, condoning and ultimately perpetuating unflattering portraits and negative character traits: cowardliness (*Fighting Is No Business,* 1914; *A Stage Door Flirtation,* 1914); foreign accents and the immigrants' inability to communicate (*Cohen on the Telephone,* 1929 talkie); deceitfulness (*The Fable of How Weisenstein Did Not Lose Out to Buttinsky,* 1916); exaggerated physical expressiveness and unethical business practices (*Cohen Collects a Debt,* 1912; *Levi's Luck,* 1914; *Toplitsky and Company,* 1913; *A Tailor Made Man,* 1922).

Though most of these early films do, indeed, show Jews as buffoons, many seem innocent and almost gentle rather than nasty, vicious, or malicious. For example, the films showing various Jewish families at play (*Cohen's Dream of Coney Island,* 1909; *Levi and Family at Coney Island,* 1910; *Cohen at Coney Island,* 1909; *Levitsky Sees the Parade,* 1909) poke gentle fun by pitting bewildered immigrants against their alien surroundings. In *Jewish Prudence* (1927), a film that treats family matters with humorous irony, a father (Max Davidson) strives to provide for his two worthless sons and pretty daughter. He refuses to allow the girl to marry a struggling lawyer until the latter wins his first case—which turns out to be a damage suit against the father and one of his sons. On the way home from the courtroom, the frustrated parent's car is struck by a truck driven by his own son, a boy he has set up in the trucking business. Here, the Jewishness is almost incidental as the age-old battle between generations receives a tender blow through the humorous aggravation created by a father who causes his own problems.

Though clearly depicted as buffoons in many of the silent comedies, the Jewish characters almost inevitably rise above their circumstances to achieve a kind of ultimate moral victory. Even in *The Airship* (1908), a film critic Josh Kanin labels inherently anti-Semitic because the Jew gets pelted with vegetables, the clownish Jewish pawnbroker emerges triumphantly (from a whale's belly no less) and dances a sailor's hornpipe to celebrate his liberation. The comedy in these films usually springs from the strangeness of Jewish life. What the moviegoer finds strange, he finds funny. The films function as kind of a Pete Smith travelogue to a foreign land, but before the last frame the initially strange Jewish figure has usually exhibited traits common enough to make him seem as human, and as American, as the audience watching his antics. Whether this final feeling remains sufficiently strong to undercut the offensive and perhaps unconscious elements of racial prejudice can best be answered by each individual. But it is clear that most comic films exploit the humor present in Jewish stereotypes without vilifying the Jew under the guise of comic invention. The films speak more clearly about attitudes toward ethnic humor during the silent era than they do about a concentrated, conscious effort to isolate one group and to hold its peculiarities up to ridicule and scorn.

Most commentators who write about Jewish silent films bemoan the fact that they present superficial portraits of Jews, and never confront actual social conditions facing the immigrants. To support this contention, writers inevitably point out that no silent films deal with the issue of American anti-Semitism. This is not strictly the case. At least two films, *The Woman He Loved* (1927) and *Welcome Stranger* (1924), present Jewish characters initially rejected by other Americans simply because they are Jewish; in both films the

Jews are eventually accepted after demonstrating their worth. However, a far greater number of silent films deal with this touchy issue set not in America but safely within foreign lands. Most often Russia is the locale, so the plight of the Russian Jews becomes a fairly prominent theme in the silent films of the twenties.

This situation suggests at least two possible interpretations. First, it might be argued that the early filmmakers had a naïve, overly optimistic vision of America that they juxtaposed with a silly, caricatured view of other countries. The films do seem part of an orchestrated effort by Jews in the film industry to convince Jewish newcomers to America that no matter how bad conditions were here, things were measurably worse in other countries. Here were poverty and crowded slums; there were harsh persecutions and death. The other, more likely reason is that though these early filmmakers remained acutely aware of American anti-Semitism and the many problems of immigrants—having themselves suffered both first-hand—they could not confront his situation directly, given the financial restrictions and artistic limitations of their medium. By and large, "social issue" films did not make an appearance until the thirties, and films dealing directly with anti-Semitism did not appear until the forties. The silent filmmakers commented on social problems in an oblique manner, much the way writers and directors of the fifties placed issues of racism and McCarthyism in the guise of Westerns and science-fiction films. The tactic of using another country, a fictive locale, or a historical setting to discuss present conditions in one's homeland is an ancient and respected literary device, so these filmmakers approached American anti-Semitism by removing it to the realm of "once upon a time, in a land far away..."

Basically, then, the films in this category revolve around anti-Semitism, interweaving in various degrees three other prominent subthemes: political activism, the breakdown of the family, and love entanglements. A ready-made subject, of course, was the infamous Mendel Beiliss case. A few films deal with it historically (*The Black 107,* 1913; *Accused by Darkest Russia,* 1913) and a few fictionally (*Prejudice,* 1922). Almost all the films in this category end with the main characters either going away or planning to leave for America. The portrayal of America as a land of democracy where the highest official takes time for the commonest of men reaches an apex with *In the Czar's Name* (1910), when a newly arrived immigrant Russian couple is actually received by President Taft.

But the most interesting film in this category, though one that fits there somewhat uncomfortably because much of its plot takes place in America, is *Vengeance of the Oppressed* (1916), a tale tracing the path of hatred and revenge from Russia to America. After a vicious pogrom instigated by Sergius Kosloff (George Routh), Aaron Markowitz (Edward Sloman) finds both his wife and mother dead. He vows revenge, rescues his daughter, Ruth, and leaves for America. Twenty years later, after becoming a wealthy international financier, Aaron learns that the Russian attaché sent to negotiate a loan with him is none other than the hated Kosloff. A series of long and complicated machinations culminate when Aaron convinces Russian secret agents that Kosloff is a spy. The Russian is killed, and Aaron dies after raising his hands to God in a prayer of thanks that his people have been avenged.

The film stresses the cruel and arbitrary violence against the Russian Jews, as well as the roles of fate and justice in the Jew's plan to gain vengeance. Again, America represents the land of opportunity in which oppressed people from foreign lands can by hard work eventually rise to positions of success and power. Aaron's uninterrupted bitterness, however, is not obliterated by his social and economic success. In fact, he goes through superhuman efforts to live and is willing to barter his daughter to a Gentile doctor to stay alive till his revenge is complete. His death after Kosloff's shows his revenge as an obsession that forces him to live in the past rather than the present. It is up to the next generation—Ruth (Francelia Billington) and her non-Jewish lover, Dr. Russell Parker—to erase the need for vengeance and enjoy the comforts and privileges of life in America. Once more, the younger generation looks forward to the fruits of tomorrow while the older remains trapped in the tragedies of yesterday.

Because of their emphasis on Jewish unity with all other Americans, these silent films support and nourish the cherished vision of America as a vast melting pot of ethnic groups who discard their individual cultural heritages to form one people. Critics like Ruth Perlmutter who attack Hollywood films because the "intricacies and real tensions of the Jewish experience are glossed over," or others like Randall Miller who complain such films "suggest the veneer of culture constitutes its substance…and rarely…treat the core of ethnic life," miss the entire thrust of these movies.[8] Not made as pseudo-documentaries to enlighten audiences about the beautiful ceremonies of Jewish religion or the more esoteric aspects of Jewish life, the films attempt to make Americans less nervous about Jews and Jews more conscious of themselves as Americans. To berate them for not dwelling on the "intricacies" or "core" of Jewish life is akin to chastizing Barbara Kopple's *Harlan County* (1977) for not dealing deeply enough with the particular lives of the mine owners. Such arguments are as futile as they are blind. The critic says what the film "should be" about and then attacks it for something it is not trying to accomplish.

Films serve a more complex function. As do all mass media and to some extent all art, they mirror the concerns of their age, reflecting conscious and unconscious aspects of the culture that shapes them. Early Hollywood movies about Jews document their socioeconomic conditions, aspects of their immigration experiences, and their steady move toward assimilation, a journey embodied in the lives of many studio heads. But in their fictive recountings the movies performed another, perhaps even more valuable, function. As historian Thomas Cripps notes, they became a conditioning factor to assimilation, so much that the screen Jew was transformed into an "icon of the ritual of Americanization." Every immigrant could share the triumphs and failures on the screen; he could feel the heartbreak and rejoice in the joys of the Jews because sitting in the darkness of the movie house he recognized screen versions of familiar aspects of his own experience. Thus, the adventures of the celluloid Jews became a common reference point for all immigrant Americans, much as Jewish writings in the sixties served a similar function for the alienated youths of the time.

But the lesson went both ways. As American audiences learned that Jews were more like themselves than they had ever suspected, so too, Jews learned to be more like their American neighbors. Any residual anxiety over the loss of a particular identity was lost in laugher at the outmoded ways of thinking—or soothed by promises tacitly given by the new order. More than simple-minded melodramas or ghostly flickerings of a now forgotten age, these films of the silent era are a rich legacy handed down from one generation to the next—irrefutable evidence of the American rite of passage.

The Timid Thirties

In the silent era America discovered its Jews and its national cinema; in the first decade of the sound era Jews virtually disappeared from America's movie screens. Thirties movie versions of literary works containing Jewish characters usually rob these figures of all telltale ethnic traces: names, mannerisms, issues. Most of the films retaining some Jews stagger beneath the weight of tired plots and heavy-handed caricatures. The broad comedies like *Gunboat Ginsburg* (1930) and the continuing "Cohens and Kellys" series simply mix worn-out situations with outdated stereotypes: a cinema feeding off its own worst products. Thirties creators of overblown melodramas like *Symphony of Six Million* (1932) and *The House of Rothschild* (1934) fashion one-dimensional Jewish central characters of little more than passing interest. The most praised film of the decade featuring a Jewish character, *The Life of Emile Zola* (1937), basically ignores Dreyfus's heritage, while the best anti-Nazi film of the era, *Confessions of a Nazi Spy* (1939), contains no Jews at all. Even the decade's most memorable Jewish-American films, *Street Scene* (1931) and *Counsellor-at-Law* (1933), gain their luster not because of their own artistic merits, but because they are something of an improvement over the general drabness surrounding them. The thirties, therefore, represent the lowest point in the history of Jewish-American films, a situation created by the position of Jews in American society during the decade, as well as by the movement of historical events during this period.

During the mid-twenties, a series of severe quota restrictions brought large-scale immigration to an abrupt halt. By 1927, Jews accounted for 3.6 percent of the total U.S. population—a proportion that remains relatively unchanged to this day. Because these ambitious immigrants wanted a higher social and economic position for their children, they struggled to provide their offspring with the best education possible to facilitate their rapid rise out of America's immigrant ghettos. And rise they did. By 1939, ten percent of American Jews were engaged in professions compared to only seven percent of the general population. The East-European Jews had, by the end of the thirties, transformed themselves from a working class into a predominately middle-class society, one composed mainly of white-collar workers, businessmen, and professionals.

Concomitant with their educational and economic gains was the geographical advance of the Jews of the thirties from the old Jewish ghetto neighborhoods. New York's Lower East Side contained 353,000 Jews in 1916; less than half that number remained at the end of the thirties. Along with the demise of the ghettos came the death of the old-world ways it sheltered. Yiddish plays lost their customers, and the Yiddish newspapers interested fewer and fewer readers with each passing year. Having successfully solved the basic problems of survival, the Jews of the thirties concerned themselves with improving the quality of their lives. They sought ways to succeed in a Gentile world and at the same time preserve a sense of Jewish identity.

The trickle of Jews moving from inner-city tenements to apartment houses and finally to suburban homes became a wave in the thirties and a virtual flood in the forties and fifties. The suburbs, however, remained out of reach for most Jews in the thirties, and they congregated mainly in large city, middle-class apartment houses. But their sense of community survived. The nicer streets with fancier names now became unofficially designated as "Jewish neighborhoods." There American values initially clashed with vestiges of ethnic traditions but eventually merged in a series of uneasy compromises. In 1935 an extensive survey in New York City revealed that 72 percent of the Jewish men and 78 percent of the women had not attended any services during the previous year. Yet in the same year over one-fourth of all school-age Jewish children received some type of Jewish educational instruction, usually in the afternoon congregational schools. Two-thirds to three-quarters received Jewish educational instruction at various points during their school years. Thus, an irony appears: these second generation parents believed Jewish education had little, if anything, to do with Jewish religion. In fact, many of these schools offered history rather than religion, and literature instead of liturgy. The split remains to this very day.

The conflict between Judaism and Jewishness suffered by the Jews of the thirties remains a crucial aspect of modern Jewish communities. However, by 1939 the combined congregations of Reform, Conservative, and Orthodox American synagogues accounted for only one and a half million Jews, a figure representing approximately one-fourth of the total number of Jews in America. Whether or not Jewishness and/or Judaism could withstand the siren song of American assimilation suddenly emerged as the central question for those who still called themselves Jews. To look at the films of the thirties is to understand their plight, for even within an industry dominated by Jews evidence of any racial or religious consciousness to help stem the tide of assimilation fails to emerge.

Just as America's Jews left behind their early confusion and alienation to achieve a more secure position of acceptance and confidence, so too America's films advanced from fledgling art form to a preeminent position in the culture of the thirties. In his short but insightful film history of this decade, John Baxter notes "of all the periods in the history of the cinema, none is more important to its growth and perfection as that of Hollywood in the thirties. In the decade between the Great Depression and World War II, American society suffered its most sweeping changes since the Civil War, changes mirrored and distorted by...the cinema."[9] Within these ten years, the all-pervasive studio system produced a series of movies that coalesced into what many have labeled "Hollywood's Golden Age." And of course, Jews ran the studios. From 1908 when Walter Selig moved his company to California until the present time, with the exception only of Darryl Zanuck who ran the town's "Goy Studio" (20th Century-Fox), Jews dominated the industry: Jesse Lasky, B. P. Schulberg, Adolph Zukor, Barney Balaban (Paramount); Marcus Loew, Louis Mayer, Irving Thalberg (MGM); Harry, Jack, Albert, and Sam Warner (Warner Brothers); David O. Selznick (Selznick International); Samuel Goldwyn (Goldwyn Pictures); Harry Cohn (Columbia); Carl Laemmle (Universal); William Fox (Fox Pictures).

But who were these men? Mostly, they were poor immigrants and sons of immigrants who saw the film business as a chance for quick profits. Their lowly origins varied but none had to worry about choking on a silver spoon. Louis Mayer started as a scrap metal dealer, and Samuel Goldwyn as a glove salesman. Carl Laemmle, Marcus

Loew, and Adolph Zukor all were former furriers. Harry Cohn eked out a living on New York City's Lower East Side as a pool hustler and song plugger. William Fox (Friedman) made dresses while Jesse Lasky sold newspapers on crowded city streets. Humble origins behind them, their power was almost absolute. When Frank Whitback, an MGM press agent, called his boss a "fat Jewish s.o.b." he was quickly informed that in the film business there was no such thing as a "Jewish s.o.b." These men never completely lost touch with their immigrant roots though they ruled over one of America's largest and most influential industries.

Jews turned to filmmaking in such large numbers for many reasons. Irving Howe concludes the business appealed to them because it was strictly cash, it needed a minimum of goods and apparatus, and it was so new there were few established Gentiles to trip over. Clearly these men possessed enough business sense to spot the potential in the early nickelodeons, turn them into a multi-million dollar industry, and maintain their grip on dream factories that mass-produced America's fondest illusion and wishes. Until television undercut the industry's power, Jews guided the destiny of America's largest propaganda machine. They put their stamp on the American mind in as significant a way as industrial giants like Henry Ford, John D. Rockefeller, and Andrew Carnegie, influencing not only the millions at home but countless more whose only view of America was cranked out by the studios of these ill-educated but street-wise immigrants. The vision of America they shared was of a country where opportunities and tolerance expanded limitlessly. It promised anyone, even newcomers, a chance to achieve the American dream. Their own lives demonstrated the possibilities for success attainable here. They had made the dream flesh.

How ironic, therefore, that a decade whose films caught the conscience of the country at this crucial juncture in its collective history almost totally ignored one of its most prominent minorities and the ethnicity of its industry's leaders. A story about Harry Cohn illustrates the prevailing attitude about Jewish actors and characters among Jewish moguls in the thirties. Director Richard Quine wanted to use a specific actor for a certain part in

his film. "He looks too Jewish," barked the irritated Cohn, adding, "Around this studio the only Jews we put into pictures play Indians." Louis Mayer obviously shared Cohn's cruder sentiments when he told a dejected Danny Kaye, "I would put you under contract right now but you look too Jewish. Have some surgery to straighten out your nose and then we'll talk." Once when an ailing studio chieftain checked into a hospital, he was questioned about his heritage. "American," he quickly responded, an answer which prompted a startled volunteer to ask, "But aren't you Jewish?" "Oh, yes," he added. "That, too."

"That, too" aptly sums up the attitude of Jews on and off the screen in the thirties. The attempt at almost total assimilation by the powerful men who ran the studios behind the cameras reflected itself in a de-Semiticizing of the action that took place in front of the lenses. Jewish character actors found little if any work during this period, and Jewish leads changed their names to de-emphasize their heritage: Julius Garfinkle (John Garfield), Emmanuel Goldberg (Edward G. Robinson), Leo Jacobi (Lee J. Cobb), Muni Winsenfreund (Paul Muni), Melvyn Hesselberg (Melvyn Douglas), Marion Levy (Paulette Goddard). Michael Blankfort, a screen writer during this era, says of the moguls who demanded this lessening of ethnic identification:

> They were accidental Jews, terribly frightened Jews, who rejected their background to become super-Americans. They were interested in power and profit. They would hardly ever touch a story with a Jewish character, and if they did, they usually cast a gentile for the part.[10]

Patronized and mocked though they may have been, screen Jews of the twenties at least existed; in the thirties they nearly vanished.

In the thirties more Jewish characters conceal than reveal their identities. In fact, Hollywood film adaptations of original works featuring Jewish characters usually eliminate the ethnic baggage of such figures. For example, George S. Kaufman's character Lehman in *The Butter and Egg Man* keeps his name when the play becomes a film in 1928, but when remade as *Dance, Charlie, Dance* in 1937, Lehman somehow becomes Morgan and

Colonel Ginsburg (George Sidney) tests out his new formula for artificial rubber in HIGH PRESSURE (1932).

when it emerges once more in 1940 as *An Angel from Texas* he becomes Allen. *The Front Page* (1931) features a governor's assistant called Irving Pincus; in its reincarnation as *His Girl Friday* (1940) Pincus is reborn as Joe Pettibone. Playwright Clifford Odets's *Golden Boy* (1937) has fight promoter Roxie Gottlieb who in the 1939 film loses his identity and is renamed Roxie Lewis. When John Howard Lawson's *Success Story* (1930).

a play with characters called Ginsburg and Glassman, gets filmed as *Success at Any Price* (1934), the characters dissolve into the ethnically neutral Martin and Griswold and the author's emphasis on the Jewish ghetto boy who "makes it" but sacrifices his heritage disappears. Irwin Shaw's drama *The Gentle People* (1939) appears in 1941 as *Out of the Fog,* his Jewish tailor, Goodman, turning into an Irish tailor, Goodwin. *Having a Wonderful Time* (1938), based on Arthur Kober's play about the Catskills, has its guests unceremoniously coverted: Stern to Shaw, Kessler to Kirkland, Aaronson to Armbruster, Rappaport to Beatty. And poor Rabbi Esdras in the 1936 adaptation of Maxwell Anderson's *Winterset* (1935) becomes just a philosophical old man. Though the tendency to eliminate as much telltale Jewishness as possible persists throughout the thirties, some Jewish figures escape and manage to survive this celluloid holocaust.

The comedies of the thirties are basically broad farces and within this area the career of veteran actor George Sidney (né Sammy Greenfield) provides a microcosm of the gradually diminishing roles available to actors who specialized in portraying Jews throughout this decade. Sidney started his career as a vaudeville and stage performer famous for his "Busy Izzy" character. His twenties performances as Abe Potash in the "Potash and Perlmutter" series and Nathan Cohen in the "Cohen and Kellys" series anointed him archetypal Hollywood screen Jew. A short, squat, balding man with frog-like eyes that seem to pop off the screen without the aid of three-D glasses, Sidney combined feverish activities, emotional gestures, and hyperactive hands to set a dubious standard for Jewish characters. Seemingly secure as the decade began, he churned out two more sequels in the continuing "Cohens and Kellys" series: *The Cohens and the Kellys in Africa* (1930) and the *Cohens and Kellys in Scotland* (1930). He and series cohort Charlie Murphy next made three other Jewish-Irish conflict films in quick succession: *Around the Corner* (1930), *Caught Cheating* (1931), and *Models and Wives* (1931). Then, by himself, Sidney starred in *The Butter and Egg Man* (1931). In 1932 Sidney completed another "Cohens and Kellys" with Murphy (*The Cohens and Kellys in Hollywood*) and had what amounted to a co-starring role with suave William Powell in *High Pressure* (1932), when he played Colonel Ginsburg, Powell's business partner in the artificial-rubber manufacturing business. In that same year, he played Mendel Marantz in Mervyn LeRoy's screen adaptation of *Mendel, Inc.,* retitled *The Heart of New York.* The last "Cohens and Kellys" feature, *The Cohens and Kellys in Trouble* (1933), proved an apt title as the once popular series ground to a merciful halt. (Jewish-Irish jokes seemed far less funny in the thirties than in the twenties, perhaps because the most highly publicized American anti-Semite of the decade was Father Coughlin, who peddled his pernicious hate campaign via the *Social Justice* magazine.)

The close of the series signaled the beginning of Sidney's rapid decline. Buried deep within the credits of *Manhattan Melodrama* (1934), a film that featured Clark Gable, William Powell, and Myrna Loy, Sidney labored away in the minor role of Papa Rosen. His part in *Diamond Jim* (1935) was so small as to be unworthy of a proper name, so the credits identified him simply as "pawnbroker." Finally in 1937, he tried to cast off his Jewish persona to play Kennedy in *Good Old Soak* with Wallace Beery, a feat akin to John Wayne playing an Indian. He couldn't. Ironically, the man who begins the decade playing Cohen ends it by playing, at least figuratively, Kelly, for Irish actors could find more work than Jewish ones. This was Sidney's last movie, and he died in 1945.

The decade's other comedies with Jewish characters prove a fairly undistinguished lot that modern reassessment can or should do little to resuscitate. Joe Smith and Charles Dale starred as two Jewish Broadway producers, the Delmans, in *Manhattan Parade* (1932). Fanny Brice made *Be Yourself* (1930), a film that did little to enhance her career. The pitiful *Gunboat Ginsburg* (1930) typifies these mundane movies. It opens with a small mustached man standing between two larger sailors as the trio sings "Sailing, Sailing." He is Jakie Ginsburg (called Ginzy) a seaman with an obvious Jewish accent and who is the almost continuous butt of his friend's jokes. The other two sailors, Swede and McGinty, drag Jakie off to Chinatown with them on shoreleave, the worried Ginzy muttering "Oy, Oy" all the way to the off-limits bar. Of course, the trio becomes embroiled in various

scrapes, the clever Ginsburg saving his friends via wit and guile. Only once does he fail them: disguised as a Chinaman, he panics and begins spouting Yiddish expressions. Later, he mournfully apologizes to his friends, saying, "I thought you was mad mitt me." No, they assure him, as they head back to the boat and presumably to further multi-ethnic adventures.

The dramatic films featuring Jews fail to generate much more interest than the comedies. A few deal with successful American Jews forced to reevaluate the price of their triumphs, but their superficial characterizations, flat visual style, and plodding story lines generally make them of little more than passing interest. *Mr. Cohen Takes a Walk* (1936)—based on a Mary Roberts Rinehart story of the same title—deals with Jake Cohen, the head of a giant London department store, whose rise from peddler to executive creates personal and family problems. Half-hearted Irish-Jewish humor crops up again in *No Greater Love* (1932) when Sidney Cohen (Alexander Carr), a cantankerous old delicatessen owner who croons Hebrew ballads, adopts crippled little Mildred Flannigan (Betty Jane Graham) after her mother dies. Eventually, Cohen sells his store to pay for an operation to restore Mildred's legs. Motivated by love, not medicine, Mildred finally does walk again, and Sidney goes on to run a bigger and better deli.

Throughout the decade, the Hollywood studios found themselves trapped in a cruel financial dilemma regarding how to depict the Nazis and their allies. How could they deal with the momentous events taking place in Europe and still remain sufficiently apolitical so as not to jeopardize their vast foreign markets? The Jewish studios heads also worried lest any mention of Nazi anti-Semitism might be construed as covert propaganda designed to edge America into the war to save their fellow Jews. The newsreels in particular found it almost impossible to report objectively on activities overseas.

Eventually, the Fascists and the Nazis solved Hollywood's problem. As early as 1936, officials of the Third Reich barred *Country Doctor,* an innocuous film about the Dionne babies, from being shown in Germany because it starred Jean Hersholt, an actor who had previously played several Jewish roles. That same year, the films of

Mendal Marantz (George Sidney) basks in the love of his family and friends in THE HEART OF NEW YORK *(1932).*

Johnny Weissmuller (an American of German extraction), Francis Lederer (a Czech), and George Arliss (known for his "Jewish" roles) were also banned. Prophets had a hard time predicting what would offend whom. For example, Mussolini outlawed *The Charge of the Light Brigade* (1936), *The Lives of a Bengal Lancer* (1935), *Lloyds of London* (1936), and *Clive of India* (1935) because they presented positive portraits of Englishmen.

Since they knew films with Jewish characters would prove difficult to market overseas, even if those characters lived in fictive locales and existed centuries ago, the Hollywood chieftains hedged their bets by creating as many nationless, raceless, and religionless characters as possible. Like the hard-headed businessmen they were, studio heads usually placed their pocketbooks above their principles or even their personal convictions. This fact, at least in part, accounts for the lack of screen Jews in the thirties, since the inclusion of even minor Jewish characters might well eliminate a film from distribution in the lucrative markets abroad. In 1939 Mussolini banned most American films, partially because Hollywood snubbed his son, Vittorio, when he was sent there to learn film-production techniques. The next year the Third Reich followed suit. Charging that the industry "stands under predominantly Jewish influence," it excluded all American films from Germany and the countries it occupied. When it did so, much of Hollywood's overseas market crumbled.

Even though Hollywood attempted to tread lightly on German issues, one of the more interesting and surprisingly early films to concentrate on the Nazi menace is photographer Cornelius Vanderbilt, Jr.'s *Hitler's Reign of Terror* (1934). The film was neither produced nor distributed by a major studio; Jewel Productions handled both functions. Today the film might be termed docu-drama, for Vanderbilt and director Michael Mindlin splice together actual newsreel footage with several staged scenes of personal interviews and incidents Vanderbilt witnessed during his tour of Austria and Germany. Meetings with the Crown Prince, between Prince Louis Ferdinand and Vanderbilt, and between the Prince, the ex-Kaiser, and Vanderbilt are all reenacted. Hitler himself is even impersonated by an actor for a few brief moments in the film. Juxtaposed with these staged sequences are actual interviews and speeches. Helen Keller, whose books are burned by the Nazis earlier in the film, talks with Vanderbilt; excerpts from speeches by Matthew Wohl (American Federation of Labor leader), Dr. John Haynes Holmes (Community Church leader), Michael Williams (editor of *Commonweal*), Raymond Moley (Undersecretary of State), and Samuel Dickstein (Congressman) are also included in the film.

Vanderbilt and Mindlin's film is the lone Hollywood indictment of the Nazi's war on the Jews in the thirties. Early in the film, they depict an eerie torchlight parade through the Berlin streets, complete with bookburning ceremony in which Nazis destroy works by Jews and others considered enemies of the state. Later, some scenes of Nazi violence against Jews and of Jews suffering in concentration camps show the dark side of Hitler's regime. Though these sequences represent just part of a whole panorama of negative images in this obviously propagandistic work, they remain an isolated attempt to depict some of the specific anti-Semitic horrors of Hitler's Third Reich.

Mention should also be made of two other attempts to present the plight of Jews under Hitler. *Professor Mamlock* (1938), a Russian import, deals with this subject from a peculiar perspective. As a non-American product, the film falls outside the concerns of this book, but it did get some play in some American theaters. In fact, *The New York Times* review complains of the lack of such subjects in our own cinema: "The film says nothing new about Nazi persecution of Jews in Germany, but that it says anything at all should be news to American filmgoers." Basically, the film follows the plight of a German-Jewish medical scientist, cruelly persecuted despite his heroic war record. *Jude* is scribbled across his surgeon's robe, and he is machinegunned to death while still proclaiming his faith in Germany. Unfortunately, the film seems more interested in casting the Communist Party as the potential savior of both Germany and the Jews than it is in depicting the plight of oppressed people. An American attempt at a similar story never made it to the screen. *Personal History*, a script about a Jewish doctor and his flight from the Nazis, was written by John Howard Lawson and assigned to director William Dieterle. Just as it was about to go into production, its sets already built and its actors hired, producer Walter Wanger called the project off. "I'm told I'll never get another penny [from the banks] if this anti-Nazi film goes into production," he explained.

The uncertainty of markets abroad contributed to the evaporation of Jews from American movie screens, but it was not the only cause. At home, the market for films about Jews seemed equally small. Thirties studio heads believed films with Jewish characters in central roles were too specialized, too exotic, for their now largely Gentile audiences. After all, films no longer played predominantly in large city nickelodeons catering to immigrant and lower-class audiences. Movies had evolved into big business, national and international products produced by gigantic assembly lines and shipped all over the world. They needed to show a profit to support the system that created them. The moguls were no longer fly-by-night operators; they were captains of industry who stood alongside the Fords, Rockefellers and Du Ponts. So what was once acceptable became unprofitable. A story set in the ghettos of New York City might fail to draw audiences in small-town America. What could be applauded and laughed about in Chicago might receive blank stares in Des Moines. The more general the topic the broader its appeal and the less likely it would be to engender controversy. Very soon, of course, Hollywood would have available a topic common to most of the countries on earth: World War II.

These historical and financial considerations are important in accounting for the banishment of Jews from American films in the thirties, but no more so than the personal motivations of the studio moguls themselves. Like many successful Jews, the studio heads had no desire to draw attention to their "otherness." The "that, too" attitude clearly dominated their thinking. As various biographies and autobiographies aptly demonstrate, the studio bosses wanted to keep whatever ethnic heritage they preserved behind, not in front of, their cameras. They were no longer simply Jews; now they were Americans. They wanted no celluloid reminders of their lean days on the New York City streets, their hunger in the little towns of Eastern Europe like Ricse (Hungary) and Krashmashilitz (Poland), or their pain in the ghettos of Minsk and Kiev. Hobnobbing with royalty and entertaining America's most powerful men, they lived in palatial estates, ate in the fanciest restaurants, and joined the most exclusive clubs. In their youth their wildest fantasies could not have envisioned such a life, and now they meant to enjoy it. Though never fully eliminating all the vestiges of their immigrant boyhoods, they plunged into the American mainstream. Many divorced their old-world wives and married Gentile beauties; others sent their children to the finest schools money could pay for. Though they all supported Jewish charities generously, anonymity was the price of their large private donations.

The Fashionable Forties

During the thirties, most Hollywood film producers attempted to ignore events in Europe as much as possible, lest they be accused of edging America into the war. Once war was declared, however, Hollywood plunged headlong into the propaganda business, much to the delight of the supportive federal government. Most of Hollywood's efforts during the war centered around doing what it did best—entertaining people. To this, filmmakers added the element of ideological persuasion. Films not only celebrated democratic virtues and goals for those at home and in allied countries, but they became two-hour furloughs for servicemen, powerful cinematic images depicting just what they were fighting to defend. *Movie Lot to Beachead,* an appreciative 1945 hymn to the movies by the editors of *Look* magazine, notes that at Bougainville battleshock was counteracted by a tent theater that projected movies continuously during the day and night.

What emerged from the war years was an acknowledgment of Hollywood's power and influence, forcing industry members and outsiders alike into an even greater awareness of film's impact on society. Concomitantly, the portrayal of ethnic minorities like Blacks and Jews was scrutinized with greater care. As film historian Garth Jowett notes, the Hollywood film industry demonstrated a conscious effort to bring about greater understanding between the various racial and ethnic groups in America. This new-found ethnic sensitivity influenced forties filmmakers and encouraged normally timid studio heads to risk production of several controversial "social issue" films during and following the war. The spirit of democracy occasioned by the great leveling forces at work during the war spilled over to create a Hollywood cinema even more resolutely dedicated to "Americanism" above all else. The "melting pot mentality" that was so prevalent in earlier movies with a focus on minority group members returned with a vengeance during and immediately following the war, and created a cinema of assimilation.

Like the silent films, therefore, most of the films of the forties featuring Jewish characters focus, in one way or another, on the continuing theme of assimilation, whether it be at home or in the armed forces. As such, Jews engage in more diverse dramatic situations than in the movies of previous eras, a reflection of their greater participation and

Chip Abrams (Sam Levene), part of a multi-ethnic fighting force, holds a light for his skipper (Humphrey Bogart) in ACTION IN THE NORTH ATLANTIC *(1943).*

visibility in American life. The largest group of films with Jewish figures, as one might expect, is the wartime action pictures like *Action in the North Atlantic* (1943) and *Bataan* (1943) in which Jews function as part of multi-ethnic platoons dedicated to preserving the American way of life and mirroring American racial harmony within their ranks. After America's entrance into World War II, filmmakers were obviously more willing to confront the Nazi horrors in Germany, and to make at least fleeting references to the persecution of Jews both in and out of the concentration camps, in films such as *Address Unknown* (1944) and *The Seventh Cross* (1944). A few directors—notably McCarey, Lubitsch, and Chaplin—focus on this painful situation in dark social comedies like *Once Upon a Honeymoon* (1942), *To Be or Not to Be* (1942) and *The Great Dictator* (1940), their laughter mingled with grief and pain.

On the homefront, Jews surface in various types of films. Entertainment biographies of famous Jewish entertainers like Al Jolson and composers like George Gershwin and Jerome Kern appear. If mentioned at all in these films, the subject's ethnic background is downplayed, and his Americanness, not his Jewishness, is emphasized. The Jews' integration into Gentile society through marriage, a popular topic in earlier films, continues into the forties via remakes of two past hymns to assimilation: *Humoresque* (1947) and *Abie's Irish Rose* (1946). In most films set in America, the Jews who appear are rarely different from the film's Gentiles. Assimilation, not individuality, becomes the thrust of the forties films featuring Jewish characters. This is particularly true of those films made during the war. So a film like *Body and Soul* (1947) which features a Jewish prizefighter almost totally ignores the character's Jewishness, preferring instead to concentrate on how he makes it in America.

Once the war ends and the soldiers return home, the American cinema enters a relatively short period when problem pictures dominate the screen. Many of these contain Jewish characters: *Pride of the Marines* (1945), *The Search* (1947), and *The Red Menace* (1949). In addition, American filmmakers shocked by the horrors of German atrocities at long last admit that anti-Semitism exists at home as well as in foreign countries. In *Crossfire* (1947) and *Gentleman's Agreement* (1947), American moviegoers receive a view of their own country's prejudice against Jews. Yet none of these films manages to delve very deeply into the problems they seek to illuminate. Instead, they offer simplistic Hollywood clichés as answers to the very complex issues they present.

In the thirties, the majority of America's Jews maintained cultural rather than religious ties to their heritage. Embarrassed by the old-world ways of their parents and intoxicated with the new freedoms of American society, they embraced its democratic values and shed their religious prohibitions. In the forties, however, many American Jews returned to the belief that Jewishness must contain some component of Judaism. This shift from Jewishness to Judaism is for the most part directly or indirectly related to the two most important events in modern Jewish history: Hitler's massacre of six million Jews and the founding of the modern state of Israel. Though each profoundly influenced the Jews of the forties—and continues to exert powerful pressure on today's Jewish-American community—the decade's moviemakers almost totally ignored both events. For our purposes, however, it is important to note that Hitler's Holocaust and the formation of Israel spurred previously uninvolved American Jews into some aspect of "Jewish action," ranging from involvement in Jewish charities to the support and construction of new synagogues.

Just as the Jews of the thirties moved out of the immigrant tenements to settle into middle-class apartment houses, so the Jews of the forties and fifties left those apartment buildings and moved to the suburbs. Their exodus to the promised land of split-level houses and lawn sprinklers increased their need for what sociologist Nathan Glazer labels "respectability." The almost totally Jewish neighborhoods these suburban Jews abandoned allowed them constant contact with things Jewish, thus lessening their need to participate in any organized religious community. Such urban areas contained vast numbers of Jews who rarely, if ever, attended services, or, for that matter, even felt compelled to join and support a synagogue. However, once Jews left neighborhoods in which

Asst. Crew Chief Weinberg (George Tobias, right) talks with John Garfield and Harry Carey in AIR FORCE *(1943).*

they made up from seventy-five to ninety percent of the population and migrated to the largely Gentile suburbs, they became more self-conscious about religion—both their own and that of their new Christian neighbors. Whereas "respectability" in the thirties meant having few or no religious ties whatsoever, in the forties and fifties it meant supporting some sort of religious causes or institutions, perhaps even joining a synagogue. Most paid at least token attention to religion, in some cases for their neighbors' benefit as much as for their own.

Like the rest of American society, the film industry of the forties was affected by an influx of highly talented immigrants. During the thirties and forties, artists like William Dieterle, Conrad Veidt (who went into exile with his Jewish wife), Billy Wilder, Lilli Palmer, Fritz Lang, and Otto Preminger all made films that enriched Hollywood. Partly because of these European immigrants, Hollywood was accused of interventionism, of edging the United States into what a substantial isolationist element labeled "Europe's War." For example, Senator Gerald P. Nye of North Dakota informed a startled radio audience on August 1, 1941, that the Hollywood studios had created films specifically designed to "rouse us to a state of war hysteria" and had inoculated America "with the virus of war." Citing the moguls by name, Nye contended that "…in this great era of world upset, when national and racial emotions run riot and reason is pushed from her throne, this mighty engine of propaganda is in the hands of men who are naturally susceptible to these emotions."

In response to the industry's charges of anti-Semitism following his speech, Nye proclaimed that "If anti-Semitism exists in America, the Jews have themselves to blame." Nye's speech caused tremors in the Hollywood community, especially among its nervous Jewish leadership, but a larger eruption occurred the next month. On September 11, 1941, America's foremost hero, Charles A. Lindbergh, charged that "the three most important groups that have been pressing this country toward war are the British, the Jewish, and the Roosevelt administration." Continuing his attack, Lindbergh singled out the Jews "as the most dangerous [because] of their large ownership and

influence in our motion pictures, our press, our radio, and our government."

Lindbergh's speech gave legitimacy to super-patriots who took it upon themselves to challenge the loyalty of the Jewish-American community: was that loyalty to the country, or to fellow Jews overseas? Jews involved in the mass media, in particular the studio heads, came under intense scrutiny from both the isolationists and the interventionists. Their movies were examined for tell-tale traces of propaganda and/or covert political sentiments. Therefore, the already nervous moguls became even more fearful of any projects that smacked, however slightly, of a message. Subsequent events proved their fears justified. A bill written by Senators Nye and Bennett C. Clark (of Missouri) charged that the film industry had been "extensively used for propaganda designed to influence the public mind in the direction of participation in the European War." In September 1941, the Senate Interstate Commerce Committee, chaired by Nye, called a hearing at which studio heads were "asked" to respond to such accusations.

To defend themselves, the moguls hired ex presidential candidate Wendell Willkie, who stated their case articulately and forcefully. Initially, he attacked the legality of the investigation, claiming that like other forms of information protected by constitutional guarantees, the movies should be free from prior censorship. He further noted that movie attendance was a voluntary act, and that the intention of the filmmakers was to make a profit, not a statement. Many of the movies criticized, Willkie said, were simply adaptations from literary sources and already in widespread circulation. The hearings ran from September 9 to September 26, 1941, after which they were halted by more pressing business. On December 8, 1941, the day after Pearl Harbor was attacked, they were permanently abandoned.

Reflecting on the late thirties and early forties with the advantage of hindsight, it now seems that the major question should have been why Hollywood did so little to alert the American people to the nature of the Fascist menace. Its films were clearly slanted to favor the allies—particularly such movies as *A Yank in the R.A.F.* (1941)—and several like *Submarine Patrol* (1938) and *Duke of West*

Job Skeffington (Claude Rains) confronts his self-centered wife (Bette Davis) in MR. SKEFFINGTON *(1944).*

Point (1938) were actually made with government cooperation. But few portrayed the Nazis in an overtly negative way. *Confessions of a Nazi Spy* (1939) and *The Mortal Storm* (1940) were the most forceful exceptions to this rule.

By the end of the war, no one seriously doubted that Hollywood had made a crucial contribution to the total war effort. Its stature was so great that it was considered the greatest educational tool of all time, one destined to alter the face of American society. "In every country liberated by Allied arms," proclaimed *Look* Magazine, "the first civilian demand was for food, the second was usually for American movies."[11] That this once scorned stepchild of American culture, an industry to which Jews had made major contributions, had evolved into such a universally acknowledged benefactor could not help but add to the stature of the entire Jewish-American community. Yet the patriotic glow in which the filmmakers and their industry basked proved short-lived. By 1947 the House Committee

on Un-American Activities (HUAC) had already begun its Communist witch hunt in the industry, an event which many came to see as inspired by anti-Semitic sentiments.

During the war years, it was assimilation, not the need to expose anti-Semitism, that dominated the thinking of the Hollywood community. American assimilation at its best appears most dramatically in the war films of that time, movies that emphasize the country's united racial front against a common enemy and show fighting units as an idealized microcosm of the entire American society. A simple roll call demonstrates Hollywood's conscious efforts to democratize celluloid warfare. The airmen in George Cukor's *Winged Victory* (1944) are Davis, Miller, Ross, Scarlono, and O'Brien, and the Marines in Allan Dwan's *Sands of Iwo Jima* (1949) are Stryker, Thomas, Ragazzi, Hellenpolis, Flynn, Choynski, McHugh, Hayes, and Stein. Tay Garnett's *Bataan* (1943) features soldiers names Dane, Ramirez, Matowski, Todd, and Feingold; Howard Hawks's *Air Force* (1943), Quincannon, Callahan, Winocki, McMartin, Peterson, and Weinberg; and Raoul Walsh's *Objective Burma* (1945) Nelson, Gordon, Miggleori, Hennessey, Nugulesco, Brophy, Higgins, Chettu, and Jacobs. One of the more popular songs of the day, inspired by movies, was titled "When Those Little Yellow Bellies Meet the Cohens and the Kellys."

In his study of war films from 1930 to 1970, Russell Shain concludes that the American war heroes of 1939 to 1947 usually shared two important similarities: 1) they were often civilians or civilians turned soldier rather than professional warriors; and 2) they felt an acute sense of responsibility for their fellow man and their country. Yet it is important to realize that such civilian patriotism and social responsibility usually evolved only during the course of the movie. Reluctant heroes became conscious of their duty; they were not born with such knowledge. As Shain points out, "The conversion caused the hero to relinquish his individualistic selfishness and to assume the role of brother's keeper regardless of nationality." Such films served as symbolic reinforcements of American foreign policy, as well as dramatic recruitment inducements. The scruffy band of ethnically separate individuals who learn to cast aside their particular prejudices and join together for the good of the country became part of America's self-generated mythology, and in this way, films presented dedicated community action triumphing over individual concerns.

Wartime action pictures showed an ethnically harmonious mix of Blacks, Jews, Irishmen, Italians, Poles, and WASPs, with the occasional Latin American. Though a few German-Americans do appear, no Asian-Americans are included in such fighting groups until *Go For Broke* in 1951. In most of these films, the various soldiers, including the Jew, have no deep ties to their ethnic culture or religion. Once again, ethnicity is superficially defined almost entirely by food preferences, attitudes, and gestures. Religious convictions as such play no part in the portraits of Jewish soldiers. Everyone in the group is seen as basically alike and with similar goals.

In the forties, Jewish survival was manifested as the need for a Jewish homeland. Toward this end, American Jews increased their pressure to make Palestine, then under British rule, the free state of Israel, under Jewish rule. Their urgings, of course, ultimately succeeded, due in part to the world's residual guilt over the fate of six million concentration camp victims. Israel became primarily a symbol rather than a homeland for Diaspora Jews. Many who had felt humiliated by the revelations of Jewish passivity in the face of Nazi atrocities gloried in the newfound image of the Jew as valiant warrior. The military might of Israel pleased even those Jewish-Americans who normally supported cuts in defense budget and nonviolent, liberal causes. Though thousands of Jews fought and died in World War II and other conflicts, it took Israel to prove that Jews could be warriors as well as scholars. For many American Jews, the litmus test of all foreign policy could be summed up in one sentence: How will it affect Israel?

Whatever else it may have done, the creation of Israel also put to rest at least one lingering stereotype: the Jew without a country. The mere fact of its existence somewhat eased the nagging insecurity created by the Holocaust and the general indifference of the Christian world to that event. To Jews, it meant there was at least one place in the world where they could not be persecuted simply because of their religion. Even for those who were completely assimilated into American life and who had little desire to emigrate, Israel provided psychological comfort. American Jews, however, never yearned for Israel with the longing so evident in the writings of other minority group authors, for they had no parents who spoke nostalgically about it as the Old Country. Many had never been to Israel and saw little need to visit. They appreciated the new state from afar as the ultimate safety valve. Short of total annihilation, they reasoned, all Jews finally had a place to which they might go. Perched on his precarious tightrope, the Jew took some comfort in knowing that at least now he had a net to catch him should he eventually tumble.

While some screen Jews fought battles against America's enemies, others suffered the cruel persecution of Hitler's policies in Germany and the countries it occupied. Before the United States entered World War II, *Escape* (1940) dealt with the situation. Director Mervyn LeRoy's faithful adaptation of Ethel Vance's best-selling novel received praise from *The New York Times* as "the most dramatic and hair-raising picture yet made on the sinister subject of persecution in a totalitarian land." The review played down *Escape's* propagandistic elements by calling it a picture "which tells a documented story." Today the film seems hardly controversial. In fact, its locale is never even specified as Germany, though the filmmakers assumed audiences would perceive it as such. The story revolves around a young German-American's (Robert Taylor) search for his actress-mother (Nazimova, in her first talking role) who he discovers has been interned in a concentration camp for her brave anti-Nazi sentiments. With the aid of the camp's doctor (Philip Dorn) and an American-born countess (Norma Shearer), he finally smuggles her out of the camp in a coffin. Though not specifically dealing with Jews, *Escape's* understated, bleak, and low-key lit scenes of a concentration camp at least provide some early recognition of their existence.

At home, the several biographies of Jewish entertainers made during this decade make up a

A non-Jewish version of HUMORESQUE (1947), starring John Garfield, Oscar Levant, and Joan Crawford.

fairly undistinguished group of films, all appearing during or after 1945. Director Irving Cummings's *The Dolly Sisters* (1945) featured S. Z. Sakall as their Jewish agent, Uncle Latsie, and he was used mainly for comic relief. The life stories of two famous Jewish composers also make their way to the screen in the forties: George Gershwin, *Rhap-sody in Blue* (1945) and Jerome Kern, *Till the Clouds Roll By* (1947). The first hardly mentioned the composer's ethnic background, and the second never mentions it at all. Actor Larry Parks, black-listed in the 1950s after admitting to his past affiliation with the Communist Party, shot briefly to fame in two films about Al Jolson: *The Jolson Story* (1946) and *Jolson Sings Again* (1949). Both films attempt to explain Jolson's life through a father-son conflict similar to that in *The Jazz Singer.*

All these films treated Judaism, if at all, only as a minor aspect of their subjects' lives. Perhaps this was actually the case of Jolson, Gershwin, and Kern; perhaps not. All that remains are these celluloid shrines to their greatness, a series of silly little parables of success that totally fail to capture the complexity of their subjects. Intent on blurring the elements that separated one nationality from another and one religion from the next, Hollywood charged ahead with its assimilation ethos of universal brotherhood, nondenominational faith in God, and ethnic invisibility. The homefront simply supported the battlefield.

The continuing emphasis on total assimilation is similarly a part of other homefront films. Jews remain practically invisible beneath their Americanized exteriors. In *Men of Boys Town* (1941), for example, Lee J. Cobb plays Dave Morris, a Jewish philanthropist, and director Norman Taurog once more recycles the old Irishman (Spencer Tracy as Father Flanagan) and Jew cooperation tale. *Margin for Error* (1943), an adaptation of Clare Boothe's play, stars Milton Berle as Joe Finklestein, a Jewish New York City cop assigned to protect a brutish German consul (Otto Preminger). Claude Rains plays a long-suffering Jewish financier married to a vain, petty, society girl. Though he has the title role in *Mr. Skeffington* (1945), Rains is lost within this Bette Davis vehicle. In the first and last of these three films, the character's Jewishness is incidental to the plot and to his personality. But in *Margin for Error*, Preminger manages to at least develop some comic tension at the expense of the Jew trapped between his professional responsibilities and his personal enmity. A Viennese Jew who barely got his family out of Europe ahead of Hitler's advancing army, Preminger's overdone performance as the despicable German consul started his career as "the man you love to hate" and opened the door for future Hollywood successes.

The three remaining homefront films simply recycle hackneyed plots. Two are remakes of previous hits: *Abie's Irish Rose* (1946) and *Humoresque* (1947). A. Edward Sutherland's production of Anne Nichols's play retells the story of Rosemary Murphy (Joanne Dru) and Abie Levy (Richard Norris), this time incorporating a wartime setting—they meet in a London hotel. Ultimately, they are married by a

Solomon Levy (Michael Chekhov) and Patrick Murphy (J.M. Kerrigan) play with their grandchildren in ABIE'S IRISH ROSE *(1946).*

priest, a rabbi, and an army chaplain who warns them not to "let outside forces touch their love." The priest and the rabbi readily accept the situation, though Solomon Levy (Michael Chekhov) and Patrick Murphy (J. M. Kerrigan) are not so forgiving. The film alternately mixes Irish and Jewish conventions: Rosie and Abie sing Irish songs to their babies, they have a Christmas tree in their apartment, she cooks ham as he places a mezuzah on the door, Murphy picks on Levy's accent, Abie gets Rosie a cross so she can pray for their baby when he swallows a pin. In the final scenes a good-natured cop sings the babies both Irish and Yiddish nursery songs, and the once cold-hearted patriarchs are warmly reconciled to the match. *Humoresque* once again pictorializes the rags-to-riches fable of a Lower East Side boy's rise to musical fame, this time, however, eliminating any of the lingering Jewish elements left over from the original film. Even the central character's name is changed, from Leon Kantor to Paul Boray, to de-emphasize his Jewishness.

The United States emerged from the war as the most powerful country in the world. However, the aftermath of Germany's mass destruction presented difficult problems for the victors as well as the vanquished. There was uncertainty about how to handle our once-arrogant enemy now that the overt hostiles were over. The standard codes of behavior for battlefield combatants proved ineffective for judging those who had herded people into cattlecars and sent them to their deaths, for those who had shot civilians, and for those who had gassed helpless inmates in the concentration camps. The question of how many should assume responsibility for the crimes of the Third Reich has not been fully answered to this day.

Sealed Verdict (1948) was Hollywood's first attempt to confront this complex issue of guilt and innocence, one that inevitably involved Germany's treatment of Jews. Based on the novel by noted war correspondent Lionel Shapiro, director Lewis Allen's *Sealed Verdict* traces the path of American prosecutor Major Robert Lawson's (Ray Milland) efforts to determine the guilt of General Otto Steigmann (John Hoyt), known as the "Mass Murderer of Leemach." Taunted by a witness who accuses him of basing his case on false testimony, Lawson seeks positive proof from the underground and finally traps the unrepentant Steigmann into a confession.

Several Jewish characters appear in *Sealed Verdict*. The Hocklands (James Bell and Elizabeth Risdon), a kindly couple, take care of the General's mother, nursing the sick old woman even though they are aware of her fanatic Nazism and her son's crimes. Jacob Meyersohn (Ludwig Donath) is a death camp survivor, a physically damaged and emotionally scarred man who retreats to the pre-war past rather than confront the realities of the present. In the figures of the Hocklands and Meyersohn, Allen presents two alternatives for Jews who survived the Nazi horrors: to rise above or to be forever trapped by their experiences. Clearly, he recommends the actions of the humane Hocklands over those of the maimed Meyersohn.

That same year Montgomery Clift starred in *The Search*, Fred Zinnemann's rather remarkable and unjustly overlooked depiction of the continuing problems faced by children who somehow escaped the Holocaust. Filmed in the American zone of Germany with a semi-documentary approach, the film revolves around a nine-year-old Czech boy, Karel Malik (Ivan Jandl), separated from his mother (Jarmila Novotna) when they were both sent to a concentration camp. After the war, the boy escapes from a Red Cross ambulance and wanders through the bombed-out streets of Germany, distrusting everyone except an American soldier (Clift) who befriends him. Finally, the tireless efforts of an alert official (Aline MacMahon) reunite the boy with his mother.

Though Malik is never actually identified as a Jew, at least one other orphan is: Joel Makowsky (Leopold Borkowski). Filled with the fear of being identified as a Jew, Joel seeks refuge as a choirboy in a Catholic church, passing himself off as a Christian. Once his true identity is discovered, however, he begins to understand that a new order has taken control of his world and that he is no longer in danger of being persecuted for his religion. Our last glimpse of Joel shows a now-smiling child happily marching off for a new life in Israel with other Jewish orphans. He has resumed his identity as a Jew and, we assume, will live and work in the new Jewish homeland. Once again, he is proud to be a Jew.

Finally, of course, the entire dirty issue of American anti-Semitism belatedly reached the screen in the decade's two most controversial films, *Gentleman's Agreement* (1947) and *Crossfire* (1947). A year later, *Open Secret* (1948) treated the same material in a far inferior manner. After years of presenting a culturally harmonious America at home and at war, Hollywood suddenly discovered chinks in the national armor; the problems rather than the promises of American society became its focus. As critic Charles Higham points out, the problem picture so fashionable during the last four years of the decade dealt with not only racial prejudice, but insanity, alcoholism, juvenile delinquency, euthanasia, and political corruption.

The problem of returning G.I.s adjusting to civilian life took a much more ominous political tone in one of the decade's last films, R. G. Springsteen's *The Red Menace* (1949). Robert Rockwell stars as Bill Jones, an ex-serviceman who decides to do something about the real-estate hustlers who fleece thousands of returning veterans with phony housing project deals. Morose, and plied with drinks by a consoling Communist Party scout (William J. Lally), Jones starts to believe that Communism provides an answer, a feeling strengthened by his growing attachment to Mollie O'Flaherty (Barbara Fuller), a party sympathizer. However, he soon learns that Communism is not the answer to his problems, and by extension those of the other returning servicemen. This lesson is driven home when he witnesses the cruel death of Henry Solomon (Shepard Menken), a talented young Jewish poet. When Solomon tries to leave the Party, he is hounded into jumping to his death from the window of an office building. Once again, the Jew becomes the screen's archetypal victim, though this time at the hands of the Communists rather than the Nazis. This brutal act motivates Jones to flee. He enlists the aid of a kindly sheriff (Robert Purcell), seeks redress for his grievances through legal means, and finds peace with another party dropout (Hanne Axman).

So a decade that began with Chaplin's gentle and humanitarian pleas for tolerance and brotherhood in *The Great Dictator* ends with the treatment of American anti-Semitism in *Crossfire* and *Gentleman's Agreement*. Along the way, Hollywood left behind its sunny simplistic vision of American racial harmony and embraced a much darker picture of a nation suffering the traumas of internal conflicts and international uncertainty. Throughout the forties, American moviemakers became even more aware of their power and of the profound influence their works could exert. In many ways, however, the films of the forties represent the industry's last period of supremacy over the minds and hearts of massive American audiences. Television would soon undercut its dominance, and the HUAC hearings would convince much of the public that Hollywood should not be trusted. The marriage between America and its movies would never be the same again.

Films of the forties, therefore, emphasized the continuing assimilation of the decade's Jews into mainstream American life. The move to the suburbs that forced many affluent Jewish-Americans to reconsider the role of Judaism in their lives never reached the nation's movie screens. Encouraged by their ambitious parents to embrace American values, the children of immigrants had thought it necessary to abandon their Judaism to better accommodate themselves to American life. This was something their heartbroken parents had never foreseen would happen. Now the children of the second-generation Jews drew their lapsed parents back to the elements of their forefathers' religion so hastily abandoned in the scramble for social and economic success. As one commentator says, "It was fine for the grandsons to remember when the sons had forgotten."

The immigrant moguls were incapable of shedding their first-generation insecurities, and their films preached accommodation to the dominant Gentile culture rather than a search for new ways to fit Judaism into it. No real approaches to what it meant to be a Jew in America were ever offered by the studio heads, even in films like *Gentleman's Agreement* and *Crossfire*. Instead, the answers of the first generation were dressed in new garb and recycled for the second and the third, sadly unmindful that the problems had changed and the audience had matured. Hollywood still refused to confront the two overriding Jewish issues of the decade in any meaningful manner: the Holocaust and Israel's creation. Perhaps the horror of the camps could not be so quickly assimilated, or perhaps the emergence of Israel as a political fact was too controversial a topic. Whatever the reasons, Hollywood basically ignored both. In *Address Unknown*, Grisella asks her hostile audience if "calling a man a Jew robs him of his humanity?" For Hollywood in the forties, one might rephrase her question: Why does identifying a character as Jewish rob him of his religion, his uniqueness, and his heritage?

The Frightened Fifties

Fifties filmmakers added little new or interesting to the image of Jews in the American cinema. "Safe" Jews, uncontroversial Jews, inhabited the decade's movie screens. With their ethnic blandness and thematic timidity, most films of the fifties resemble those made during the low-point in the history of the Jewish-American cinema, the thirties. A fear of presenting anything too new, anything too different, marks both decades as periods dominated by uncertainty and apprehension, a fact symbolized by the remake of *The Jazz Singer* in 1953. Few films of the fifties, therefore, confront contemporary problems faced by the Jewish-American community or deal with painful topics like the Holocaust. In fact, the total number of films featuring Jewish characters produced during this decade is smaller than in any other except the thirties, and most fifties screen Jews have even more minor roles than their celluloid predecessors. Fifties filmmakers simply dusted off old stereotypes and retreated to worn-out clichés, placing their Jewish characters into bloated Biblical epics, conventional war sagas, sanitary biographies, and syrupy melodramas.

Only a few films venture beyond these safe boundaries. One of the decade's more intriguing treatments of Communist witchhunts, *Three Brave Men* (1957), features a Jewish protagonist, though it concentrates more on his patriotism than his Jewishness. Two other pictures—*Never Love a Stranger* (1958) and *Home Before Dark* (1958)—deal with the familiar theme of inter-faith love, but add some surprisingly different twists to the typical pattern of most such stories. While Hollywood's belated recognition that Jews had entered new occupations and industries is reflected in several films featuring Jewish record executives and writers, as well as doctors and garment workers, the decade's major contribution to the Jewish-American film genre are a film about Israel (*The Juggler,* 1953) and the presentation of the new Jewish-American woman (*Marjorie Morningstar,* 1958) inspired by Herman Wouk's best-selling novel.

Like the fictional Marjorie Morningstar, the American Jew of the fifties, both on and off screen, looked, spoke, and acted far more like his Gentile neighbors than his immigrant ancestors. Following World War II and into the next decade, government attempts to eradicate some of our society's racial

Accused of espionage, Bernie Goldsmith (Ernest Borgnine) attempts to convince his neighbors he is innocent in THREE BRAVE MEN *(1957).*

Jerry Golding (Danny Thomas) embraces his mother (Mildred Dunnock) as his approving father, Cantor Golding (Eduard Franz), looks on in THE JAZZ SINGER *(1953).*

and religious barriers eased his progress into once-forbidden areas of American life: universities, medical school, politics, and industry. In addition, the educational provisions of the G.I. Bill of Rights made it possible for more members of minority groups to attend colleges formerly outside their financial reach. While the Supreme Court's famous Brown decision in 1954 was primarily directed against ending "legalized" racial segregation, it put the power of the federal government squarely behind minority rights. The democratizing effects of the war and these specific actions destroyed many of the country's unspoken barriers to social and economic achievement.

The progressive breakdown of discrimination in occupational and educational opportunities signaled a similar lessening of restrictions in residential areas, and the Jewish exodus from the cities to the suburbs increased. Urban sections once predominantly Jewish evolved into neighborhoods populated by newer arrivals such as Blacks and Puerto Ricans. Only Orthodox and Hassidic Jews stubbornly clung to the old neighborhoods, either because they could not afford to move or because they feared religious contamination in suburbs more sparsely inhabited by Jews. However, in the fifties and sixties the suburbs, rather than the cities, became home for many of America's Jews who at first tried to blend inconspicuously in with their Gentile neighbors, but soon felt the need for greater religious identification. Thus, a growing emphasis on various cultural aspects of Jewishness was paralleled in the fifties by an equally increasing acceptance of Judaism's role as a religious force in suburban life. Motivated by painful memories of the Holocaust and aided by the renewed emphasis on Jewish identity engendered by the creation of Israel, suburban Jews now sought ways to express their ethnic values.

The apparent social and economic acceptance of Jews by the Gentile world failed to allay their nagging self-doubts about their position in society. Sociologist Herbert J. Gans in *The Levittowners* (1967) concludes: "Jews often move into communities where the median income is lower than their own, partly because some prefer to spend a lower share of their income on housing, partly because they fear rejection from their non-Jewish neighborhood of a similar income and education." Sociologist John P. Dean's 1958 surveys in a town of 50,000 that included 1,500 Jews reveal that only nine percent of the Gentiles said they felt differently about Jews than about other Gentiles, but that 39 percent of the Jews thought Gentiles treated them differently. Whether as the result of paranoia or objective experiences, the suburban Jew of the fifties felt a gap between himself and his Gentile neighbors. Perhaps the bitter lesson of the assimilated German Jews of the Holocaust kept him wary, perhaps he was actually excluded from certain social and fraternal organizations, or perhaps he feared a loss of Jewish identity. Whatever his reasons, the suburban Jew often restricted his personal relationships to other Jews, and his social activities to the synagogue.

In the entertainment field, as in literature and the other arts, Jews continued to make inroads. Indeed, Jews dominated the so-called Golden Age of television whose stars were Milton Berle, Jack Benny, and Sid Caesar—all of whom had received their early training in the hotels of the Catskill Mountains, a circuit called the Borscht Belt. Caesar, whose writers included future celebrities such as Mel Brooks, Carl Reiner, Howie Morris, and Neil Simon, even peppered his act with Yiddishisms. Some commentators argue that the pervasiveness of television in living rooms across the country edged heartland America into a greater acceptance of all types of ethnic diversity, particularly Jewish humor. Irving Howe concludes that such an outpouring of Yiddish humor reflects "the rise of a large and affluent middle-class Jewish audience…which could now share with the comics a display of precisely the 'Jewish vulgarity' earlier generations had been so intent upon keeping under wraps." There was a soft, comfortable feeling about such humor, a warm nostalgia for the days most third-generation Jews had only heard about.

The energetic Jewish moguls who had succeeded the first generation of Fox, Laemmle, and Zukor could not survive in this new era, and as stockholders sought scapegoats for dwindling profits they found themselves being pushed out of the very studios they had nurtured for two decades. In 1951, the lordly Louis B. Mayer, then sixty-three years old, was fired from MGM. He became an advisor to Cinerama Corporation and spent his remaining years in a futile attempt to regain control of the studio. David O. Selznick made his last film, *A Farewell to Arms,* in 1957, and Samuel Goldwyn his last, *Porgy and Bess,* in 1959. Harry Cohn died in 1958. In 1956, Harry and Albert Warner sold the majority of their shares in Warner Brothers. Their brother, Jack, stayed on as studio chief until 1967, when Seven Arts Productions purchased the studio that had introduced the talking film. As the decade continued, the studios became more important as backers of independent producers than as creators of their own films. Some auctioned off properties and huge back-lots to the highest bidders. Distribution, not production, became their major business.

The financial woes of those remaining in the production business were compounded by the increasing dominance of television. In 1948 television became a true mass media. That year the number of stations on the air jumped from 17 to 41, and television sets sold represented a 500 percent increase over 1947. This trend continued throughout the next decade. In 1948, there were 250,000 sets in use; by 1952 there were fifteen million. The laying of the coaxial cable linking East and West coasts in 1951 allowed the television industry to develop large, national networks that progressively eroded the financial basis of the movie industry. By the end of the fifties, Hollywood realized the sad truth of Samuel Goldwyn's 1950 prediction: "After the silent period, and the sound era, Hollywood is about to enter the third stage of its development—the television age."

Still another event, the House Un-American Activities Committee (HUAC) investigation into alleged Communist activities within the movie industry, which lasted from 1947 to 1952, did even greater damage, psychological this time: it convinced many Americans they could no longer trust their filmmakers. Though it had displayed a united front against earlier government investigations into its alleged pro-war propaganda, the industry disintegrated into bitterly opposing factions in the face of these new attacks. The Motion Picture Alliance for the Preservation of American Ideals, an organization of politically conservative moviemakers, provided HUAC with inside testimony about industry activity. Twenty-three friendly witnesses appeared before the committee, including Gary Cooper, Ronald Reagan, George Murphy, and Robert Montgomery. As a result of their testimony and other evidence, eleven other witnesses were subpoenaed to testify. One, Bertolt Brecht, answered inquiries and then quickly returned to Europe. The other ten men—who became known as the "Hollywood Ten"—refused to answer the committee's questions about their various political activities. After being cited for contempt, two served six-month prison sentences, and the other eight were jailed for a year.[12]

Hollywood's Jews, in particular, felt vulnerable to the political investigations into the "un-American" aspects of the industry during this period, and with good reason. After all, many of them were immigrants—often from Russia or nations within what was known as the "Soviet bloc"—and because of this many outsiders saw the industry as dominated by foreigners. Before the war the moguls sensed the comforting support of many Americans who applauded their pro-Allies, anti-Nazi films. When in 1945 HUAC member John J. Rankin of Mississippi unleashed his blatantly anti-Semitic attack on Hollywood, punctuating his words with expressions like "kikes" and "yids," many of his colleagues defended Hollywood and denounced his racism. On November 24, 1947, Rankin rose from his seat once again to read into the Congressional Record a list of Hollywood people opposed to the HUAC investigation. During his speech, he paused dramatically after reciting names like Edward G. Robinson, Danny Kaye, and Melvyn Douglas to inform fellow lawmakers that their real names were Emmanuel Goldenberg, David Kaminsky, and Melvyn Hesselberg. This time no one rose to dispute his clear implication.

Hollywood Jews feared that the public would equate the Hollywood Ten, six of whom were Jewish, with the industry as a whole, seeing all filmmakers as dangerous, leftwing propagandists. Their worst fears seemed justified when thirteen of the first nineteen people subpoenaed were Jewish. It increased when Samuel Ornitz, one of the Ten, declared he felt it necessary to address the committee as a Jew, "because one of its leading members is the outstanding anti-Semite in the Congress and revels in that fact."

The moguls feared that a blanket equation of Communists with Jews could destroy them and their industry. To counteract this impression, some of the industry's most powerful Jews, including studio heads like Mayer and Jack L. Warner, led the witch hunt, and many of their victims were Jewish writers, performers, and directors. The unity that once allowed the conservative producers and the radical workers to sit down together at the studio to collect money for the United Jewish Appeal during the war could hold no longer. As HUAC's attacks on the industry and its Jews intensified, filmmakers grew increasingly reluctant to present Jews in their movies, fearing that such characters would inevitably attract criticism from all sides.

What of the growing emphasis on Judaism as a religion during the fifties, that emphasis spurred by the horrors of the Holocaust and the hope of Israel? On the screen, there was little mention of the new Jews, or of their search for an accommodation between their new-found Judaism and more traditional aspects of American life. Intermarriage, once the focus of many movies, almost evaporated as an issue in films of the fifties in spite of its increasing incidence. The plight of older Jews trapped in rapidly deteriorating urban areas was never confronted. The perceptions of Jewish-American intellectuals and writers who interpreted society from the viewpoint of a different heritage failed to impress Hollywood filmmakers, who dismissed them simply as East Coast intellectuals with no mass-audience appeal. So the fifties blacklisted Jews in front of the camera as well as behind it.

The decade's war films are indicative of the Jew's diminishing role on screen. Most of them simply recycle clichés and situations familiar from past movies. Rudy Maté's The Deep Sea (1958) is a case in point. In it, a Quaker naval officer (Alan Ladd) is rejected by his crew because of his pacifism. Only Shapiro (William Bendix), a bosun's mate, supports him. He tries to explain to the men how the officer is not a coward but a man of conviction. Finally, Ladd gains the respect of his crew by an act of heroism, thereby justifying Shapiro's evaluation of his character. Though Shapiro has a sympathetic role in the film, no attempt is made to explain or explore his stand. He is simply more sensitive than the film's other sailors.

The Jewish issue most present in these war films is anti-Semitism. Though never the central focus, as in *Gentleman's Agreement* and *Crossfire,* its presence contradicts the image of peaceful minority co-existence so prevalent in forties combat pictures, and provides a more realistic portrait of the racial tensions in World War II platoons. Films with a Jewish character usually also include a bully waiting to pounce on him. For example, in *The Naked and the Dead* (1958), Sergeant Croft (Aldo Ray) delights in baiting Roth (Joey Bishop) and Goldstein (Jerry Paris) with racist remarks. Confronted with such overt bigotry, the Jew—usually presented as quiet and sensitive—must prove his manliness in physical combat with his oppressor.

It's a Big Country (1951), *Me and the Colonel* (1958), and *The Diary of Anne Frank* (1959) use the war as a backdrop for more personal stories, emphasizing the civilian rather than the military side of the conflict. An interesting view of American religious prejudice is found in *It's a Big Country.* During one sequence, a Jewish veteran visits a Gentile soldier's mother, only to find her bigoted attitude a shocking contrast to her dead son's humanity. *Me and the Colonel*—based on a Franz Werfel play—stars Danny Kaye as S. L. Jacobowsky, a kindly Jewish refugee who joins forces with an anti-Semitic Polish aristocrat, the arrogant Prokoszny (Curt Jurgens), to escape the Nazi army marching on Paris. By the end of the film, Prokoszny develops a grudging admiration for the spunky Jacobowsky, who refuses to abandon his fellow refugee even though it would have been easier, and far safer, to travel alone. In *The Diary of Anne Frank,* the Frank family in Nazi-occupied Amsterdam spends two years in hiding only to be discovered at last.

The popularity of war movies continued during the fifties, but filmgoers also witnessed a comeback of lavish Biblical epics, including *David and*

Anne Frank (Millie Perkins) and Peter Van Daan (Richard Beymer) find love amidst the horrors of World War II in THE DIARY OF ANNE FRANK *(1959).*

Bathsheba (1951), *The Ten Commandments* (1956), and *Solomon and Sheba* (1959). Each of these films contains Jewish characters safely distanced by the passing of centuries. As usual, such pictures concentrate on sprawling spectacles, luxuriant sets, and expensive costumes that mask superficial ideas, cardboard characterization, and weak dramatic development. Jews generally appear as mere historical necessities, and filmmakers Henry King, Cecil B. DeMille, and King Vidor make no attempt to understand the Jewish religious or cultural heritage.

Directors of several film biographies of famous contemporary Jews during this period are equally unwilling to explore their subjects' Jewishness. For example, *The Eddie Cantor Story* (1953), featuring

Entertainer Eddie Cantor (Keefe Braselle) hams it up in the EDDIE CANTOR STORY *(1953).*

Keefe Brasselle as the saucer-eyed entertainer, never mentions his Jewish heritage, though it does explore his ghetto background. *Somebody Up There Likes Me,* Robert Wise's 1956 film biography of the Italian-American boxer Rocky Graziano, never mentions that his supportive wife is Jewish, though it does include his Jewish manager, Irving Cohen (Everett Sloane), as well as the kindly candy-

store owner (Joe Buloff), who helps Rocky go straight. Both films concentrate on how the characters "make it," not on their origins. *Compulsion* (1959), based on Meyer Levin's 1957 play (which Levin adapted from his own novel), recounts one of the most famous murder trials in American history—the Leopold and Loeb case. Director Richard Fleischer changes the defendants' names to Artie Straus (Dean Stockwell) and Judd Steiner (Bradford Dillman), but he keeps intact most of the events of the case: two brilliant college students attempt to commit the perfect crime in order to demonstrate their elitist disgust for American society and to realize their Nietzschean fantasy. The act they commit is the brutal murder of an innocent, arbitrarily chosen fourteen-year-old boy. Ultimately, thanks to the impassioned argument of their brilliant defense lawyer (Orson Welles), the pair receive life sentences rather than the expected death penalty.

Unlike these film biographies, *The Benny Goodman Story* (1956) pays at least passing attention to its subject's Jewishness. With Steve Allen cast as the famous musician, the movie contains several scenes that document Goodman's Lower East Side origins and his problems with intermarriage. When he falls in love with Alice Hammond (Donna Reed), a rich society girl, Benny's mother (Bertha Gersten) initially describes the situation as "a knife in my heart." In fact, she is more opposed to the match than are Alice's wealthy and socially prominent parents. However, in true Hollywood fashion, Mrs. Goodman eventually comes around, playing matchmaker to Benny and Alice, worrying only that her son "should be happy." As in the silent films, the dictates of the heart remain more important than the prohibitions of religion.

Many of the decade's films reflect the occupational diversity of the era's Jews. At the start of the fifties, *Detective Story* (1951) includes a philosphical Jewish police reporter (Luis Van Rooten). *The Big Knife* (1955) features a Jewish Hollywood agent, Nat Danziger (Everett Sloane), and a Jewish producer, Stanley Hoff (Rod Steiger). In *Never Love a Stranger* (1958), the head of a multimillion-dollar liquor racket (John Drew Barrymore) is Jewish, though a new twist is added to an old plot:

the Jewish gangster grows up as a non-Jew in a Catholic orphanage and only discovers his true heritage as an adult. In most of these films, Jews are simply secondary characters included for atmosphere, not for exploration. But their very presence adds to the growing number of occupations available to celluloid Jews in the fifties, a number that will expand dramatically in the sixties and seventies.

This is not to say that moviemakers of the fifties ignored more traditional occupations for their screen Jews. *I Can Get It For You Wholesale* (1951), based on Jerome Weidman's novel and Abraham Polonsky's script, focuses on garment workers. Paddy Chayefsky's *Middle of the Night* (1959) uses the same milieu as the setting for a romance between Fredric March, a lonely Jewish garment manufacturer, and Kim Novak, a twenty-four-year-

old divorcee. *The Proud Rebel* (1958) includes a traditional Jewish shopkeeper (Eli Mintz), thereby becoming one of the earliest films to acknowledge the presence of Jews in the Old West.

Jewish doctors appear in several films during this decade. *Not As a Stranger* (1955), Stanley Kramer's first directorial effort, features Broderick Crawford as Dr. Aarons, mentor to the cold, unfeeling Lucas Marsh (Robert Mitchum). Only once does Aarons allow his bitter resentment over exclusionary racial policies at his school to bubble to the surface. He tells Lucas that as a Jewish doctor he, Aarons, is "part of the five percent they let in here because they can't keep us out entirely." *Say One*

For Me (1958), a Bing Crosby musical directed by Frank Tashlin, includes a Jewish doctor in a bit part, and *The Last Angry Man* (1954) focuses on Dr. Samuel Abelman (Paul Muni).

The films of the fifties comprise a relatively unfruitful period in the history of the American cinema's screen Jews. Partially, this results from the continued assimilation of Jews into American life, and partially, from the fear of anything too different that permeated the Hollywood community, as well as much of the nation, during the decade. Except for the low-budget *The Juggler,* the subject of Israel never surfaces in the movies of the 1950s. No fifties pictures attempt to confront the horror of the Holocaust and its traumatic effect on the lives of those who experienced it. Safe Jews dominate Jewish-American films through the era. Though nagging doubts about anti-Semitism become secondary themes in some war films like *The Young Lions* and *The Naked and the Dead,* Jews always emerge victorious in their battles with the dark forces of ignorance and prejudice, a triumph often unmatched in offscreen confrontations. Intermarriage receives scant celluloid attention, and those films which do discuss the issue continue the Hollywood tradition of presenting only the assimilationist point of view. None of the caustic and bitter humor of anguished Jewish performers like Lenny Bruce is reflected in the fifties films. Hollywood virtually ignores the increasing role Judaism played in the lives of many of the decade's Jews, as it does the growing influence of Jewish intellectuals who filtered their insights about the American experience through a decidedly Jewish perspective. When Hope Plowman's father tells Noah Ackerman in *The Young Lions* that he "never knew a Jew before," his ignorance extends to the decade's moviegoers, whose main images of Jews had little in common with the actual members of America's Jewish community.

The Self-Conscious Sixties

Fifties films with Jews rarely ventured very far beyond conventional situations and stereotypical characters. Such was not the case in the sixties when a new generation of filmmakers delved into areas of Jewish life previously and studiously avoided: Jewish criminal figures, the Holocaust, and the plight of alienated Jewish intellectuals. As such, the movies of the sixties mirror the growing ethnic consciousness that marks this period in American history. The United States of the sixties prized individuality over sameness. The notion of a "Great Melting Pot" that reduced everyone into blandly similar types, therefore, held little interest for those people needing to proclaim their uniqueness. To discover who they were, many reached back to their ethnic origins, back to the customs and traditions that made their heritage distinctive. And they liked what they found. Many saw ethnic identification as an alternative to a modern, computerized world that encouraged uniform conformity. Ethnic affiliation, a pride in belonging to a minority group, became an important feature of sixties life, one crucial element in what amounted to a decade-long obsession with ethnicity.

Such an obsession was not ignored by the decade's moviemakers, who were desperately trying to entice people out of their living rooms and into the theaters. One way to do this was to appeal to various special-interest groups. Freed from a monolithic studio system that cranked out predictable assembly-line films supporting white, middle-class, Christian values, the "new Hollywood" felt free to strike out in different directions. One such direction was the ethnic films that appealed to a smaller but still sizeable audience. Thus, an emerging ethnic concern that lasted the entire decade, the destruction of the old studio system, and the need to reach more specialized audiences inspired sixties film producers to transcend moribund racial stereotypes and to create a cinema that attempted to confront ethnic issues and characters with greater understanding, sensitivity, and sophistication.

Jews, as well as other minorities such as blacks and native Americans, suddenly found themselves scrutinized under the lenses of America's movie cameras, their traditions explored and their psyches dissected. During these ten years, Jewish figures appear in more films than ever before.

Dolly Gallagher Levi (Barbra Streisand) is lavishly greeted by her many admirers in HELLO, DOLLY! *(1969).*

Their various roles show the broad involvement of Jews in American life during the sixties, as well as the country's increasing interest in its Jews. Comedies, as in earlier periods, dominate this era. But there are significant differences between the simple-minded plots and antics of *Captain Newman, M.D.* (1963) and *John Goldfarb, Please Come Home* (1964) in the first half of the decade and the incisive satire of *Bye Bye Braverman* (1968), *The Producers* (1968), and *Goodbye, Columbus* (1969) in the second half. These latter films display Hollywood's maturing ethnic consciousness. In

fact, a decidedly Jewish, comic perspective informs a broad range of subjects in the sixties: show business (*Enter Laughing,* 1967); hippie culture (*I Love You Alice B. Toklas,* 1968); horror films (*The Fearless Vampire Killers,* 1967); search for identity (*Me, Natalie,* 1969); the detective film (*No Way To Treat A Lady,* 1968); the musical (*Hello, Dolly!,* 1969). More than those of any other decade, the movies of the sixties offer filmgoers a series of diverse Jewish portraits ranging from the troubled to the timid to the terrible.

Hollywood's broadening ethnic concern eventually led filmmakers beyond comedy. Noteworthy attempts to confront the pain and trauma of the Holocaust were made in *Judgment at Nuremberg*

(1961), *Lisa* (1962), and *The Pawnbroker* (1965). The formation of a Jewish state emerged as a suitable subject in *Exodus* (1960), *Cast a Giant Shadow* (1966), and *Judith* (1965). Jews are also shown demonstrating a concern for society's social and ethical problems. A Jewish lawyer helps Father Charles Clark set up a halfway house in *The Hoodlum Priest* (1961) and another defends the religious rights of a Christian Scientist in *Walk in the Shadow* (1962). At the start of the decade, a typical show business biography, *Act One* (1963), almost totally ignores its central character's ethnicity, but by the end of the decade *Funny Girl* (1968) luxuriates in Fanny Brice's Jewish background. Sixties filmmakers also adapt several important novels with Jewish characters: Bernard Malamud's *The Fixer* (1968), Katherine Anne Porter's *Ship of Fools* (1965), John Le Carre's *The Spy Who Came in From the Cold* (1965), and James Joyce's *Ulysses* (1967)—without robbing these characters of their heritage. Even Dickens's *Oliver Twist* was resurrected, this time around as the musical *Oliver!* (1968).

Sixties films displaying such an unparalleled range of Jewish characters and situations reflect the feelings of acceptance and confidence prevalent among the majority of America's Jews during this period. Many reasons account for their sense of well-being, particularly at the start of the new decade. The economic prosperity the American-Jewish community had experienced in the fifties continued unabated into the sixties. Jews at the nation's most prestigious universities became an accepted fact, as did the presence of Jewish doctors, lawyers, and teachers. Also, the sometimes traumatic exodus from the cities to the suburbs was basically complete as the decade began. Most of the problems occasioned by the post-World War II mass migration had been solved, and Jewish suburbanites felt relatively comfortable in their affluent surroundings.

Though American Jews started the decade with a sense of security rarely eqalled in the long history of their people, the relative calm of the decade's

Fiedler (Oskar Werner), the brilliant Jewish spy eliminated by his superior, a double agent, in THE SPY WHO CAME IN FROM THE COLD *(1965).*

first years quickly gave way to a period of internal turmoil and tension within the Jewish community, as well as the country as a whole, unmatched since the Great Depression. At first, the shooting of John F. Kennedy seemed like a cruel but isolated intrusion on American complacency. Those shots, however, signaled the start of a time in which, as Black militant H. Rap Brown put it, "violence was as American as apple pie." The country's growing involvement in the Vietnam War resulted in escalating bloodshed, political upheaval, and social un-

Moss Hart (George Hamilton) leaves his Brooklyn home in ACT ONE *(1963), another biography which ignores its subject's Jewishness.*

rest. The shocking assassinations of Robert F. Kennedy and Martin Luther King, Jr., in 1968, along with the violent clashes between anti-war protesters and Chicago policemen at the Democratic National Convention that same year, provided vivid evidence of the powerful, internal pressures that threatened to push the country toward anarchy. Many affluent, suburban Jews suddenly found themselves caught up in the tensions of the time. They became the targets of their own children who assailed their materialistic ethos and rejected their cautious, liberal approach to politics. Like the rest of American society, Jews experienced an intense sense of culture shock as the sixties progressed.

Many of the conflicts that threatened the Jewish-American community, however, proved to be boons as well as curses. The Black Power movement, for example, often caused bitter clashes between black activists and liberal Jews fearful of the movement's growing anti-Semitism. Respond-

ing to this, many Jewish civil-rights advocates ceased active support of integration; others were expelled from organizations they had kept financially solvent for years. Some Jews who had once strongly supported desegregation in public schools withdrew their children and enrolled them in private institutions less vulnerable to the perpetual violence of city schools.

But Black demands for ethnic recognition had another side to them: they helped legitimize Jewish claims for individuality. If black was beautiful, so too was Jewish; taking their lead from Blacks in Afros and dashikis, many Jews began to acknowledge and then celebrate their own cultural heritage. Ethnic pride thus grew steadily during the 1960s, the desirability of cultural pluralism replacing the earlier goal of total assimilation. To be a hyphenated American endowed one with a source of pride, a feeling of uniqueness, and a particular perspective from which to view the confusing events of a troubled decade. It gave one a natural sense of his roots, a steady center that would hold amid the passionate intensity and mere anarchy that had been let loose upon the world of the sixties.

Added to these turbulent domestic issues was a major foreign policy problem: the 1967 Israeli War, with its frightening potential for the destruction of a centuries-old dream—a Jewish homeland. Jewish pride became particularly important during this war. Unlike earlier generations, the Jewish-Americans of the sixties vocally, as well as financially, supported Israel during this difficult period. Their boldness came partly from Jewish pride and ethnic identification and partly from another seemingly divisive aspect of sixties life: student radicalism. Many of the campus activist leaders such as Abbie Hoffman, Mark Rudd, and Jerry Rubin were Jewish. Their membership in organizations like the Students for a Democratic Society, the Yippies and the Weathermen was a logical outgrowth of their liberal and even socialist backgrounds. Because of their vehement opposition to America's military role in Vietnam, one would have assumed these radical Jews would be equally opposed to fighting in the Middle East. This, however, was not the case. Many Jewish members of radical organizations rallied to Israel's defense, their deep-seated fear of Israel's demise triumphing over their anti-military feelings. In this way, student radicalism was often channeled into Israel activism, and many of these young Jews deserted radical organizations that supported the Arabs over Israel.

Because of their opposition to the Vietnam War, a great many Americans—Jews and non-Jews alike—found themselves alienated from their government's policies abroad, as their personal beliefs clashed with society's demands. How much could a government require of its citizens? What values could a citizen place above the demands of his country? These questions stretched the fabric of American society until it appeared ready to rip apart at the seams. A sizable segment of the population, therefore, assumed the status of marginal men and women trapped between two worlds with different values. Feeling a sense of aloneness and alienation, of not belonging, they became outsiders within their own country, assuming the position occupied by Jews over the centuries. In effect, then, the internal conflicts of many Americans during the sixties were mirrored in those of the Jew.

Appropriately, the Jewish fiction dealing with the issues of exile and alienation, of conflicts between personal and public obligations, became the dominant literature of the sixties. Saul Bellow, Philip Roth, Bruce Jay Friedman, and Bernard Malamud moved to the center of American fiction. Such Jewish-American novelist portrayed the anxiety of the age, the often painful quest for some sort of accommodation between personal identity, private morality, and public activity. Suddenly, it was "in" to be Jewish, for as poet Delmore Schwartz prophesied, "to be born a Jew was to have been thrust into a condition that all men in time are destined to enter…the sense of being an outsider, the sense of being homeless and in exile." No longer was the Jewish experience exotic; now it had become the sixties American experience. The Jew, in effect, became the Everyman who embodied the trauma of a decade in his own private psychological dilemma.

America's turmoil during the sixties was reflected in Hollywood both on and off the screen. Though familiar emblems of the once-powerful studios still introduced films on movie screens across the nation, the studio system as it operated during its heyday in the thirties and forties simply ceased to exist. Studios in the sixties had no distinctive style, no roster of brandable stars, and no stable of contract players. As the decade progressed, sagging profits turned studios into easy targets for merger-hungry conglomerates: Paramount became part of Gulf & Western Industries, United Artists of Trans-America Corporation, Warner Brothers of Seven Arts (then of Kinney National Services, Inc.), Universal of Decca (then of MCA), and MGM of hotel magnate Kirk Kerkorian's growing empire. By 1971, only Columbia and 20th Century-Fox were independent filmmakers rather than a part of some sprawling conglomerate of which film production was only one segment of the total economic output. Even these two companies sought ways to diversify during the sixties. By the end of the decade, the corporate mentality ruled American filmmaking, replacing the instinctive approach to moviemaking that characterized the work of eccentric Jewish moguls of a previous era.

The death of Harry Cohn on March 2, 1958, signaled the end of one-man studio rule in Holly-

Ari Ben Canaan (Paul Newman) and his father (Lee J. Cobb) survey the scene in EXODUS *(1960).*

wood. Although Adolph Zukor lived until 1976 and Samuel Goldwyn until 1974, they retained little actual power. Many of those who replaced the old moguls in the industry's hierarchy were Jewish, but they were American-born and had radically different world-views than their immigrant predecessors. Men like Robert Evans at Paramount, Richard Zanuck at Fox, Frank E. Rosenfelt at MGM, and David Picker at United Artists typified the new breed of Hollywood film producers. Some had degrees in management and accounting; most were college educated. All were far removed, both physically and psychologically, from the old-country *shtetls* and immigrant experiences that had shaped

the dictatorial Jewish moguls. To their moviemaking, these newcomers brought a sophistication, as well as a confidence about themselves and their heritage. Though some in Hollywood looked back nostalgically to the paternalistic studios and their erratic, colorful chieftains, most realized that those days were ancient history. Hollywood during the sixties was not quite sure where it was going, but it was positive about where it would never return.

The differences between the films created by these new producers and those of their predecessors is apparent in all movie categories. Most earlier film biographies, for example, spotlighted popular Jewish entertainers (Al Jolson, Benny Goodman, Eddie Cantor), role models of decency and courage (Alfred Dreyfus) or success stories (the Rothschilds, Benjamin Disraeli). The sixties, however, widened the area of Jewish screen biographies to include some far less savory characters.

A House Is Not a Home (1964), for example, presents an alien character to the screen: the Jewish madam. Loosely based on the autobiography of Polly Adler, the film follows the story of a young Polish immigrant (Shelley Winters) who is raped and, when her guardian refuses to believe her story, driven from her home. To survive, Adler becomes a madam who furnishes girls to racketeers. Eventually, Polly loses her chance at happiness when her musician/lover, Casey Booth (Ralph Taeger), can't accept her past and deserts her. Director Russell Rouse, who clearly remains sympathetic to the clever Adler throughout the film, cannot avoid the inevitable moral. After losing Booth, a saddened Adler admits that she "pins her diamonds on her loneliness and despair." If Adler's Jewishness is not a central part of the story, the very image of a Jewish prostitute seems shocking in a cinema whose major Jewish female protagonists had been Molly Goldbergs and Marjorie Morningstars.

In the sixties Hollywood responded to the Holocaust by dealing with the Jewish victims of the past and also by portraying the Jewish heirs of the future. In particular, the decade's filmmakers paid increasing attention to the Jewish battle to create and then to maintain the state of Israel, a psychological and geographical safety valve for survivors of Nazi atrocities. In *Operation Eichmann* (1961), for example, director R. G. Springsteen highlights the morality of the Israelis in contrast to the animal savagery of the Nazis. After the fall of the Third Reich, the founding of Israel allows Jews "to leave behind forever the despair and hopelessness that had been their heritage." Their new life, however, does not mean they have forgotten their Nazi oppressors. After Israeli agents spend ten years searching for Eichmann, they are faced with the moral question of what to do with this monster. "Try him six million times for six million lives" screams one woman. Others want to murder him.

Bertha Jacoby (Rosalind Russell) falls in love with Koichi Asano (Alec Guinness) in A MAJORITY OF ONE *(1961).*

John Goldfarb (Richard Crenna) prays for divine intervention as his Arab footballers tackle Notre Dame in JOHN GOLDFARB, PLEASE COME HOME *(1964).*

Some devise gruesome tortures for Eichmann. Finally, however, Eichmann is given a fair trial, allowed a chance to defend himself, and executed for his war crimes.

Mickey Marcus in *Cast a Giant Shadow* and Ari Ben Canaan in *Exodus* are fighters involved in the battle to establish a Jewish state, and Hollywood fit them quite neatly into prepackaged soldier stereotypes and stock war film situations. The terrain might be a Mideastern desert rather than an Italian beach or a Pacific Island, but the basic plot elements, as well as the personal characteristics of the soldiers, remain quite similar to those found in our own war films. In fact, Hollywood continued to fight World War II during the sixties. A number of Jewish characters appear in these war movies though most play fairly minor roles. *Captain Newman, M.D.* (1963) features Tony Curtis as Corporal Jackson Laibowitz, a clever aide to a kindly psychiatrist, Captain Newman (Gregory Peck), who treats battle-fatigue patients at a large army base during the war's final years. It is Laibowitz who finds a way to help Newman circumvent the rules and regulations that hamper his healing. In *Tobruk* (1966), German-born Palestinian Jews aid British commandos in capturing and holding a crucial gun emplacement against superior Nazi forces.

While Biblical films featuring Jewish characters all but disappeared from Hollywood during the sixties, pictures featuring Jewish/Gentile romances continued to flourish throughout the decade. Two films put a Jewish/Gentile romance at the center of their stories: *A Majority of One* (1961) and *No Way to Treat a Lady* (1968). In *A Majority of One* director Mervyn LeRoy, who had made a far better story of Jewish and Gentile outsiders united against an alien world (*Home Before Dark,* 1958), loses his way. The sentimental yarn of a lonely Brooklyn widow, Mrs. Bertha Jacoby (Rosalind Russell), who meets and falls in love with a Japanese gentleman, Koichi Asano (Alec Guinness), when her son-in-law (Ray Danton), a diplomat, is assigned a post in Tokyo, fails to hold much interest beyond its initially unique premise. Like the Leonard Spiegelgass hit play it was based on, the movie's theme is the triumph of common sense over diplomatic nonsense. Mrs. Jacoby's humane sensitivity toward others is recommended over the bureaucratic silliness insisted upon by her protocol-conscious son-in-law. "Cutting through red tape," as *The New York Times* review notes, "is as easy for Mrs. Jacoby as the recipe for gefilte fish." In the end, Mrs. Jacoby's democratic openness triumphs over stuffy rituals.

The compassionate humor of *A Majority of One* and the black comedy of *No Way to Treat a Lady* represents the two opposite approaches sixties filmmakers employed to deal humorously with the Jewish-American experience throughout the decade. In the films of the first type like *John Goldfarb, Please Come Home* (1964), *Enter Laughing* (1967), and *Me, Natalie* (1969), moviemakers filter a broad range of situations through a Jewish comic perspective. *John Goldfarb, Please Come Home,* for example, examines American/Arabic relations in this manner. A Jewish-American spy plane pilot, John Goldfarb (Richard Crenna), crashes in the oil-rich Arab country of dictatorial King Fawz (Peter Ustinov), a nutty ruler who rides around his palace on giant toy trains and keeps a bikini-clad harem. When Fawz's son is cut from the Notre Dame football team, the king forces Goldfarb to organize an Arab squad of footballers and challenges Notre Dame to a game. Throughout the film, there is a series of running jokes about Goldfarb being Jewish. Early, Fawz asks Goldfarb, "Are you Jewish?" He replies "Yes," and Fawz responds, "Funny, you don't look Jewish." From that point on, the king refers to Goldfarb as "a nice Jewish boy."

The football game becomes a slapstick superbowl of various religions: the Islamic players and their Jewish coach against the Irish-Catholic Notre Dame team. At one point during the contest, Goldfarb gets so wrapped up in the game that he screams at his players to "Kill the infidels! Remember the Crusades!" Released in 1964, *John Goldfarb, Please Come Home* pays scant attention to Arab-Jewish hostilities, though in a few short years the 1967 Middle-East War would vividly remind the world of the hatred between the two. The picture's humor springs from director J. Lee Thompson's satiric portrait of an oil-rich sheik with so many Petrodollars he doesn't know how to spend them.

In the final analysis, the arrival of all types of Jews on America's movie screens was inevitable. The sixties was a time when private problems were made public, when cries for ethnic individuality outshouted pleas for bland assimilation, and when searches for personal identity become more important than material successes. Needless to say, such values stimulated a bitter clash between an emerging youth culture and a powerful establishment both within and without the Jewish-American community, a conflict that flowed over into family gatherings, the streets of Chicago, the jungles of Vietnam, the music of the age, and the movies of an era. The series of culture shocks that reverberated throughout the decade caused a complacent country to re-evaluate its priorities.

The most common image of Jews in the World War II films of the sixties is the same as in previous battle dramas: the Jew as victim. *Lisa* (1962) once again treats the plight of Jewish refugees after the war. Desperately trying to reach Palestine so she can begin a new life, an Auschwitz survivor (Dolores Hart) is aided by a kindly Dutch police inspector (Stephen Boyd) who risks his life and career in that effort. The episodic adventure directed by Philip Dunne traces the refugee's journey through London, Amsterdam, Venice, Morocco, and finally to Palestine. *The Saboteur: Code Name Morituri* (1965) provides an interesting twist to the issue of Nazi anti-Semitism. A German merchant marine officer, Captain Mueller (Yul Brynner), is a staunch anti-Nazi, but the German government forces him to transport rubber for the army by threatening to kill his family. Ironically, the American survivors Mueller picks up after their ship sinks are far more anti-Semitic than most of the Germans in the movie. "Your kind always wind up living rich," one of the Americans tells a fellow survivor, Esther Levy (Janet Margolin), unaware that she is a former concentration camp inmate who suffered sexual horrors while imprisoned. Later the Americans, not the Germans, rape Esther before they riot and destroy Mueller's ship.

While Biblical films featuring Jewish characters all but disappeared from Hollywood during the sixties, pictures featuring Jewish/Gentile romances continued to flourish throughout the decade. Two films put a Jewish/Gentile romance at the center of their stories: *A Majority of One* (1961) and *No Way to Treat a Lady* (1968). In *A Majority of One*

director Mervyn LeRoy, who had made a far better story of Jewish and Gentile outsiders united against an alien world (*Home Before Dark,* 1958), loses his way. The sentimental yarn of a lonely Brooklyn widow, Mrs. Bertha Jacoby (Rosalind Russell), who meets and falls in love with a Japanese gentleman, Koichi Asano (Alec Guinness), when her son-in-law (Ray Danton), a diplomat, is assigned a post in Tokyo, fails to hold much interest beyond its initially unique premise. Like the Leonard Spiegelgass hit play it was based on, the movie's theme is the triumph of common sense over diplomatic nonsense. Mrs. Jacoby's humane sensitivity toward others is recommended over the bureaucratic silliness insisted upon by her protocol-conscious son-in-law. "Cutting through red tape," as *The New York Times* review notes, "is as easy for Mrs. Jacoby as the recipe for gefilte fish." In the end, Mrs. Jacoby's democratic openness triumphs over stuffy rituals.

The compassionate humor of *A Majority of One* and the black comedy of *No Way to Treat a Lady* represents the two opposite approaches sixties filmmakers employed to deal humorously with the Jewish-American experience throughout the decade. In the films of the first type like *John Goldfarb, Please Come Home* (1964), *Enter Laughing* (1967), and *Me, Natalie* (1969), moviemakers filter a broad range of situations through a Jewish comic perspective. *John Goldfarb, Please Come Home,* for

In the final analysis, the arrival of all types of Jews on America's movie screens was inevitable. The sixties was a time when private problems were made public, when cries for ethnic individuality outshouted pleas for bland assimilation, and when searches for personal identity become more important than material successes. Needless to say, such values stimulated a bitter clash between an emerging youth culture and a powerful establishment both within and without the Jewish-American community, a conflict that flowed over into family gatherings, the streets of Chicago, the jungles of Vietnam, the music of the age, and the movies of an era. The series of culture shocks that reverberated throughout the decade caused a complacent country to re-evaluate its priorities.

In turn, such shocks forced the Jewish-American community to examine the principles that had guided its growth from the mass migrations of the 1880s onward and to assess what had been lost and gained in the rapid assimilation of Jews into American life. Along the way, Jews asked the troublesome questions so often ignored in their rush to become Americans: What does it mean to be a Jew in the United States? How are we different from the surrounding Gentile world? How can we salvage something meaningful from the past and integrate it as a valuable part of our present? Ignored in the fifties, these topics dominate the Jewish-American cinema of the sixties. We should not be too hard on a decade of films because it provides few answers to these disturbing inquiries. Sixties filmmakers had, at least, started to ask the right questions and to honestly investigate the course American Jews had chosen to follow. The eighties filmmakers would provide some answers.

The Self-Centered Seventies and the Emerging Eighties

Jews increasingly appeared on America's movie screens in the seventies. Lush musicals like *Fiddler on the Roof* (1971), *Cabaret* (1972), and *Funny Lady* (1975) spotlight Jews. *The Big Fix* (1978), a low-key detective movie, focuses on a Jewish shamus, and Jewish gangsters have important roles in *The Long Goodbye* (1973), *The Godfather, Part II* (1974), and *Lepke* (1975). In *The Frisco Kid* (1979) Jews finally go West. *Norma Rae* (1979) has a tough Jewish textile union organizer as its male protagonist. Jews also have major parts in horror films (*Love at First Bite,* 1979), reporter films (*All the President's Men,* 1976), animated pictures (*Fritz the Cat,* 1972), boxing movies (*The Main Event,* 1979) and the suspense thriller (*The Last Embrace,* 1978).

Bloodline (1979) a glossy melodrama, features a Jewish heiress. Even the flashy, rock music fantasy, *Who Is Harry Kellerman and Why Is He Saying Those Terrible Things About Me?* (1971) centers on a neurotic Jewish songwriter who cannot accept his own success.

The presence of Jewish characters in traditionally non-Jewish genres is one distinctive feature of the decade's cinema. Another is a wave of nostalgia that swept through Hollywood in the seventies and influenced all American films—including those with Jewish characters. The turmoil and strife of the sixties drove moviemakers, as well as much of American society, back to less complicated periods with far clearer issues and

To unravel a mysterious death threat, Harry Hannan (Roy Scheider) and Sam Urdell (Sam Levene) journey to an old synagogue on the Lower East Side in THE LAST EMBRACE *(1979).*

answers. Times that seemed rough when they were happening, appeared almost gentle in comparison with what the nation had just experienced, so Hollywood turned back its clock. The result was a series of films bathed in the warm glow of sentimental nostalgia. Pictures like *Fiddler on the Roof* (1971), *The Way We Were* (1973), *Hester Street* (1975), *Hearts of the West* (1975), *Lies My Father Told Me* (1975) and *Julia* (1977) all display a desire to find refuge in past events and all have central Jewish figures.

Seventies filmmakers, however, did not totally ignore the concerns of contemporary Jews. The continuing animosity between Jews and Blacks surfaced in *The Angel Levine* (1970) and *Boardwalk* (1979). Audiences were reminded of how the horrors of Nazi Germany affect modern life in *The Man in the Glass Booth* (1975), *Marathon Man* (1976), and *The Boys From Brazil* (1979). The worries of modern Jewish businessmen were central in *Save the Tiger* (1973) and of modern Jewish marriages in *The Diary of a Mad Housewife* (1970) and *Blume in Love* (1973). In the seventies, Hollywood even made a conscious effort to explore the implications of aging, using Jewish characters to capture the joy and pathos of growing old—*Kotch* (1971), *Harry and Tonto* (1974), *The Devil and Sam Silverstein* (1975), and *Boardwalk* (1979).

One of the tragedies of sixties life was the widening "generation gap" between the young and the old, children and their parents. In the seventies, parent/child conflicts dominated a number of films, inlcuding *Where's Poppa?* (1970), *Portnoy's Complaint* (1972), *The Apprenticeship of Duddy Kravitz* (1974), *The Gambler* (1974), and *Sheila Levine Is Dead and Living in New York* (1974). Sometimes love problems plagued young people as a result of their meddling parents, as in *Made for Each Other* (1971), *The Heartbreak Kid* (1972), *The In-Laws* (1979) and *Voices* (1979). These pictures, however, depicted the conflicts between children and their parents in a far gentler manner than did sixties movies like *No Way to Treat a Lady* (1968).

Blume (George Segal), Elmo (Kris Kristofferson), and Nina (Susan Anspach) become strange bedfellows in BLUME IN LOVE *(1973).*

Dr. Sheldon Kornpett (Alan Arkin) holds tightly to the top of a speeding cab while escaping South American gunmen in THE IN-LAWS (1979).

Lester Karp (Jack Warden) and his wife Felicia (Lee Grant) share a tense meal in SHAMPOO (1975).

Like their predecessors in the silent era, seventies screen parents are narrow-minded, parochial, and inflexible; they are not evil. In the end, it is the children who teach their parents about love and acceptance.

Though many Jewish-American films of the seventies, following the lead of the sixties, investigated serious concerns such as intermarriage, aging, and parent/child conflicts, comedies did not totally disappear from America's movie screens. Woody Allen's *Annie Hall* (1977) and Mel Brooks's *Blazing Saddles* (1974) juxtaposed Jewish humor and heartland America's values. Neil Simon's *The Sunshine Boys* (1975) treated old age comically but with tenderness. *Minnie and Moskowitz* (1971) approached mixed marriage with gentle humor, *Meatballs* (1979) parodied summer camps, and *Shampoo* (1975) surveyed the Hollywood sex scene. Each film contains at least one important Jewish character. Even America's energy crisis was ridiculed in *Americathon* (1979), as a United Hebrab Republic (composed of Israelis and Arabs) strives to take over the United States. Though all these movies deal with basically serious subjects, their approach is humorous, offering audiences a spoonful of sugar to help the medicine go down.

This serio-comic approach to life and its problems becomes the hallmark of two major Jewish-American filmmakers who rose to prominence during the seventies: Woody Allen and Paul Mazursky. Both populate their films with the Jewish characters and both offer audiences a Jewish slant on American life. *Annie Hall* (1977), in particular, demonstrates Allen's urban, Jewish consciousness, in a series of extended Jewish jokes that become the daily life of his screen persona. In *Next Stop, Greenwich Village* (1976), Mazursky proves himself a sensitive satirist of American life, as he reveals the foibles of his Jewish and Gentile characters with penetrating wit. Allen becomes the Isaac Bashevis Singer and Mazursky the Bernard Malamud of the screen during the seventies, and their movies help move the Jewish-American film to the center of American cinema. Like the novels of the sixties, these films show that the Jewish-American experience had become an intrinsic part of the total American experience.

Sociologist Sidney Goldstein's 1970 demographic study suggests several factors present at the start of the decade that led to a lessening of distinctions between Jews and non-Jews. First, significant alterations within the Jewish-American community broke down barriers between Jews and Gentiles: continuing suburbanization of urban Jews, relocation of Jews away from traditional Jewish centers in the Northeast and toward new areas in the South and West, occupational changes that moved Jews into roles as salaried professionals and managers. Second, change within the Gentile community forced Jews and non-Jews into greater contact: the national emphasis on higher education, the move toward urban areas for work and toward suburban areas for residence, the rising economic standards achieved by Gentiles. Such migration patterns, economic developments, and educational emphasis encouraged increased mingling of Jews and Gentiles at home, in schools, and on the job, resulting in more interaction between them than in previous eras. All these factors contributed to the higher rate of intermarriage in the seventies. They also reduced both groups' impulses toward ethnic separation. Goldstein concludes, "the Jews' direction of changes appears to be the adjustment of American Jews to the American way of life, creating a more meaningful balance between Jewishness and Americanism."

Many segments of American society, as Goldstein notes, experienced prosperity during most of the seventies, including the Jewish-American community. The Census Bureau's 1972 survey shows that of the eight ethnic groups studied, Jews had the highest median family incomes, the highest percentage of high school and college graduates, the highest percentage of white collar workers, and the highest percentage of prestigious occupations. In the academic world, a Carnegie Commission on Higher Education study noted the increasing number of Jews prominent in the country's leading universities. Citing information from these studies as well as from his own research, sociologist Andrew Greeley, a Jesuit priest, concluded in his report to the Ford Foundation that "the Jews are America's most impressive success story" and wondered aloud if "the so called Protestant work ethic had not merely been refuted but reversed" by their rise to success in American life.

Such an "impressive success story" masks two seemingly antithetical movements within the Jewish-American community that characterize the seventies. On the one hand, the emphasis on ethnic uniqueness begun during the sixties continued unabated in the seventies. It was apparent in the growing number of Jewish country clubs, increasing enrollments in Jewish day and Sunday schools, expanding contributions to Jewish charities, and founding of more and more Jewish social clubs. All these trends seemed to create greater Jewish separateness from the surrounding Christian world. On the other hand, many American Jews of the seventies became more involved than their predecessors in life outside their ethnic community, participating in everything from national political conventions to local building drives. Sociologist Melvin Tumin describes this apparent conflict between Jewishness and Americanism as a particularly Jewish challenge to American Society: "Jews are now asking the American community to respect their rights to establish as full-bodied an identity as they care to contrive, and at the same time, to act as though such an identified group does not exist." Jews sought cultural pluralism without cultural prejudice, a kind of selective ethnicity that allowed them to celebrate their heritage with whatever degree of intensity they deemed appropriate while still participating fully in American life. Such a demand called upon American society to be flexible enough to respect the differences between people and tolerant enough to accept them.

Jews had ruled the movie industry during the heyday of the vast studio empires, and they maintained their positions of authority throughout the seventies. As we have seen, however, the new Jewish chieftains did not possess the absolute power of their immigrant predecessors. The movie business had changed. Most of the major studios were now part of large conglomerates, and the studio head had a boss of his own: the company president. The presidents, in turn, had to justify company policies to their stockholders. Such a hierarchy encouraged caution, resulting in film studios making fewer and fewer movies in the decade's early years. Both Fox and MGM auctioned off their props and wardrobes early in the decade.

Mel Brooks directs Clevon Little as sheriff Bart in BLAZING SADDLES *(1974).*

The latter, once the most prestigious dream factory in the world, ceased almost all its film production and distribution activities during the seventies, though it did still invest in a few films each year. In the first part of the decade, the studios seemed like dinosaurs watching over their own extinction.

One of the most significant trends in moviemaking during the seventies was that the impetus to make pictures came from a variety of sources, not just from the large companies that now owned the studios. Agents, for example, become powerful figures in Hollywood. Because financial backing for a project was often predicated on the commitment of a star, those who guided the destinies of

their highly sought-after clients became almost as powerful as the performers themselves. Six of the decade's top production chiefs were ex-agents: David Begelman (Columbia), Mike Medavoy (Orion), Alan Ladd, Jr. (Fox), Ned Tanen (Universal), Martin Elfand (Warners), and Richard Shepard (MGM). Another three—Daniel Melnick (Columbia), Mike Eisner (Paramount), Barry Diller (Paramount)—came from television production. Of these nine executives, six were Jewish (Tanen, Begelman, Elfand, Melnick, Eisner, Diller), continuing the tradition of highly placed Jews within the industry.

When Jews first appeared in seventies sagebrush sagas it was not in heroic or romantic roles; rather, they were used for comic relief. In *The Duchess and the Dirtwater Fox* (1976), for example, two con men (George Segal and Goldie Hawn) stumble into a Jewish wedding while trying to elude their pursuers. There they listen to a silly speech delivered by a frontier rabbi who advises his congregation to "wear long underwear on the range so not to catch a cold." To avoid capture, the two join the dancing celebrants and finally escape by disguising themselves as the Jewish newlyweds. This scene is a small and relatively insignificant part of *The Duchess and the Dirtwater Fox,* but it at least shows Hollywood's recognition that Jews, as well as other minority groups, did live and work in the Old West.

Mel Brooks's *Blazing Saddles* (1974) also recognizes this fact. Though the film's central character, Sheriff Bart (Cleavon Little), is Black, the intolerance he encounters in the supposedly democratic West reveals Brooks's understanding of the prejudice that all minorities faced on the frontier. Brooks's bold, scatological humor masks some serious observations about our heritage, much as his slapstick comedy in *The Producers* (1968) hides some trenchant comments about America's preoccupation with the Third Reich. His portrait of the bigoted Western townspeople of Rock Ridge attacks the "frontier ethics" that helped forge our traditional American value system, showing them tainted with the poison of prejudice, hypocrisy, and intolerance. In fact, the entire film reverberates with the Jewish sense of alienation that leads Brooks to focus on the problems faced by outsiders in the Old West, those segregated by race, color, or religion. Jews, as such, never really appear in *Blazing Saddles,* though one of the picture's funniest moments occurs when an Indian chief (played by Brooks) begins speaking Yiddish. Somehow, it seems comically appropriate that the West's most conspicuous outsider, the Indian, should speak in the tongue of history's traditional outsider, the Jew.

The harmonious balance between old and new seems conspicuously absent in the animated Jewish characters who populated Ralph Bakshi's *Fritz the Cat* (1972). The first of Bakshi's Jewish characters is the police sergeant who, along with his partner Ralph, breaks up Fritz's orgy. Fleeing, Fritz ends up a "fucking fugitive," hiding in a synagogue and disguised in the long, flowing beard of a rabbi. Ralph and the sergeant search the synagogue for

Marcus Rottner (Michael Brandon) enjoys a carefree moment in Venice with his high-society girlfriend (Tippy Walker) in JENNIFER ON MY MIND *(1971).*

Fritz, and the Gentile cop asks his partner if this place is "some kind of hippie church." When they discover Fritz molesting a buxom Jewish woman in the ladies room, they chase him around the synagogue, only to have their pursuit halted by a newscast announcing that the President of the United States has just sent more arms to Israel. The overjoyed rabbi and his congregation begin to dance as Bakshi pokes fun at the supposedly pious Jews who celebrate the delivery of guns that will kill more people. Later, Fritz "bugs out for the West coast" with Winston Schwartz, a boisterous Jew who prefers Howard Johnson's ("You can always count on Howard Johnson's") to the freedom of the open road. From the befuddled police sergeant, to the blood-thirsty synagogue congregants, to the lascivious Jewish matron, to the obnoxious Winston Schwartz, Bakshi's *Fritz The Cat* presents a series of unsympathetic, unattractive portraits of Jews.

Dr. Jeffrey Rosenberg (Richard Benjamin) confronts his arch-enemy, the suave Count Dracula (George Hamilton) in LOVE AT FIRST BITE *(1979).*

Equally unsympathetic and unattractive Jews appeared in the decade's gangster films, perpetuating the trend begun with *The King of the Roaring Twenties: The Story of Arnold Rothstein* (1961). In several films, Jewish gangsters play minor roles. Marcus Rottner, a character in *Jennifer on My Mind* (1971), holds imaginary conversations with his dead grandfather, an immigrant Jew who arrived at Ellis Island with only thirteen cents in his pocket. The Orthodox old man quickly accustomed himself to American life and became a millionaire via racketeering and bootlegging. In Elaine May's *Mikey and Nicky* (1976), Dave Resnick (Sanford Meisner), a Jewish neighborhood boss, puts out a contract on Nick Godolin (John Cassavetes), a small-time bookie. Desperate to escape, Godolin calls on his long-time friend, Mike Mittner (Peter Falk), to help him, and the two embark on a frantic journey through the night.

In the horror films in which Jews appear during the seventies, moviemakers use an element of the Jewish consciousness, humor, to add to the genre's appeal, much as it did earlier in *The Little Shop of*

Horrors and *The Fearless Vampire Killers* (1967). The decade's best example of this tendency is director Stan Dragoti's fetching little spoof of the vampire film, *Love at First Bite* (1979). Among the humorous touches, such as swinging modern girls who think Dracula's (George Hamilton) bite is just another kinky sexual activity, Dragoti includes Richard Benjamin as Dr. Jeffrey Rosenberg, a Jewish descendant of Dr. Van Helsing, Dracula's arch-enemy. Rosenberg persists in confusing the various means of vampiricide. In one memorable moment, he reaches underneath his shirt to extract an amulet to ward off Dracula's advances. The audience, as well as the Count, assumes a cross will be forthcoming; instead, Rosenberg brings forth a Star of David, a symbol which has no effect on the bemused Dracula. So unlike his illustrious and successful ancestor, Rosenberg cannot defeat his sharp-fanged opponent, who escapes at the film's conclusion with his willing bride (Susan St. James).

Another reversal of sorts occurs in *The Main Event* (1979), directed by Howard Zieff, in which a Jewish businesswoman and a rundown fighter team up. Barbra Streisand plays Hilary Kramer, a perfume magnate who discovers she is suddenly broke when her trusted accountant embezzles her money and leaves the country. All Hilary has left is the ownership of one Eddie Scanlan (Ryan O'Neal), also known as Kid Natural, an over-the-hill pugilist with no desire to enter the ring ever again. In a sense, *The Main Event* becomes a kind of modern *Pat and Mike* (1952), with Streisand playing the Tracy role and O'Neal the Hepburn part. Together, the two train, fight, and of course, eventually fall in love.

Zieff opens the movie with a closeup of Streisand's nose, a sly visual joke on those who seem obsessed with its size and shape. In fact, Hilary's nickname in the perfume trade is "the nose," and it stems from the superior sense of smell that has made her fortune. The whole Scanlan/Kramer romance is not only a reverse in sexual roles; it is also a turnabout on the traditional Jewish boy/Irish girl setup so predominant in Jewish-American films throughout the decades, and probably the brainchild of the film's witty scriptwriter, novelist Gail Parent. The movie's other Jewish elements, however, are more felt than featured. Streisand runs through her repertoire of shrugs, facial expressions, and body movements, making O'Neal function more like a prop than a person.

Hilary Kramer (Barbra Streisand) congratulates her fighter Eddie Scanlan (Ryan O'Neal) after his boxing victory in THE MAIN EVENT *(1979).*

The musical genre also contained its share of Jews during the seventies. In 1975, Streisand continued the Fanny Brice saga in a $7.5 million sequel to *Funny Girl* (1968) entitled *Funny Lady.* This time, however, her director was not William Wyler, but the far less accomplished Herbert Ross. The story begins in 1948 during Brice's radio stint as Baby Snooks, and then flashes back to follow her life in the thirties. After being rejected by her gambler/husband Nicky Arnstein (Omar Sharif),

Billy Rose (James Caan) directs his most famous star, Fanny Brice (Barbra Streisand), in FUNNY LADY *(1975)*

High Priests Caiaphas (Robert Bingham)
and Annas (Kurt Yaghjian) listen as Judas
(Carl Anderson) betrays his master in
JESUS CHRIST SUPERSTAR (1973).

she meets and marries Jewish impressario Billy Rose (James Caan). Eventually, she also loses Rose, who falls for a younger, prettier girl. "When you're a star, everything you do is magic," says Fanny, an ironic comment on her loss of Rose. For all its lushness (one commentator counted forty-two lavish Streisand costumes), *Funny Lady* fails to match the life and spirit of its predecessor. The story of the Brice-Rose affair never equals the Brice-Arnstein romance, and Brice is far less interesting as an established star than she was on-the-rise. Whereas the first Brice picture stressed Fanny's Jewishness, made it part of her very essence, the second barely mentions it. Grandiose sets, ornate musical numbers, and five new songs never compensate for the heart and soul so evident in *Funny Girl* and so absent in *Funny Lady*.

The original Brice film caused something of a stir within the Jewish community because of its casting of Sharif, an Egyptian, as Nicky Arnstein, a Jew. The sequel caused no such controversies. But another of the decade's musicals, the rock opera *Jesus Christ Superstar* (1973), infuriated many Jewish-Americans. It was directed by Norman Jewison, who in 1971 had given us *Fiddler on the Roof.* And the film *does* perpetuate the notion that Jews were responsible for Christ's death. The high priest Caiaphas (Robert Bingham) and his cohort Annas (Kurt Yaghjian) convince the Jewish council that this "hero of fools" must die. When their paid informant, Judas (Carl Anderson), reveals that Jesus (Ted Neeley) will be "…where you want him, far from the crowds, in the Garden of Gethsemane," the scheming duo orders soldiers to drag Christ to Caiaphas's house for questioning. When the high priest asks if he is the son of God, Jesus responds, "That's what you say. You say that I am" —enough of an admission for them to order him taken to Pilate. In this sense, then, the Jews who fear Christ's power, popularity, and promise, are shown as clearly responsible for his death. Though they don't commit the actual murder, the film's Jews manipulate the Roman authorities into killing Jesus.

Movies about contemporary Israel, as opposed to those set in the Middle East of the past, virtually disappeared from America's theater screens. Only two films about Israel, both readily forgettable, surface during the entire decade. Director John Flynn's *The Jerusalem File* (1971) involves a Yale student (Bruce Davidson) who gets caught up in the Israeli-Arab conflict by befriending a Palestinian partisan, Raschid (Zeev Revah). Torn between the entreaties of an Israeli secret agent (Donald Pleasance) who wants him to inform on his friend, and the warnings of his professor (Nicol Williamson) who advises him to stay uninvolved, the student eventually sets up a peace meeting between the Arabs and the Jews so they can resolve their differences. His naïve romanticism results in tragedy. *Children of Rage* (1975) focuses on a humane Israeli doctor (Helmut Griam) who sneaks off to tend Palestinian refugees in Jordon, his Arab girlfriend (Olga Georges-Picot), and her terrorist brother (Richard Alfieri). Director/writer Arthur Allan Seidelman moves what little action there is around a series of set pieces in which various characters mouth a spectrum of Arab and Israeli political positions.

The lack of films about Israel during the seventies seems due to several factors. In the first place, few filmmakers wanted to risk Arab boycotts by making pro-Israeli pictures. Some Jewish moviemakers feared charges of bias, or even racism, if they made films that depicted positive Jewish characters clashing with evil Arabs. On the other hand, a film that showed the Arab side of the Mid-Eastern problem ran the risk of inciting the wrath of American Jews, as well as of vocal Jewish organizations like the B'nai B'rith. To these pressures was joined the fact that the American attitude toward Israel seemed less clear in the seventies than it had been in the sixties. Many in this country viewed Israel as the obstacle to a comprehensive peace settlement in the Middle East. Others supported the claims of the Palestinian refugees. In addition, some argued that America's support of Israel could provide an excuse of oil-rich Arab countries to stop the flow of desperately needed fuel to our own shores. It was conceivable that a film about Israel could so incense the Arab world that it would simply turn off the pumps for a while; no producer or filmmaker wanted that on his conscience. So with typical Hollywood fortitude, industry filmmakers simply chose to avoid the entire subject of Israel, figuring that no movies were better than potentially explosive movies.

In the seventies there were also few biographical films with Jewish subjects. Only one major film, director Bob Fosse's *Lenny* (1974), even attempted to tell the story of a real-life Jewish personality—comedian Lenny Bruce—and it downplayed the title character's Jewishness. Fosse never delves very deeply into Lenny Bruce's (Dustin Hoffman) traumatic childhood or the deep resentment he felt for his overbearing mother, Sally Marr (Jan Miner). Perhaps the film's producers feared legal repercussions from Marr, or perhaps they just did not feel this aspect of Bruce's life was particularly important to his development as a performer. Whatever the reasons, Fosse glosses over Lenny's early days. In fact, the film never captures much of Bruce beyond his cabaret persona. Bruce intuitively recognized the pervasive hypocrisy that characterizes much of American life, the gap between what we say in public and what we do in private. His bitter, comic routines shocked complacent Americans because he frankly

Axel Freed (James Caan) toasts his immigrant grandfather, A.R. Lowenthal (Morris Carnovsky), during a birthday celebration in THE GAMBLER *(1974).*

Minnie Moore (Gena Rowlands) and Seymour Moskowitz (Seymour Cassell) become a mismatched couple in MINNIE AND MOSKOWITZ *(1971).*

Drew Rothman (Michael Ontkean) brings a romantic present to his deaf girlfriend Rosemary Lemon (Amy Irving) in VOICES *(1979).*

Writer Neil Simon, author of PLAZA SUITE *(1970),* THE SUNSHINE BOYS *(1975),* THE GOODBYE GIRL *(1977), and* CALIFORNIA SUITE *(1979).*

confronted issues polite people never discussed openly: racism, drugs, religion, sex hang-ups. The routines are in the film, but not the reasons Bruce felt the need to bare his, and the country's, soul. Fosse's Lenny becomes simply a naughty, clever little boy rebelling against his stuffy society with drugs and dirty words, much as Arnold Rothstein and Lepke Buchalter rebelled against their restrictive worlds with bullets.

The family conflicts which Fosse ignores in *Lenny* erupts in a series of films that spotlight clashes between Jewish children and their parents. *Sheila Levine Is Dead and Living in New York* (1974), like *Me, Natalie* (1969), explores a young girl's (Jeannie Berlin) journey toward independence, despite the objections of her clinging, Jewish parents (Sid Melton and Janet Brandt). Pandora Gold (Renée Taylor) in *Made for Each Other* (1971) spends her childhood studying Rita Hayworth movies to appease her star-struck mother (Helen Verbit). Axel Freed (James Caan) has trouble relating to his doctor mother (Jacqueline Brooke) and his merchant-king grandfather (Morris Carnovsky) in *The Gambler* (1974), his obsession with betting is one result of the pressure his family puts on him to succeed.

Just as parent/child conflicts remained a popular subject in the Jewish-American films of the seventies, so too did romantic involvements between Jews and non-Jews. For the most part, the problems are created by the couple's parochial parents. *Made for Each Other* (1971), for example, unites Pandora Gold (Renée Taylor) with Giggy Pamimba (Joseph Bologna), two lonely souls who meet in group therapy. "If you marry her you can forget about skiing," Giggy's father yells at him, "the Jews don't like the cold." Giggy and Pandora ignore their parents and find happiness together. The same holds true for Minnie Moore (Gena Rowlands) and Seymour Moskowitz (Seymour Cassell) in John Cassavetes' *Minnie and Moskowitz* (1971). The contrast between their backgrounds becomes apparent in Cassavetes' portrait of Minnie's and Seymour's parents: the very WASPish Mrs. Moore (Lady Rowlands) and the very Jewish Mrs. Moskowitz (Katherine Cassavetes). Like Giggy and Pandora, Seymour and Minnie find more that joins

than separates them, and ignoring their parents' warnings, they resolve to stay together. In *Voices* (1979) Drew Rothman (Michael Ontkean) faces more than parental displeasure in his affair with the Gentile Rosemary Lemon (Amy Irving). Rosemary is deaf, so Drew must find nonverbal ways to communicate his feelings for her and to gain her trust. Eventually, of course, he does, and they become lovers.

Throughout the seventies an increasing amount of women of all faiths sought equal rights, Jewish women being among the most outspoken. A group of Jewish women founded Ezrat Nashim ("helper of woman") in 1971, an organization dedicated to expanding the role of Jewish women in all aspects of religious life. Characteristically, the group displayed a healthy sense of Jewish humor about their grievances, sporting buttons that read, "It's Not Just Tallis Envy," to underline their demands.[13] Later, in 1974, the Jewish Feminist Organization was founded, and it claimed over 1,500 members by 1976. Other activities signaled the advance of Jewish feminism: Haggadahs (prayer books for the

Passover seder) were rewritten to provide women with larger roles; *Lilith,* a Jewish women's periodical, appeared in 1976; ceremonies for female babies were created; more female Reform rabbis were ordained; the Bat Kol Players, a woman's acting group, toured cities with plays featuring Jewish Biblical heroines and then led discussion groups about these women; *havurahs,* study and worship groups with men and women, accorded females larger roles in religious ceremonies. Other women's groups revived old services discarded by men, such as the Ceremony of the New Moon that celebrates the rebirth of life in female and lunar cycles. As with any new movement, the Jewish feminists had their problems with more traditional segments within the Jewish-American community, but their achievements assured them a reassessment of the traditional, subservient role women have played throughout much of Jewish history.

David Kessler (David Naughton) gets bitten by a werewolf and becomes a savage beast in AN AMERICAN WEREWOLF IN LONDON *(1981).*

Such a new feminine consciousness surfaced in many of the films of the seventies featuring Jewish women. A few, like *Made For Each Other* (1971), *Sheila Levine Is Dead and Living in New York* (1974), *Funny Lady* (1975) and *The Main Event* (1979) have already been mentioned. At least two other movies, however, demand more attention: *The Way We Were* (1973) and *Julia* (1977), particularly the latter. Directed by Fred Zinnemann, *Julia* dramatizes the deep bond between writer Lillian Hellman (Jane Fonda) and her childhood friend Julia (Vanessa Redgrave), who becomes a dedicated anit-Nazi in the days prior to the war. Its high point is Hellman's willingness to act as a secret courier in order to bring Julia, now a fugitive from the Germans, $50,000 to pay for the release of Third Reich prisoners. Her act is particularly courageous because, as a Jew traveling through Hitler's Germany, Hellman is particularly vulnerable. Through the character of Hellman, Zinnemann shows how a generation abandoned its innocent isolationism to fight the evil that threatened to destroy them.

Seventies filmmakers did not totally ignore the funny side of Jewish-American life. Woody Allen and Paul Mazursky, the decade's best Jewish-American moviemakers, played important roles in the American cinema of the seventies and assured film audiences a steady diet of laughs. In addition, the prolific Neil Simon contributed a number of film scripts to the screen, most with Jewish characters: *Plaza Suite* (1970), *The Out of Towners* (1970), *Last of the Red Hot Lovers* (1972), *The Prisoner of Second Avenue* (1975), *The Sunshine Boys* (1975), *The Goodbye Girl* (1976), and *California Suite* (1978). In just twenty years, Simon produced over twenty plays, many of them turned into successful films. Critic Daniel Walden recently argued that the style of Simon's comedy "comes right out of the Eastern-European experience, is consistent with the humor in stories of Mendele, Sholem Aleichem, and Pertz, and is part of a tradition that includes Abraham Cahan, Saul Bellow, Bernard Malamud, and Philip Roth." Such humor is clear at moments, as in the Walter Matthau/Elaine May segment of *California Suite:* a Jewish New Yorker who comes to Los Angeles for his nephew's bar mitzvah is tricked into sleeping with a hooker and his wife

Teteh (Mandy Patinkin), a Jewish immi-grant turned filmmaker in RAGTIME *(1981).*

The famous Jewish radical Emma Gold-man (Maureen Stapleton) in REDS *(1981).*

Doris Feinsecker (Maureen Teefy) auditions to enter the High School of Performing Arts in FAME *(1980).*

finds the two in bed the next morning. But unlike Allen and Mazursky, Simon is not an *auteur;* he does not have the artistic control over his works as do those writers who also direct. In essence, Simon remains a man of the theater, where words dominate, rather than of the cinema, where images dominate, which is one reason why his successful Broadway plays have made unimpressive films lacking both visual appeal and thematic interest.

The success of *Annie Hall,* in particular, proved that a vast number of Americans could appreciate overt Jewish humor. The groundbreaking attempts at more realistic and complex portraits of Jewish characters begun in the sixties reached its fruition in the seventies. The celluloid Jew, though still alienated, came of age in a diverse series of films that covered a broad spectrum of Jewish-American experiences. Controversial subject areas like the conflicts between Blacks and Jews and painful topics like the plight of elderly Jews in urban America were deemed worthy of presentation during this decade, a sign of the increasing confidence as well as the acceptability of Jews in all parts of the country. Though they continued to appear in comic roles, Jews emerged as legitimate subjects for serious film parts as well. This trend continued on into the next decade, but with some variations in emphasis. "Surviving, that's my career," says old David Rosen in *Boardwalk* (1979). That, too, was the career of America's screen Jews, as they emerged as fully developed characters in the films of the seventies.

In the sixties, when Hollywood responded to the country's growing obsession with ethnicity, filmmakers presented Jews in a number of new roles. The movies of the seventies continued in this direction, expanding their range and exploring their characters more fully. If the first five years of the eighties proves an accurate indicator of Hollywood trends, Jews will figure even more prominently on celluloid during the rest of the decade. Many Jewish characters have already appeared, some in the most unlikely of places. In *Fort Apache, The Bronx* (1981), an Orthodox Sergeant Applebaum (Irving Metzman) lectures the multi-ethnic cops of the beleaguered 41st precinct, and in *Sharkey's Machine* (1981) Burt Reynolds is aided by his Jewish boyhood friend, an electronic genius

The Angel Beach High theatrical ensemble featuring Brian Schwartz (Scott Colomby, second from left) awaits word of their show's fate in PORKY'S II *(1984).*

John Landis, director of AN AMERICAN WEREWOLF IN LONDON *(1981) and* TWILIGHT ZONE, THE MOVIE, PART ONE *(1983).*

(Right) Mickey Goldmill (Burgess Meredith), Rocky Balboa's trainer and good friend in ROCKY III *(1982).*

Max Herschel (Alan King) meets his match in Seymour Berger (Keenan Wynn), a shrewd movie mogul in JUST TELL ME WHAT YOU WANT (1980).

Max Herschel (Alan King) takes it on the chin from his glamourous mistress (Ali MacGraw) in JUST TELL ME WHAT YOU WANT (1980).

(Right) David Levine (Michael Huddleston), the comic Jewish member of a high school gang in FOUR FRIENDS (1981).

Estelle Rolfe (Anne Bancroft), a dying eccentric whose last wish is to meet her favorite moviestar in GARBO TALKS *(1984).*

Bearded Daniel Issacson (Timothy Hutton) is joined by his wife (Ellen Barkin) and family friends as they bury his sister next to his parents in DANIEL *(1983).*

Saul Benjamin (Dudley Moore), a psychiatrist in love with his patient, consults the ultimate father figure, Sigmund Freud (Alec Guinness), in LOVESICK *(1983).*

Kathy Gunsinger (Jill Clayburgh) tries to explain her feelings to Ben Lewin (Michael Douglas) in ITS MY TURN *(1980).*

Marshall Brickman, frequent collaborator with Woody Allen and director of SIMON *(1980) and* LOVESICK *(1983).*

named Nosh (Richard Libertini). Arthur Rosenberg (Robert Balaban) assists Dr. Eddie Jessup (William Hurt) with his religious hallucinatory experiments during *Altered States* (1981). Seymour Goldfarb, Jr., playboy son of a wealthy girdle manufacturer and a competitor in *The Cannonball Run* (1981), pretends to be suave actor Roger Moore (who actually plays this role). A young American Jew (David Naughton) traveling in England gets bitten by a werewolf and turns into a savage best in *An American Werewolf in London* (1981). Mr. Blumenthal (Eli Wallach), the cynical and tightfisted bailbondsman in *The Hunter* (1980), provides bountyhunter Ralph Thorsen (Steve McQueen) with most of his assignments.

Ragtime (1981) contains an interesting, if brief, portrait of a Jewish immigrant turned filmmaker (Mandy Patinkin), and *Reds* (1981) shows glimpses of the famous Jewish radical Emma Goldman (Maureen Stapleton). One of the Angel Beach boys in the *Porky's* series (1982, 1984, 1985) is Brian (Scott Colomby). A clever Jewish highschooler, he is first a victim of anti-Semitism but later proves his manhood and is accepted in the gang. Much to the amazement of audiences, Rocky Balboa's seemingly Irish trainer and friend, Mickey (Burgess Meredith), turns out to be Jewish in *Rocky III* (1982). A former Jew turned cult member (Nick Mancuso) is captured and deprogrammed by his concerned parents in *Ticket to Heaven* (1984). Jews even enter a new genre in the eighties, science-fiction films: the archetypal scientist from early serial days becomes a Jewish Dr. Hans Zarkov (Topol) in the campy, updated *Flash Gordon* (1980), a Jewish secretary is abducted by a lascivious robot in *Heavy Metal* (1981), and the first two segments of *Twilight Zone—The Movie* (1983) contain Jewish characters.

The Jewish characters in these films are mainly secondary figures, but the very fact that identified Jews function as commonplace inhabitants of the vastly different environments in these diverse pictures shows that much of the "exoticness" so evident in earlier movies is no longer a necessary component of Jewish celluloid portraits in the eighties. American filmmakers apparently feel confident that their audience will not find it strange or disconcerting to discover Jews almost anywhere, from the Harvard of *Altered States* to the alien planets of *Heavy Metal* to the reform school of *Bad Boys* (1983) to the suburbs of *Compromising Positions* (1985) to the city streets of *Quicksilver* (1986), and even in *The Twilight Zone*.

In the eighties Jews are not relegated to minor roles. Ralph Bakshi's *American Pop* (1981) follows the saga of a family of Russian immigrants in the United States, as does the first Jewish Christmas movie, *An American Tail* (1986). *It's My Turn* (1980) presents a female protagonist, Kathy Gunsinger (Jill Clayburgh), who tries to assert herself in her professional and personal life, while *Fame* (1980) concentrates on a Jewish girl, Doris Feinsecker (Maureen Teefy), who tries to make it in show business. *Eyewitness* (1981) reverses the typical Jewish male/Irish female romance by having a cultured, upper-class Jewish reporter (Sigourney Weaver) become involved with a blond, working-class Irishman (William Hurt). Neil Diamond remakes *The Jazz Singer* (1980), this time with a rock score, and Alan King plays an egotistical Jewish tycoon in *Just Tell Me What You Want* (1980). Dudley Moore is a Jewish psychiatrist involved with his patient in *Lovesick* (1983), Michael Huddleston a sensitive Jewish youth in *Four Friends* (1981), Timothy Hutton the son of Jewish radicals in *Daniel* (1983), and Anne Bancroft an eccentric Jewish mother whose dying wish is to meet the elusive Greta in *Garbo Talks* (1984). In *Private Benjamin* (1980), Goldie Hawn struggles with her parents and the United States Army, in *Ordinary People* (1980) Judd Hirsch ministers to an ailing WASP family, and in *S.O.B.* (1981) Robert Preston plays a hip, Beverly Hills physician.

A trio of talented Jewish filmmakers make new movies in the eighties: Woody Allen *(Stardust Memories,* 1980; *Broadway Danny Rose,* 1984; *Zelig,* 1983; *Hannah and Her Sisters,* 1986), Paul Mazursky *(Willy and Phil,* 1980; *Tempest,* 1980; *Moscow on the Hudson,* 1984; *Down and Out in Beverly Hills,* 1966), Mel Brooks *(History of the World, Part One,* 1981; *To Be or Not to Be,* 1983). Unfortunately, while many of these films deal with Jewish problems and all contain Jewish characters, most lack the openness of the sixties films about Jews and the sophistication of the seventies

Professor Bobby Fine (Ryan O'Neal) learns why his father (Jack Warden) needs him to take over the family fashion firm in so FINE (1982).

Dr. Irving Feingarten (Robert Preston) with his perscription for happiness in s.o.b (1981).

91

movies. Instead, the directors and writers of the eighties often fall back on stereotypes.

Stereotypes were a problem both on and off the screen at the dawn of the eighties. Harold E. Quinley and Charles Y. Glock's *Anti-Semitism in America* (1979) concludes that "anti-Semitism today largely involves the harboring of a negative image about Jews." It also provides the Jews of the eighties with some disconcerting news: while very few non-Jews favored overt discrimination, a third of the Gentile Americans surveyed viewed Jews with suspicion and distrust, seeing them as "deceitful and dishonest in business, clannish in their behavior toward others, pushy and aggressive, vain and conceited, and controlling or having disproportionate influence over the media, motion picture, and banking industries." Another poll conducted during the last month of 1980 showed that one-third of those surveyed believed Jews were more loyal to Israel than to the United States. For the Jewish-American community, therefore, the new decade brought an increased awareness of their "otherness," and a series of shocking and disturbing incidents testified to a renewed spirit of anti-Semitism in American life. In 1980, the Anti-Defamation League of the B'nai B'rith reported a three-fold increase in anti-Semitic "episodes" in just one year, including arson, firebombings, and death threats. The resurgence of the Ku Klux Klan and the American Nazi Party, both of which ran somewhat successful candidates for public office in the last election, contributed to Jewish fears.

Many movies of the eighties containing Jewish characters follow familiar patterns begun in the sixties and developed in the seventies, including the appearance of more films featuring female protagonists. One such film is director Alan Parker's *Fame* (1980). His central character, Doris Feinsecker (Maureen Teefy), becomes part of a talented group of students assembled at New York City's High School for the Performing Arts. Afraid her talents are inferior to those of her classmates, Doris starts her freshman year as a shy and detached introvert. Her aggressive Jewish mother (Teresa Hughes) harbors no such fears. She pushes Doris to enter the highly competitive school, books her daughter to sing at kiddie birthday parties, and remains convinced that she will one

day be a star. But when Doris wants to change her name to the more theatrical Dominique Dupont, Mrs. Feinsecker is mortified. "I don't mind being Jewish," Doris says later, "but it's not all I am." By the end of the film, Doris has proven her worth as a human being and her talent as a performer. Graduation day finds her secure in her accomplishments but frightened about what lies ahead in a show-business world even more competitive than the classroom.

Like most of the other screen Jews of the eighties, male and female, Doris Feinsecker is not ashamed of being Jewish. She does not attempt to hide her heritage or to pass as a Christian in a Gentile world. But her Jewish consciousness never overwhelms her, never locks her into the uncomfortable positions assumed by Neil Klugman in *Goodbye, Columbus,* or by Alexander Portnoy in *Portnoy's Complaint.* Her recognition that being Jewish is "not all I am" stands as a motto for most celluloid Jews of the new decade: they accept their heritage as a valuable part of their lives, but they seek more. Screen Jews of the early eighties don't turn into something other than Jews; rather, they become something in addition. Jewish teachers *(It's My Turn, Willy and Phil, Simon),* Jewish psychiatrists *(Ordinary People),* Jewish filmmakers *(Stardust Memories, Ragtime),* Jewish doctors *(S.O.B.),* Jewish businessmen *(Just Tell Me What You Want),* Jewish performers *(The Jazz Singer)* and even Jewish undertakers *(Four Friends).*

Eighties filmmakers whose comedies depict Jews have failed to equal Woody Allen's or Paul Mazursky's technical skill and thematic depth. Director Gary Weis's *Wholly Moses* (1980), which Orthodox Rabbi Abraham Hecht denounced as "a savage mockery of our God, Bible…and our teacher and prophet Moses," is more silly than sacrilegious. With Dudley Moore as Herschel, Moses' ill-fated brother-in-law who keeps thinking that it is to him God is speaking, the picture functions as nothing more than a pointless and drawn-out Biblical parody. In director Hal Needham's *The Cannonball Run* (1981), Seymour Goldfarb, Jr. (Roger Moore), ignores his true identity as the son of a wealthy Jewish manufacturer by passing himself off as film star Roger Moore, despite the protestations of his overly protective

Jewish mother. Director Gerald Potterton in the animated *Heavy Metal* (1981) includes one segment in which a Jewish secretary is kidnapped by a sex-starved alien robot, and rejects his marriage proposal because "mixed-marriages don't work." Finally, she agrees on two conditions: he gives her "a large Jewish wedding" and he gets circumcised. *So Fine* (1982) showcases the generaton gap between Jack Fine (Jack Warden), the hustling head of Fine Fashions, and his son Bobby (Ryan O'Neal), a professor of comparative literature more concerned with Dreiser than with Dacron. When Fine Fashions falls on hard times, Bobby leaves the halls of Ivy for the cutting rooms of Seventh Avenue. Accidentally, he creates a new fashion craze: de-

Masha (Sandra Bernhard), a wealthy Jewish groupie, can't believe Rupert Pupkin (Robert De Niro) has a meeting with a famous talk-show host in THE KING OF COMEDY *(1983).*

signer jeans with see-through back pockets. About all these films do is contribute to the growing visibility of Jews on screen in the films of the early eighties.

Director Blake Edwards makes more of his Jewish character, Dr. Irving Feingarten (Robert Preston) in *S.O.B.* (1981). A pillpopping, vitamin freak, Feingarten joins with the film's other admirable characters (William Holden and Robert Webber) to take revenge on some sadistic Hollywood studio heads who have destroyed their friend, producer Felix Farmer (Richard Mulligan). Beneath his cynical, hip exterior, Feingarten displays the morals of a concerned man disgusted by the crass commercialism and heartless hypocrisy that dominates Hollywood. His decision to help right the wrongs done to his friend Felix represents an ethical choice, as well as an attack on the Hollywood establishment he despises. There is something of the old Dr. Abelman (*The Last Angry Man,* 1959) still very much alive in the modern Dr. Feingarten; both are Jewish physicians who obey the dictates of their consciences instead of simply protecting their own interests.

Another attempt at humor, this time modern screwball comedy, revolves around Max Herschel (Alan King), a Jewish business tycoon, and his affair with the aggressive Bones Burton (Ali MacGraw), a successful television producer in director Sidney Lumet's *Just Tell Me What You Want* (1980). Max is a lovable louse who spouts Yiddish curses and treats his lovers like an overprotective Jewish father: he finances their college educations and has an orthodontist straighten their teeth. His own daughter, now grown up and married, is still called "Baby," though Max barely tolerates her professor husband. In the film's slapstick climax, Bones beats up Max in Bergdorf Goodman's. Though the cowardly Max hides under a display case to avoid her blows, he nevertheless ends up in the hospital, where he insists on tipping Jewish workers fifty dollars more than Christian workers.

Director Lumet has never been known for his light touch, and *Just Tell Me What You Want* adds little to his reputation. However, the picture does contain one notable Jewish characterization: Keenan Wynn as Seymour Berger, the head of International Pictures. In the person of Berger, Lumet fashions a complex portrait of the oldtime Jewish movie mogul, alternately charming and vicious. For example, Berger tearfully spins out a poignant yarn about his family for Max, which we later discovered is simply a clever ruse to save the studio for his homosexual nephew (Tony Roberts). Berger thus bests Herschel at his own game of manipulating money and people to gain power. But he is more than just a shrewd old con man. The tired mogul outsmarts Max not because he likes his nephew but because he feels a responsibility to

provide for his family members. Never the same since the death of his beloved wife, Berger carries around her ashes with him wherever he travels. The film's tenderest moment comes between Berger and Bones, not between Bones and Max, as the old Jew and the young girl sit and talk quietly about their loves and losses. For once, both drop their protective shells and speak freely about their loneliness and pain. This placid, fleeting moment in an otherwise loud and frantic movie stands alone, an isolated encounter of tenderness shared by two near strangers.

Finally, the eighties provides two different, but equally intriguing, comedies: *Diner* (1982) and *The King of Comedy* (1983). The former stars Steve Guttenberg as Eddie, a totally assimilated Jew of the early sixties and part of a gang of five Baltimore buddies. Eddie seems blithely unaware of his heritage. A football fanatic, he demands everything at his wedding be decorated in blue and white, not for Israel but for his beloved Colts. The latter film, directed by Martin Scorsese, remains one of the most underrated works of the decade. A wonderfully wry piece of painful satire, it stars Robert De Niro as Rupert Pupkin, a comic obsessed with getting on television. His partner is Marsha (Sandra Bernhard), a rich, neurotic Jewish girl who forever hangs around theater exits waiting to get autographs of famous people. Desperate to be "somebody," the two kidnap talk show host Jerry Langford (Jerry Lewis). Their ransom is a spot on the show for Rupert's comedy skit. In the movie's finest scene, a bound and gagged Langford sits numbly staring at a seductive Marsha who delivers a seriocomic monologue about her fantasies and frustrations. Even the film's motto echos its Jewish sense of humor: "Better to be a king for a night than a schmuck for a lifetime."

To date, the films of the eighties have not matched the raw power of the sixties movies or the thematic sophistication of seventies pictures; however, they have been filled with portraits of Jews. Sadly, most of these Jewish characters have been negative, from the lost immigrants of *American Pop* (1981) to the immature professional of *It's My Turn* (1980), to the spoiled "JAP" of *Private Benjamin* (1980), to the gangsters of *The Cotton Club* (1984), to the fat brat of *Goonies* (1985). Most ominous of all is the picture of the suave but fanatical Israeli murderer in *Eyewitness* (1981), the first negative portrait of an Israeli in Hollywood history. The strongest positive images of Jews in the eighties have come in the form of the kindly psychiatrist of *Ordinary People* (1980), the Jewish cantor who becomes a rock star in *The Jazz Singer* (1980), and the adolescents of *The Chosen* (1982). In these films there does seem to be some meaningful union of the past and present, of the traditional and the new.

Throughout the history of Hollywood, celluloid Jews have been pilloried, chastised, praised, victimized, ridiculed, and admired. Hollywood filmmakers acknowledged their positive values, such as a dedication to a warm homelife and a deep love of learning, as well as their more negative manifestations: the overbearing Jewish mother and the spoiled Jewish-American Princess. All became part of American culture, as easily recognizable as hot dogs and apple pie.

NOTES

1. Stuart Fox's 1970 bibliography compiled under the auspices of The Hebrew University (Abraham F. Rad Contemporary Film Archives), The World Zionist Organization (Dept. of Organization and Information), and the University of Southern California (Division of Cinema), lists over 700 feature films containing Jewish characters of various types. Since the list was completed, a substantial number of other titles could be included. Fox's groundwork in this field proved an invaluable starting point for my own work, as well as a useful compilation of information.

2. Milton R. Konvitz, "The Quest for Equality and the Jewish Experience," in *Jewish Life in America* (ed.) Gladys Rosen (New York: KATV, 1978), p. 43.

3. Israel Zangwell, *The Melting Pot* in *The Collected Works of Israel Zangwell* (New York: AMS Press, 1969), p. 95.

4. Stuart Samuels, "The Evolutionary Image of Jews in American Films," in *Ethnic Images in American Film and Television,* (ed.) Randall Miller (Philadelphia: The Balch Institute, 1978), p. 23.

5. This isn't to say there was no concern on the part of Jews in the industry. As James Yaffe points out in *The American Jews* (New York: Random House, 1968), the Anti-Defamation League of the B'nai B'rith organized several theater owners in a boycott of movie companies that made the infamous Rosenstein films early in the 1900s. These were two-reel melodramas in which Rosenstein, a villainous miser and jewel fence, appeared rubbing his hands together and grinning evilly as he bilked poor Christian widows and orphans out of their life savings (p. 39).

6. The Motion Picture Project, originally funded by National Jewish Organizations and now called the Jewish Film Advisory Committee, was formed according to its president, Allen Rivkin, because of "two despicable films *[Abie's Irish Rose* and *The Cohens and The Kellys]*...inimical to Jewish interests." Specifically, Rivkin goes on to note, "it was the task of the Motion Picture Project to convince producers by persuasion and information to tone down such films."

7. Sig Altman, *The Comic Image of the Jew* (Rutherford: Fairleigh Dickinson Press, 1971), pp. 11, 49, 50.

8. Both comments are found in *Ethnic Images in American Film and Television,* Randall Miller (ed.) Philadelphia: The Blanche Institute, 1978), p. 37, p. XIV.

9. John Baxter, "The Thirties" in (ed.) Peter Cowie, *Hollywood 1920-1970* (London: The Tantivy Press, 1977), p. 69.

10. Quoted in Tom Tugent, "The Hollywood Jews," *Davka* (Fall 1975), p. 5.

11. *Movie Lot to Beachhead* (New York: Doubleday, Doran and Co., 1945), p. 216.

12. The "Hollywood Ten" were Dalton Trumbo, Albert Maltz, Edward Dmytryk, Ring Lardner, Jr., Lester Cole, Samuel Ornitz, Herbert Biberman, Alvah Bessie, John Howard Lawson, and Adrian Scott.

13. A *tallis* is a prayer shawl worn by Conservative and Orthodox Jewish males in obedience to an ancient biblical law. Reform Judaism has eliminated the use of the *tallis* at general worship, though some Reform rabbis still wear it over their gowns while conducting services.

Judith (Blanche Sweet) beautifies herself to ensnare the Assyrian King Holofernes in JUDITH OF BETHULIA *(1914).*

Chapter 2

The Silents

Silent films featuring Biblical Jewish figures form a rather sizable category, though they are among the least interesting because of their pedestrian aesthetics, insensitivity to historical accuracy, heavy-handed morality, and simplistic character development. Nevertheless, all the Jewish figures one would expect appear: Saul, Moses, Abraham, Cain and Abel, David, Noah, Esther, Joseph, and Samson. In addition, figures like Bar Kochba, the Maccabees, Judith, and Elisha also spring to life in

the silent films of early directors. Taken as a whole, this relatively undistinguished group of movies contains only two films—Griffith's *Judith of Bethulia* (1914) and Curtiz's *Noah's Ark* (1929-part talkie)—of real interest and that mainly for events outside the films themselves.

Judith of Bethulia remains an important film primarily because it shows early evidence of the power and talent so abundantly clear in later Griffith works such as *The Birth of a Nation* (1914) and *Intolerance* (1916). Biograph's failure to support the venture properly, a costly $36,000 four-reel feature produced at a time when films customarily were less expensive and ran only two reels, finally convinced Griffith to forsake that studio and move on to Reliance-Majestic where he could make longer, more expensive projects. Based on the story from the Apocrypha, the film tells the emotional story of Judith, a virtuous Israelite, who murders Holofernes, a fierce leader of the attacking Assyrians, and saves her people. In fact, what finally motivates Judith to slay Holofernes is a vision of her people being slaughtered by a merciless enemy. The Jews are portrayed as a nation composed predominantly of potential victims rather than of fierce warriors. They rely on a woman who seduces a man and then cuts off his head, securing by guile a victory they are unable to attain in manly combat. Thus, the Jewish nation survives through trickery rather than heroic action on the battlefield of honor. Though perhaps not worthy of all the praise it subsequently received as the culmination of Griffith's Biograph years, and qualifying neither as the first feature film in American cinema nor as the longest film made to that date as some critics believe, *Judith* does provide ample evidence of Griffith's rapidly maturing talents as well as his ability to manipulate large-scale action scenes with an ease and assurance unmatched by other silent directors. The film further demonstrates Griffith's superb sense of cinematic rhythm and movement in both the

Judith (Blanche Sweet) getting Holofernes (Henry Walthall) drunk before beheading him in JUDITH OF BETHULIA *(1914).*

action inside and between the frames. (Griffith instructed theaters showing *Judith* to play excerpts from Rossini's *William Tell* in conjunction with certain scenes.)

Japheth (George O'Brien) watches Miriam (Dolores Costello) rather than the sheep in the Biblical section of NOAH'S ARK *(1928).*

David Cominsky (Rudolph Schildkraut), the old-world patriarch in HIS PEOPLE *(1925).*

Curtiz's *Noah's Ark* is equally interesting to film historians—but for very different reasons. The director parallels a classic Biblical tale with a World War I love story. Most of the actors play dual roles, one in the Biblical and one in the modern story: Dolores Costello (Mary/Miriam), George O'Brien (Travis/Japheth), Noah Beery, Sr. (Nickoloff/King Nephiliu). Though the necessity of a strong, enduring faith in God remains the ultimate message in both stories, some odd permutations in character occur. For example, a clearly Jewish maiden like Miriam in the Biblical section of the film becomes just as clearly a non-Jewish character when she surfaces in the modern segment of the film. It is somehow acceptable for a heroine to be Jewish if she lives in Biblical times, but the same role played for the same themes and set in modern times demands a non-Jewish heroine. Clearly, contemporaneity makes Jewishness in a heroine far less desirable.

Sammy Cominksy (George Lewis) and Mamie Shannon (Blanche Mahaffey) declare their love in HIS PEOPLE *(1925).*

Two totally overlooked films of this period, *His People* (1925) and *Surrender* (1927), present an exemplary mixture of many plots and preoccupations of silent films about Jews. Edward Sloman, the director of both, is a man whose work has long since been forgotten, ignored in catalogues of trivia and in most scholarly works on the silent era. Only Kevin Brownlow shows passing interest in his work by devoting a chapter to Sloman in *The Parade's Gone By* (1969). In addition to enjoying a rather successful stage and screen acting career, Sloman directed over fifty features between 1916 and 1938 including: *The Embodied Thought* (1916), *Westerners* (1919), *We Americans* (1928), *The Kibbitzer* (1930), *Puttin' on the Ritz* (1930) and *A Jury's Secret* (1938). This list fails to qualify Sloman for a spot in Andrew Sarris's famous "Pantheon" or perhaps even for a place in his "Miscellany," but the technical excellence of *His People* and *Surrender* combined with their sophisticated character insights and complex themes make them neglected examples of film artistry. As such, they deserve a larger viewing and sympathetic rediscovery.

David Cominsky (Rudolph Schildkraut) hears his son Morris (Arthur Lubin) deny him to impress his upper-class friends in HIS PEOPLE *(1925).*

His People opens with a series of New York City ghetto shots emphasizing the El train cutting through the city, and immigrant children playing in the crowded streets. Its first title hints at the romantic, melodramatic flavor that seasons the entire picture: "Scattered for centuries, these people have come from the four corners of Europe, each bringing a dream of prosperity and happiness." Newcomers often find these two dreams mutually exclusive, and Sloman strives throughout the film to unify them in a particularly American manner. Quickly, and with little unnecessary exposition, he introduces the film's leading characters. The Shannons are "foreigners in the neighborhood" of Eastern-European Jews, and Mamie (Blanche Mahaffey) is characterized as "so sweet you'd never think she's Irish." Juxtaposed with the Shannons are the Cominskys. David (Rudolph Schildkraut), the father, was a student in Russia but finds "no market for his knowledge here;" Rose (Rosa Rosanova), his wife, is a stereotypical *Yiddishe mama* whose large heart is matched only by the size of her enormous bosom; Sammy (George Lewis) dreams of being what Papa contemptuously labels a "box fighter;" Morris (Arthur Lubin), "the pride of the Cominsky household," studies to be a lawyer.

The film's opening moments clearly establish

Sammy Cominsky (George Lewis) orders his brother Morris (Arthur Lubin) home to their Lower East Side tenement in HIS PEOPLE *(1925).*

Happy Mama Cominsky (Rosa Rosanova) reconciles her two sons (George Lewis/ Arthur Lubin) in HIS PEOPLE *(1925).*

99

the familiar conflicts between the strict discipline of old-world religious traditions and the intoxicating freedoms of New-World life in America. Though Papa dutifully kisses the mezuzah upon entering his tenement apartment, he agrees to stay home from synagogue on the Sabbath because his busy day selling linens exhausts him. The nascent affection that will develop into interracial love between Manie and Sammy surfaces as they shyly share an ice-cream cone. When he saves his studious brother from the local bully, Izzy Rosenblatt, Sammy displays physical strength superior to Morris's, and when the latter tattles on his defender for fighting, Sammy's moral superiority is also clear. Of course, the mother defends Sammy from the father's wrath by quickly lighting the Friday night candles and reminding her husband it is the Sabbath, a day of restful peace.

The sharp cut from the family's Sabbath meal to a similar scene ten years in the future provides some convincing evidence of Sloman's technical competence. He presents the family in a complex deep-focus shot with all planes of action visible throughout much of the scene. The fore and midground contain most of the action with Mamie dominating the background by remaining in an open window across the alley. Sixteen years before Gregg Toland's experiments for Orson Welles in *Citizen Kane,* Sloman's shot emphasizes the interaction between fore, mid, and background activities, with Mamie a constant presence in the Cominsky household through her presence in the scene. A series of important exchanges within the relative stasis of the setup deepen character relationships through verbal and visual motifs. Morris, now that he has graduated from law school with honors, feels smugly superior to Sammy, who remains a lowly newsboy; Mama, however, tactfully reminds him that it was Sammy's earnings that put him through law school.

Sloman continues to develop the scene with a series of sharp and expertly handled crosscuts. As Papa gives the traditional blessing over the Sabbath wine, Mamie whistles for Sammy to join her. The scene thus becomes symbolic of the conflict between the observance of traditional religion and the pull of the new world. When Sammy goes to the window, his irritated father drags him back to the table by the ears. He accedes for the moment, but Mamie eventually lures him away and he joins her on the fire escape. America wins.

Both of Papa's sons desert the Sabbath rituals: Sammy to be with Mamie, and Morris to join his fancy uptown friends. Morris, as we later learn, is courting former Judge Stein's beautiful daughter, Ruth. At the judge's home, Sloman again employs the deep-focus technique to create simultaneous action with all planes constantly in focus. When the Judge asks to meet Morris's parents, the young lawyer's embarrassment at their lowly status overwhelms him, and after telling how he put himself through college, he concludes, "I am quite alone. I have no parents."

Sloman pushes the action forward with a series of carefully executed juxtapositions enlarging on the difference between Morris and Sammy, as well as on David's misreadings of his sons. For example, after Papa trudges through a terrible snowstorm to pawn his most prized possession (a Russian fur coat) so Morris can have a new suit, Morris decides that the outfit is too shabby and heartlessly tosses it into the nearest ash can. Meanwhile, Sammy bills himself as "Battling Rooney" and wins a series of fights. Even when his father discovers the ruse and banishes him from the house, Sammy continues to slip Mama money to help pay the bills.

These conflicts culminate in one of the film's most painful scenes. Morris ignores an urgent note from his mother asking that he visit his sick father; he chooses instead to go out with Ruth and her rich, German-Jewish friends. Sammy, however, rushes to his ailing father's sickbed. In the badly lit apartment, David mistakes him for Morris and delivers what he thinks is his final blessing on the wrong son, a parody of the Biblical tale of Jacob and Esau. With a grieving heart, the son who loves him accepts the father's blessings for the absent son who rejects him.

But Sloman does not end the story on this ironic note. Thanks in part to huge doses of corned beef and cabbage supplied by Mrs. Shannon, David recovers, though the doctor warns Mama, "He won't last six months unless he moves to a better climate." Sammy, therefore, undertakes a championship fight to obtain the needed money. Midway through, after a bloody beating, he rouses himself

from the canvas, galvanized by Mama's tearful, "Get up so papa won't die!" He does and wins. Meantime, a shocked David reads in the paper about Morris's engagement and wonders why his son is erroneously described as an orphan. Traveling to the opulent Stein household, he finds the newly engaged couple celebrating their betrothal. In the film's most powerful moment, David confronts his son, only to have Morris self-righteously tell Stein, "I never saw this man in my life." Again Sloman uses effective crosscutting to convey the emotional distance between the now-distraught David journeying home in a deserted subway, and the unfeeling Morris enjoying dinner with his prospective in-laws.

Sloman moves to resolve the situation in a typical Hollywood manner. When Sammy hears of his brother's cruel treatment of their father, he rushes to the Stein mansion, drags Morris away, and hustles him back to their Lower East Side tenement. There Morris tearfully begs his father's forgiveness, vowing to "make it up to him." David now realizes Sammy's true worth and devotion: "I thought success only came through learning," says David ruefully, "but in this country success can even mean a box fighter." Following this admission, the entire family embraces and Sloman shows that, given a correct vision of the new world's pressing demands, prosperity and happiness can be achieved in America.

His People warrants treatment in detail because it encompasses so many of the central themes dealt with in silent Jewish-American films: Irish-Jewish and Gentile-Jewish relationships, ghetto melodramas, East-European (Cominskys) versus German (Stein) Jews, family interaction, conflicts between traditional and newly emerging values, religion versus commerce, generational disagreements, and monetary problems. In addition,

Rabbi Lyon (Niger DeBrulier) is almost driven to murder Constantine (Ivan Mosjukine) to protect his daughter (Mary Philbin) in SURRENDER *(1927).*

The Jewish townspeople beg Lea Lyon (Mary Philbin) to save them from death in SURRENDER *(1927).*

Sloman's early use of deep focus, his expert crosscutting for emotional impact and thematic emphasis, his ability to create character depth and complexity within the confines of standard melodrama, his skillful plot manipulations, his movement within and between scenes, and his compelling vision of the painful depths and joyous heights of immigrant life endow the film with an exuberant vitality that captivates modern film-goers and enlightens film historians. Sloman's exploration of ghetto life manages to avoid trivializing the experience, while his union of form and content moves the film out of the category of superficial melodrama.

Surrender is equally as intriguing as *His People,* though far less popular in its day. Based on a 1915 Alexander Brody drama, the story allows Sloman to put in the foreground the issue of intermarriage, since the action is set in a faraway land. Mary Philbin, best known for her role opposite Lon Chaney in *The Phantom of the Opera* (1925), plays Lea Lyon, daughter of Rabbi Mendel Lyon (Nigel DeBrulier), spiritual advisor of a small town near the Austrian/Russian border. By chance, she meets Constantine (Ivan Mosjukine), a Russian prince who engages her in a bit of harmless flirtation. Objecting to these happenings, the rabbi insults the Russian and sends him away. Later, war is declared and the Russians, under Constantine, take over the town. Now the head of an occupying force, Constantine searches the town for Lea and, upon finding her betrothed to Joshua (Otto Matieson), confronts the town and its rabbi with an excruciating moral dilemma: he will lock the Jews in their houses and burn down the village if Lea does not sleep with him. Lea refuses, thus stirring Constantine's deeper affections. When the victorious Austrian army regains the town, Lea, now in love with the Russian, hides him until he can escape. The furious townspeople drive her from the village and begin to stone her. Her distraught father dies saving his daughter's life. After the war, the lovers are reunited.

Sloman goes to great length early in the film to demonstrate the rabbi's exalted position in the town. In the opening scene, he "administers justice and the wisdom of ancient laws," as he solves a heated dispute between two brothers over their father's estate. But he is compassionate as well as wise. Sloman's tracking shot follows the venerable rabbi on a walk through his beloved village. Along the way, he hears the cry of a little girl. He kindly gives her an apple to make her forget her broken doll. Sloman's visual construction, as Patricia Erens correctly notes, unites the apple, child and village into a single deep-focus shot far beyond the technical powers of most silent film directors.

Constantine's introduction in the subsequent scene allows Sloman to display more of his tech-nical virtuousity. He opens with a long shot of the nobleman and his servant hunting in the woods. Sloman fades to a closeup of Constantine's face, his gun poised to shoot. He then fades to an extreme closeup point of view shot, looking down the gun barrel. Next, he tracks down the barrel to a closeup of the hunter's prey: a small squirrel. Sloman now crosscuts between the hunter, his intended victim,

Lea Lyon (Mary Philbin) cradles her father (Nigel DeBrulier), who dies saving her from being stoned, in SURRENDER *(1927).*

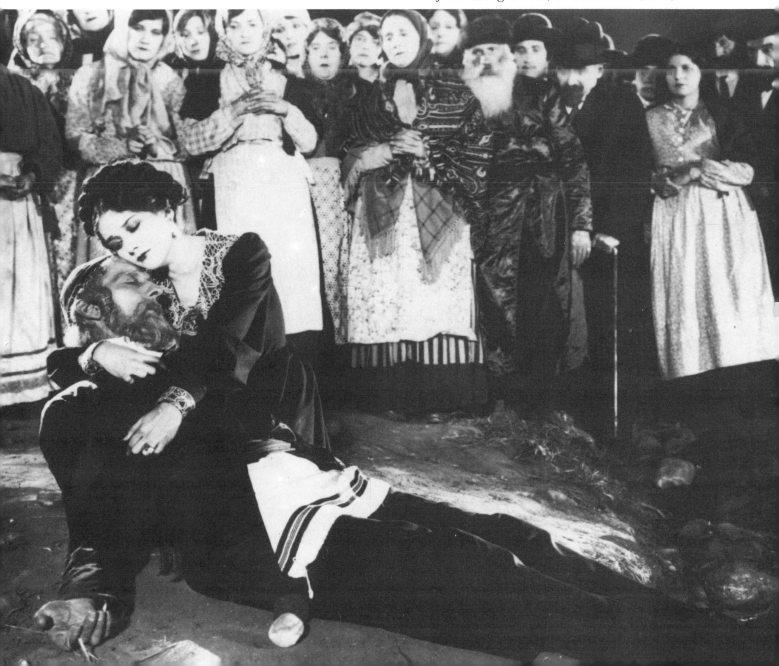

An early advertisement for THE COHENS AND THE KELLYS *(1926).*

and his faithful hunting dog. Finally, Constantine gently smiles, lowers his rifle, and watches the squirrel run away into the bushes. The scene is thematically significant, since it establishes Constantine's unwillingness to destroy helpless victims. As he does with the squirrel, so too he will let the defenseless Lea live. In fact, Sloman makes the relationship between Lea and the animal quite explicit. Constantine's hunting dog runs after the animal and returns with Lea's shoe, an event which initiates the chance encounter between the prince and the beautiful Jewess.

When Lea and Constantine next meet it is as World War I antagonists. The rabbi hides his daughter in the holy ark, where the Russian's soldiers find her huddled in a corner. She emerges, vilifying him and screaming how she hates the uniform of his cossacks, who "persecute us and makes the streets run red with our blood!" While this is happening the distraught rabbi removes a knife from the Sabbath bread and moves menacingly toward his enemy. But, as he seems ready to stab Constantine, he hears sounds that signal the start of the Sabbath and remind him of his sacred duties.

Sloman follows this scene of high tension with one of the most remarkable depictions of religion's power found anywhere in the Jewish-American cinema. Lea, her father, and Constantine sit together during the Sabbath meal. She lights the Shabbas candles and recites the traditional prayers. (The words of the prayer appear superimposed over her image, not on a separate title card.) Sloman slowly takes us through the ancient rituals of the Sabbath meal, as Rabbi Lyon and his daughter share their modest food with their mortal enemy. The director's use of spatial relationships establishes the prevailing anxiety in the room: the unwanted guest sits between the rabbi and Lea, dividing father and daughter as he will later in the film.

Finally, however, Sloman moves the film toward its emotional and moral climax. Constantine demands that Lea sleep with him or he will "burn the people like rats in their homes." The frightened people clamor in front of Rabbi Lyon's house. A spokesman reminds Lea that Esther, the great heroine of Jewish history, "surrendered" herself so that others might live. "The sin is on his head," he argues, "not on yours. You'll be blessed for saving one thousand lives." To this logic, the rabbi responds: "Jews have been martyrs all through the ages. Must we bow our heads and do less than those who have gone before us?" Thus, the film plays out the ethical battle between the Jews and their oppressors within a sexual allegory. Will the Jews save their lives at the price of betraying their ethical values? Lea must choose between public sin and individual morality. Her ultimate decision to reject Constantine's demands represents a realization that personal morality is the basis for public action. Communal standards must evolve naturally from private morality.

Yet, Sloman is not content to rest with an uncomplicated little melodrama. He must further test his characters, as well as his audience. When the Austrians retake the town, some of the Jews turn into a bloodthirsty lynch mob. Joshua informs the rabbi not only that Lea has protected the Russian but that she now wears his ring. The anguished father cries out against his daughter: "Out of my sight! You are a traitor to your father, a traitor to your people, and a traitor to your God!" But as an angry mob drives Lea from the town and begins to hurl rocks at her, the rabbi runs to

The Cohens and the Kellys square off, once again, in THE COHENS AND THE KELLYS (1926).

*Izzy Goldberg (George Jessel) romances
Eileen Cohannigan (Patsy Ruth Miller) in*
PRIVATE IZZY MURPHY *(1926).*

protect his beloved daughter. He dies when hit by a
stone meant for her. Years later, Constantine and
Lea meet on a bridge, symbolic of their joining
together halfway between two worlds. Though
certainly not enough of an achievement to rank
Sloman with the masters of silent film art, *His
People* and *Surrender* forcefully demonstrate the
considerable talents of an early and now neglected
filmmaker who deserves better from history.

The first film featuring Jewish-Irish interaction
is *Levy and Cohen—The Irish Comedians* (1903).
Usually, Jewish-Irish interaction center around love
relationships. The earliest film on the topic, *Becky
Gets a Husband* (1912), establishes the basic pattern found in most interreligious romances: Jewish
and Irish children fall in love, the parents object,
the couple marries anyway, the parents are even-

tually reconciled to the match. Of the many films in
this category, *The Cohens and The Kellys* (1926),
Private Izzy Murphy (1926), and *Abie's Irish Rose*
(1928) are the most representative. In fact, the
three are cousins, for though a screen version of
Anne Nichols's fantastically successful 1924 play
was not made until 1928, the Universal series and
the Warner Brothers film clearly spring fullblown
from its head.

The most interesting of all Jewish-Irish films
from a contemporary perspective is *Private Izzy
Murphy,* in which a zany confusion of ethnic identities so entangles the two cultural groups as to
make them almost inseparable. Soon after Isadore
Goldberg (George Jessel) arrives from Russia, he is
well on his way to earning enough money to send
for his parents, even though a persistent marriage
broker (Nat Carr) continually dangles eligible girls
before him. An eviction notice forces Izzy to
relocate, and finding the only available spot in the
middle of an Irish neighborhood, he quickly

changes his name to I. Patrick Murphy and attracts hordes of customers with his charming manner. Soon he becomes enamored with Eileen Cohannigan (Patsy Ruth Miller).

The arrival of Izzy's parents coincides with the United States' entrance into World War I. After patriotically enlisting, even though it means leaving his confused parents alone, Izzy becomes a hero with the 69th Brigade, an all-Irish regiment of daring fighters. Returning, he finds a group of neighborhood Irishmen led by Cohannigan come to honor him. But Roger O'Malley, who also loves Eileen, sees pictures of Izzy's parents and scorns him as a Jew, causing Cohannigan to reject him. All is finally resolved, however, when nine of Izzy's war buddies burst in, keep Cohannigan and O'Malley prisoner, and advise their friend to marry Eileen. He does so, while the matchmaker faints in despair.

The film presents a typical Jewish-Irish pattern of initial distrust between members of two minority groups, some events which cause each to reevaluate the situation, and eventual acceptance. Stronger in this film than in most others is the almost complete obliteration of ethnic identity for business interests and then for love. The point is made that little difference exists between good men of any religion: whether his name be Izzy Goldberg or I. Patrick Murphy, in the final analysis a man's character is more important than his nationality or religion. Izzy's acceptance by men on the battlefield is democracy in action, and their final defense of him at the expense of narrow-

Much to their distaste, Patrick Murphy (J. Farrell MacDonald) and Solomon Levy (Jean Hersholt) find themselves related to each other in ABIE'S IRISH ROSE *(1928).*

Jakie Rabinowitz (Al Jolson) torn between his religious obligations and his singing career in THE JAZZ SINGER *(1927).*

minded individuals like Cohannigan and O'Malley shows the triumph of republicanism over prejudice; what a man can do is more important than his origins.

The opening scenes in *The Cohens and The Kellys* also rely on the initial enmity between the two immigrant families forced to live across the hall from each other in their tenement. First the dogs bark and fight, then the two children tussle, then the mothers (two similarly hefty women with coarse features and dark hair pulled back into a tight bun) yell and scream at each other, and finally the fathers (an ethnic Laurel and Hardy with the tall, thin Kelly and the squat, fat Cohen) argue violently and for little apparent reason. The picture goes on to become a virtual compendium of previously discussed themes including the clever/

sneaky Jew (Cohen outsmarts his business competitor by cheating), the sudden, undeserved riches (Sadie Greenbaum leaves Cohen—and then Kelly—a fortune), interracial romance (Nannie Cohen and Terry Kelly), ghetto life, and Jews as butts/creators of humor. More importantly, the film perpetuates ethnic stereotypes still with us today. Kelly, the tough Irish cop, never lets his sensitive emotions show, except for a solitary tear which he decorously shakes off while his back is to the intruding camera. On the other hand, Cohen gives way to almost constant emotional displays of crying, swearing (which appears on the screen as Hebrew gibberish), and elation. Of course, the film concludes on a note of joyous reconciliation and friendship, Cohen playfully donning Kelly's cop outfit, Kelly proposing a partnership to Cohen, and Cohen wondering if it's "legal" to use the names Cohen and Kelly together. Starring George Sidney as Cohen and Charles Murphy as Kelly, this successful film spawned sequels showing the pair in *Paris* (1928), *Atlantic City* (1929), *Africa* (1930), *Scotland* (1930), *Hollywood* (1932), and *Trouble* (1933).

Abie's Irish Rose (1928) stands out as an equally, if not more, impressive Jewish-Irish film success. Despite the fact that most theater reviewers severely panned Nichols's play, it staggered through 2,327 Broadway performances, two movie versions (1928 and 1946), a radio serial, and even television stepchildren like "Bridget Loves Bernie." The now-classic story revolves around a Jewish-Irish romance between Rosemary Murphy (Nancy Carroll) and Abie Levy (Charles Rogers), a romance bitterly opposed by her father (J. Farrell MacDonald) as well as by his (Jean Hersholt). *New York Times* critic Mordaunt Hall cited director Victor Fleming's "admirable and meticulous care in reproducing the Jewish home" and praised the film for its overall "good taste," but later commentators have been far less kind, seeing it as a sorry collection of bad Irish and Jewish jokes.

Though *The Cohens and The Kellys, Private Izzy Murphy,* and *Abie's Irish Rose* remain the most characteristic examples of Jewish-Irish films, a number of other films on interfaith love were made: *Cohen's Outing* (1913), *For the Love of Mike and Rosie* (1916), *Second Hand Rose* (1922), *Fool's Highway* (1924), *One of the Bravest* (1925), *Sweet Daddies* (1926), *Kosher Kitty Kelly* (1926), *Clancy's Kosher Wedding* (1927), *The Shamrock and The Rose* (1927), *Frisco Sally Levy* (1927), *The Rawhide Kid* (1927), and *Flying Romeo* (1928). In almost all these films, humor arises at the expense of the intractable immigrant parents who refuse to understand the mores of their new land. Their annoyed and/or humiliated offspring may choose either to ignore or to criticize their parochial parents. The ultimate point of the films, particularly because of their parents' eventual acceptance of their children's decisions, is that a new generation of American-born-and-bred children will forget their religious differences to join hands and create a new nation, a true melting pot in which cultural differences matter no more than the color of one's hair.

According to these films, the easiest way to become Americanized is to marry a Catholic girl, enter into a partnership with an Irishman, or adopt

Jakie Rabinowitz (Al Jolson) fulfilling his religious responsibilities by singing the Kol Nidre service in THE JAZZ SINGER *(1927).*

Jakie (Al Jolson) comforts his dying father, Cantor Rabinowitz (Warner Oland), in THE JAZZ SINGER *(1927).*

a Gentile baby. These Jewish/Irish romance films reign as the assimilationist films par excellence, castigating old world ways, supporting those who turn from the traditional to the modern, and apotheosizing those who consign custom to the history books in their headlong dash to become true Americans. Both the fear of being different and the unlimited education opportunities available in this country created a generation of immigrants who fostered the assimilation of their children into American society. Ironically, the immigrant parents themselves became the victims of the trend they nurtured. But then, it was their kids who went to the movies.

Another film about conflicts between the past and present, *The Jazz Singer* (1927), is a fitting transition between the silent film era and the beginning of sound films in both theme and technique. According to legend, this movie ushered in the sound era some fifty-three years ago. Actually, however, it was not the first sound picture, it relied on no specifically new technical devices, and it instigated no immediate revolution. In fact, as originally conceived the picture had singing but no talking sequences, though Jolson's exuberant ad libs were left in, much to the delight of audiences and reviewers. Nonetheless, *The Jazz Singer* occupies a special place in the history of American cinema. Its predominant theme of the bitter conflict between old ways and new ideas remains symbolically apt for the role it played in replacing silent film with sound film.

According to Samson Raphaelson, the story's original author, the initial inspiration for the tale struck him when as a student in 1917 he saw Jolson in *Robinson Crusoe, Jr.*:

> When he finished, I turned to the girl beside me, dazed with memories of my childhood on the East Side....My God, this isn't a jazz singer. This is a Cantor! This grotesque figure in blackface, kneeling at the end of a runway which projected him into the heart of his audience with a prayer—an evangelical moan—a tortured imperious call that hurtled through the house like a swift electrical lariat with a twist that swept the audience right to the edge of that runway. The words didn't matter, the melody didn't matter. It was the emotion—the emotion of a cantor.

Years later (1922) Raphaelson wrote a story about a Lower East Side kid, Jakie Rabinowitz, who forsakes his religious duties to pursue a singing career. He called it "The Day of Atonement," eventually turning the story into a play (1925) and selling it to producer Al Lewis, who christened it *The Jazz Singer* and used it as a vehicle to launch the dramatic career of George Jessel. The play turned into the surprise box-office hit of the year. Partly because they had Jessel under contract, Warner Brothers bought the film rights for him. Through several strange twists of fate no one is very sure about, Jessel soon gave way to Jolson who signed for $75,000 plus $10,000 per week for any runover time past eight weeks of production.

The rest, as they say, is history. On October 6, 1927, *The Jazz Singer* premiered at Warners theaters in New York, complete with a souvenir program that included an English glossary of the film's Yiddish terms. Upon viewing it, critic Robert Sherwood prophetically declared "the end of the silent drama is in sight." By late 1928/early 1929 the end was not only in sight but had arrived. Warners continued to release a series of popular talkie winners (including Jolson's all-talking *The Singing Fool,* 1928), Fox announced it would produce only talking films from then on with its more convenient Movietone system, and even stately MGM started producing talkies, the first being *The Broadway Melody* (1929) which won the year's Academy Award as Best Film. The silent film rapidly became a historical artifact.

Some brief comments on *The Jazz Singer's* now disreputable use of blackface are necessary. Today most people associate the blackface tradition with minstrel shows, and more particularly with Al Jolson. In actuality, many Jewish performers gained early and continued success using it. Sophie Tucker was billed as the "World Renowned Coon Shouter" or more euphemistically as the "Manipulator of Coon Melodies." Eddie Cantor played Salome in drag and blackface, while George Burns often toured with an even more comically stylized blackface than Jolson's. Later George Jessel often joined Eddie Cantor on stage in various classic blackface routines.

Why should Jews, in particular, have made such widespread use of blackface? Irving Howe, in *The World of Our Fathers,* provides at least one answer:

When they took over the conventions of ethnic mimicry, the Jewish performers transformed it into something emotionally richer and far more humane. Black became a mask for Jewish expressiveness, with one woe speaking through the voice of another....Blacking their faces seems to have enabled the Jewish performers to reach a spontaneity and assertiveness in the declaration of their Jewish selves.

This sympathetic interpretation provides part of the answer but is not totally sufficient. In today's world of greater ethnic sensitivity such an appropriation of another group's cultural traits with a leering emphasis on its socially comic elements appears blatantly offensive. Indeed, it is too easy to ignore the derogatory aspects of such activities, the unconscious racism accepted and nourished by such cruel parodies, by citing historical contexts. The undisguised elements of ridicule in such blackface portrayals by Jews mimicking the outlandish stereotypes of Blacks now looks suspiciously like one group's desperate need to assert its own superiority by mimicking another. Such a motivation while perhaps unconscious is nonetheless hard to ignore.

The Jazz Singer for all its latent racism is nevertheless a forceful summation of the assimilationist tendencies present throughout the Silent Era, and, indeed, that dominate this genre in films such as *Gentleman's Agreement* (1947) and *Marjorie Morningstar* (1958) right up until the sixties. Raphaelson states that he wrote the original story partly as a direct response to the offensiveness of *Abie's Irish Rose* and partly to provide a more sincere portrait of the Jewish immigrant family in crisis. Director Alan Crosland and production supervisor Darryl F. Zanuck, however, had other ideas. By ending the picture with Jakie singing "Mammy" to an adoring Winter Garden audience instead of taking his place in the synagogue, as both Raphaelson and scriptwriter Alfred A. Cohen had intended, Crosland and Zanuck transforms the film's message from "a fable of adjustment...to a more characteristically American fable of success...open revolt against tradition...and the replacement of the values of the old by the values of the new." Even more to the point, Jakie becomes a

Sara Rabinowitz (Eugenie Besserer), the screen's archetypal Yiddishe Mama in THE JAZZ SINGER *(1927).*

Disraeli (George Arliss) as loving family man with his adoring wife (Florence Arliss) in DISRAELI *(1929).*

ages," Jack and his generation feel that "jazz is the sacred music" of the new America.

Another major theme in *The Jazz Singer* is the potentially suffocating attention of the Jewish mother. Later, in the turbulent sixties, the kindly Sara Rabinowitz metamorphoses into the castrating Sophie Portnoy, though without straining one can find seeds of Roth's destructive mother-figure in Crosland's Sara. Sara's dominant activities throughout the film are crying, sighing, pleading, and suffering. In the scene in which she desperately tries to convince Jack to sing the Yom Kippur service in his father's place, Sara pulls out all the manipulative emotional stops: tradition ("For generations...a Rabinowitz sings every Day of Atonement"); religion ("God is used to it"); pathos ("Maybe our papa is dying and will have to tell him his only son is singing in a theater"); feigned acceptance ("Here he belongs"); calculated resignation ("If God wanted him in His house, He would have kept him there"); guilt ("Tell him maybe he can see papa anyway before it's too late"). It is this type of intense cajoling in the name of love and obligation that foreshadows the more destructive Sophie Portnoy. Jakie gently ignores his mother's pleas and becomes a successful jazz singer. Alex Portnoy tries to ignore his mother and ends up an Oedipal wreck.

Though *The Jazz Singer* breaks with the silent films in its addition of sound segments, its thematic emphasis remains similar to the concerns of most silent films dealing with Jews, as well as many sound movies. The idea that success in America depends on a severe curtailing, if not a total rejection, of traditional Jewish values is eventually accepted. Though Jakie painfully waivers between the obligations of his religion and the demands of his singing career, the audience feels no real doubt as to which will triumph. Alienation and ridicule result from strict adherence to a cultural identity; acceptance and admiration come from accommodation to the new values and beliefs. The unbending morality and strict religious prohibitions of the older generation must give way to the moral freedoms and democratic principles of the younger. Just as the silent films themselves quickly degenerated into period pieces in the faster-paced thirties, so too the centuries-old traditions of Jewish life, at least as portrayed in the movies, were

success by directly defying his father's wishes and rejecting his traditional values. "You're of the old world," he lectures the heartbroken old cantor, "tradition is alright, but this is another day." Even his relationship with the Gentile girl Mary Dale (May McAvoy) symbolizes the dominance of love—a democratic American ideal—over duty—a religious prohibition. Though Jakie may sing with a "tear in his voice" and at times feel the "call of the trundled out only for ceremonial occasions, if not entirely forgotten. In depicting this cultural transformation, *The Jazz Singer* is a summary of the silent era and a transitional bridge to the sound films. Al Jolson's promise that "You ain't heard nothing yet" became a prophecy both for talking pictures and Reform Judaism. Within *The Jazz Singer's* frames are the last vestiges of religious discipline already outdated in a modern world.

By far the most popular historical Jew of the silent period is the nineteenth century's most famous politician, Benjamin Disraeli (Earl of Beaconsfield) whose life seemed a natural subject for screen biograhies. Elected to Parliament in 1837, he became Prime Minister of England in 1868 and and again from 1874-1880, founded the modern Conservative Party in Britain, and was important in England's gaining control of the Suez Canal. His baptism in 1817 owing to a bitter dispute between his father and the Sephardic synagogue of Bevis Marks is an ironic fact that allowed him to become a member of Parliament from which, as a Jew, he would have been barred until 1858. Disraeli's pride in and insistence upon his Jewish heritage culminated in his 1847 vote for removal of bans against Jews who desired government offices.

Three separate, though closely-related, films, each entitled *Disraeli,* focus on this extraordinary politician's life. The first, scripted by Louis N. Parker and based on his play, was distributed in 1917. The second, written by Forrest Halsey and released in 1921, draws on Parker's play. It stars George Arliss (who made the role famous on stage) and his wife, and centers on Disraeli's ultimately successful attempts to finance the Suez Canal. The third, made in 1929, again stars Arliss in a sound version of the previous production scripted by Julian Josephson. Nowhere is the Jewishness of Disraeli more evident than in this final version, which begins as a Hyde Park speaker castigates Disraeli because he is an "outsider and a Jew whose grandfather was a foreigner." The film subsequently traces Disraeli's many problems with the Bank of England, whose governor calls him a "dreamer and a dangerous visionary," and his parliamentary disputes with his Liberal archrival Gladstone; it also provides intimate glimpses of the private man as a gentle family partriarch and a loving husband. The sympathetic portrait of Dis-

An angry Benjamin Disraeli (George Arliss) as public figure in DISRAELI *(1929).*

raeli emerging from the film shows him as a benevolent man possessing the foresight to see beyond his time and the heroic fortitude to lead England to great world power. Financially successful and critically acclaimed, the 1929 film received an Academy Award nomination for the Best Picture (although it ultimately lost to *All Quiet on the Western Front*) and earned Arliss an Oscar as the year's Best Actor.

The various films of the silent era about Jews stress economic success, intermarriage, freedom, and accommodation to American middle-class values. Religious scholarship, parochialism, duty and uniqueness represent outworn notions associated with foreign countries and bygone times. Though such films often begin by accentuating the differences of Jews—speech, dress, custom, diet— they usually end by proclaiming their more important similarities to other Americans—love of family, financial distress, generational differences. Only superficial, outward elements distinguish Jews from their neighbors; inner strengths bind them to all Americans.

Chapter 3

The Thirties

The two most interesting thirties films about Jews are both based on the works of Elmer Rice, one of the decade's most famous dramatists: King Vidor's *Street Scene* (1931) and William Wyler's *Counsellor-at-Law* (1933). An important Jewish character in *Street Scene,* Abraham Kaplan (Max Montor), first appears sanguinely reading his Yiddish newspaper (a neighbor can't understand how anyone can read this gibberish). Soon he interrupts his repose to debate with a rich socialite, advising her to read about the life of Christ for an economics lesson. "Listen who's talking about Christ," cackles Jones, the resident American who perceives everyone else as a foreigner. Undaunted, Kaplan launches into a socialist diatribe about "oppressors of the working class" and the rich do-gooders who "steal millions of dollars and give to the poor thousands. So long as institutions of private property exists," continues Kaplan resolutely, "workers will be at the mercy of the property owning classes. Putting industry in the hands of the working class can only be accomplished by revolution."

Kaplan's revolutionary sentiments enrage Maurrant (David Landau), an ardent supporter of capitalism who later murders his wife. He calls Kaplan "a dirty Bolshevik" and lambastes him with a now familiar cry: "If you don't like it here, why don't you go back where you came from. We don't want no foreigners coming here and telling us how to run things." These opening exchanges between Kaplan, a rich socialite, and Maurrant represent the first Hollywood presentations of the Jew as socialist, a depiction later regretted when Senator McCarthy and others attacked the industry for harboring Communist sympathizers.

The attitudes of Kaplan's American-educated son, Sammy (William Collier, Jr.), continue the theme of generational conflict so prominent in the silent films. Oblivious to his father's partisan politics, he remains more interested in studying law

Abraham Kaplan's (Max Montor) socialist views infuriate Frank Maurrant (David Landau) in STREET SCENE *(1931).*

and listening to Beethoven, whom he claims "expresses the emotions of the human soul." He is also depicted as a coward. Early in the film, Jones's son taunts Sammy by calling him a "little kike" and a "yid." Then he beats Sammy up and sarcastically crowns him "the pride of Jerusalem." As will generally be the case with screen Jews until the late forties, when films about Israel start to appear, Sammy is shown as a thinker rather than a fighter.

The film encourages us to appreciate his finer instincts, his intellectual achievements, but we cannot help but be put off by his refusal to defend himself against Jones's bullying. *Street Scene* thus reinforces one of the major stereotypes of the silent movies: the clever Jew who lets physically stronger adversaries humiliate him. This attitude, of course, culminates in these films which deal with Jews as the victims of Nazi oppression, for

Lena Simon (Clara Langsner) comforts her troubled son George (John Barrymore) in COUNSELLOR-AT-LAW *(1933).*

they imply that, at least in part, the Jew is responsible for his own fate at the hands of the Germans.

The film's romantic intrigue centers on another interracial love affair, this time between Sammy and Rose Moran (Sylvia Sidney). The older generation is not as opposed to the match as Sammy's sister Shirley (Anna Kostant), who worries lest Rose distract Sammy from his schoolwork. At one point, Sammy lectures Shirley, an old maid school teacher who sacrifices her life and earnings to put Sammy through law school, and attacks her religious chauvinism with American democratic ideals, saying, "Jews are not better than anyone else." Yet at the film's end there is no joyful reconciliation of the races as in the simpler silent films. Rejecting as romantic nonsense Sammy's offer to run away with her, Rose leaves him and goes off to face the world alone.

Though *Street Scene* broaches the issue of American anti-Semitism and introduces anti-Jewish words like "kike" and "yid" to the screen, *Counsellor-at-Law* deals with the issue in a more subtle,

complex manner. Helped by Rice's own strong screenplay, the film follows the career of George Simon (John Barrymore), a very successful lawyer who rises above his immigrant beginnings but finds time only for work. Director William Wyler, himself a German Jew and distant cousin of Carl Laemmle, recalls wanting to use a Jew for the lead part and going to producer Samuel Goldwyn with that suggestion. "You can't have a Jew playing a Jew," scolded Goldwyn, "it wouldn't work on the screen."

Wyler tackles the delicate subject of anti-Semitism obliquely through Simon's snobbish wife (Doris Kenyon) and her children who continually snub their stepfather because he is Jewish. Finally, after his wife fails to stand by him when he is threatened with disbarment for shielding his old friend Breitstein (John Qualen), Simon accepts the healing affection of his loyal secretary, Regina Gordon (Bebe Daniels). Seen today, *Counsellor-at-Law* remains remarkably powerful. Only Clara Langsner's portrayal of Simon's protective Jewish mother strikes the modern viewer as vastly overdone, perhaps because such attitudes have become part of the "Jewish Mother" syndrome. Her visits to her son's office appear more like intrusions on his privacy than affectionate interludes.

The decade's most direct attack on anti-Semitism once again sets its action safely on foreign soil. The yellow passport or yellow ticket designating a "public woman" who could remain outside the so-called Russian "Pale" inspired two silents—*The Yellow Passport* (1916) and *The Yellow Ticket* (1918)—based on the plight of respectable Jewish women forced to apply for such a passport in order to travel beyond the area in which Jews could legally reside. In 1931, Raoul Walsh remade the latter film for 20th Century-Fox (the only non-Jewish Hollywood studio) with a script by Jules Furthman, based on Michael Morton's play and starring Elissa Landi, Lionel Barrymore, and Laurence Olivier. In many of Walsh's other films dealing with social pressures, his characters are forced to commit desperate, anti-social acts. So it is in *The Yellow Ticket* when the film's gentle Jewish heroine, Marya Kalish (Landi), eventually kills her tormentor, the cruel aristocrat Baron Andreff (Barrymore). The film's context, however, justifies her

Suave Julian Rolfe (Laurence Olivier) converses with Marya Kalish (Elissa Landi) and Baron Andreff (Lionel Barrymore) in THE YELLOW TICKET *(1931).*

act. Initially forced to obtain the dreaded yellow ticket to visit her sick father in prison, Marya finds him dead and herself unable to wash away the ticket's evil stigma. She joins forces with British journalist Julian Rolfe (Olivier) to write a series of scathing articles exposing the conditions of life in Russia. Andreff accuses her of spying for Rolfe, noting that "it is one of the pleasures of despotism that we can act without proof." When he attempts to rape her, Marya kills him and flees to England with Rolfe. Interestingly, throughout the film, Andreff compares himself to Holofernes and Marya to Judith of Bethulia, and like her Biblical counterpart, she too murders the persecutor of her people.

Seen today, *The Yellow Ticket* suffers from overdone music and overblown acting. Nevertheless, its denunciation of brutal Russian anti-Semitism remains strong and vibrant. Early in the film courageous Jews huddle together in ghettos, managing within their squalid rooms to maintain their dig-

nity and their love of learning despite the repressive environment. One can imagine modern encounters between Jewish dissidents and Russian secret policemen foreshadowed in Marya's bitter conflict with Andreff, who heads the police force. A spirited woman, Marya maintains her purity in the face of Russian licentiousness and her truthful patriotism in a world of lies; thus, she asserts the moral and ethical superiority of the Jews over their despised oppressors. The film equates political corruption with depraved and hypocritical sexual morals. The barometer of a state's righteousness is its attitude toward sexuality, and Andreff's lustful pursuit of Marya contrasts starkly with Rolfe's respectful love and Marya's own chastity.

The interplay between personal heroism and historical inevitability manifests itself here as a

Baron Andreff (Lionel Barrymore) thinks he has Marya Kalish (Elissa Landi) in his power in THE YELLOW TICKET *(1931).*

conflict between free will and fate. Such a clash produces tension between individual acts and societal norms that remains central in many of Walsh's other films. Furthermore, the rhythm of the film, like so many of his others, displays Walsh's ability to unite strong narrative movement with dramatic character tension. The emphasis on a female rather than male protagonist, used again in his later films where the woman's capacity for flexibility eludes her male counterparts, also persists here. In fact, feminist critics like Pam Cook and Claire Johnson, who disagree that Walsh's female characters present positive alternatives to his male figures, would do well to give *The Yellow Ticket* a second viewing. Andreff's petty cruelty and Rolfe's rather superficial suaveness pale before Marya's vigorous intellectual capacities and resolutely passionate actions. The Jewish heroine, not the men, forces fate to do her bidding by rejecting passivity in favor of action; this is in contrast to the central male characters in most other Jewish-American films. Although *The Yellow Ticket* at first appears as a somewhat atypical Walsh film, a

closer analysis of its themes, rhythms, textures, and characters align it with his better-known works and establish its kinship to Walsh's major achievements.

Another film dealing with inter-faith relations is *The House of Rothschild,* which won a 1934 Academy Award nomination for Best Film of the year. Director Alfred Werker surrounds the love affair between Captain Fitzroy (Robert Young), dashing aide to the Duke of Wellington (C. Aubrey Smith), and Julie (Loretta Young), lovely daughter of Nathan Rothschild (George Arliss), with historical events relating to the famous banking brothers' fortune. After the anti-Semitic Prussian ambassador, Baron Ledrantz (Boris Karloff), scornfully rejects his bid to restore France's economic security, Nathan forbids Julie to marry Fitzroy and plots his revenge for Ledrantz's insult. History grants him a chance for vengeance when Napoleon escapes. Ledrantz and other government representatives beg financial aid from the brothers, who agree to provide it with one provision: the allies must sign an agreement guaranteeing Jewish citizenship in their countries. Eventually, Nathan singlehandedly saves the English stock market from crashing, heroically risking his fortune by buying while others are selling. With the news of Napoleon's defeat at Waterloo, the market rises dramatically and the Rothschild fortune is assured. England's grateful ruler publicly honors Nathan who finally consents to the marriage of Julie and Fitzroy.

In terms of Jewish elements, *The House of Rothschild* displays some confusing ambiguities. Early in the film, old Papa Rothschild is shown hastily putting away a roast and then cunningly pleading poverty to an official tax collector. Nathan apparently prevents Julie's marriage to Fitzroy out of pique rather than religious concerns. Once fully accepted by Gentile society, he quickly agrees to marriage. The brothers seem genuinely interested in gaining rights for other Jews; however, they do so for personal instead of for racial reasons. Nathan's rescue of the English stock market also scrambles personal and patriotic motivations. In fact, *The Rothschilds,* a 1940 German film combining anti-Semitic with anti-British sentiments, uses the same events with different emphasis, showing the bankers profiting "while nations are bleeding on the battle fields," describing England's

victory over Napoleon as "a victory for the Star of David," and arguing that the Rothschilds purposefully spread news of a Napoleonic victory to make millions in the market. Even in the American film, the family's relationships suggest a meeting between stockholders in a multinational corporation more than a loving Jewish household. Finally the brothers' inventive method of receiving advance information smacks of the "clever/sneaky" Jew syndrome in the silent films. All in all, *The House of Rothschild* sends mixed messages. It overtly intends to glorify the Rothschilds. But its covert innuendos replace positive images with troubling doubts, as if a totally positive portrait is impossible.

Approached in varying degrees in *The House of Rothschild, Counsellor-at-Law,* and *The Yellow Ticket,* anti-Semitism as a topic almost disappears in the decade's most popular film featuring Jewish characters. One of the most praised films of the thirties, *The Life of Emile Zola* (1937) received Academy Award nominations for Best Picture (it won), Best Actor (Muni lost to Spencer Tracy), Best Supporting Actor (Joseph Schildkraut won as Dreyfus), Best Director (Dieterle lost to Leo McCarey), Best Assistant Director, Best Original Story and Screenplay, Best Interior Design, Sound Recording, and Musical Score. Dieterle, a German refugee and former student of Max Reinhardt (with whom he co-directed *A Midsummer Night's Dream),* had a distinguished career in the thirties and forties with such films as *The Story of Louis Pasteur* (1936), *The Hunchback of Notre Dame* (1939), *Juarez* (1939), *All That Money Can Buy* (1941), *Love Letters* (1945), and *Portrait of Jennie* (1949). Throughout the thirties Dieterle and his wife Charlotte came to the aid of many German refugees, such as Bertolt Brecht, and he was considered the quintessential "liberal" director of the decade, partially because of his staunch anti-Nazi stand.

A furious Emile Zola (Paul Muni) addresses the court in THE LIFE OF EMILE ZOLA *(1937).*

The Life of Emile Zola meanders through the writer's long career from his start as a struggling novelist to his accidental death from carbon monoxide fumes. The film's dramatic center is the famous "J'Accuse!" editorial in which Zola charged the French authorities with trying to railroad Captain Alfred Dreyfus, a Jew, on charges of espionage. (It was the newspaper article that made Zola, in the words of Anatole France, represent "a moment in the conscience of man.")

Unfortunately, the movie lacks any conscience of its own. It almost totally ignores the blatant anti-Semitism that destroys Dreyfus's career. Though Dieterle claims he did use the word and it was cut out by the studio, "Jew" is never heard in the movie. So in 1937, two full years after Hitler proclaimed the anti-Semitic "Nuremberg Laws" on September 15, 1935, Warner Brothers produced a universally acclaimed film about the famous Dreyfus case that failed to emphasize why he was singled out, how he could be so unjustly accused, and why people were so willing to believe him guilty.

Thus, the dramatic films featuring Jews fail to generate much interest during the thirties The few films that focus on Jewish characters simplify, sanitize, and de-Semiticize. A few deal with successful American Jews forced to reevaluate the price of their triumphs, but their superficial characterizations, flat visual style, and plodding story lines generally make them of little more than passing interest. For example, director Gregory La Cava's *Symphony of Six Million* (1932), based on Fanny Hurst's story, details a surgeon's (Ricardo Cortez) rise from the ghetto to Park Avenue and finally back to the ghetto to help his people. Its highlight is a sentimental speech in which a penitent Dr. Klauber proclaims: "I dedicate these two strong hands to service—that the lame may walk, the halt may be strong—tending the needy and comforting the dying. This is my oath in the temple of healing." Hurst's tale reflects a nostalgia for ghetto life, a time of sacrifice, love and accomplishment. In particular, she shows how those who have "made it" have a responsibility to help those they left behind.

This refusal to confront the unpleasant realities of anti-Semitism remained a stubborn part of the Hollywood thirties mentality, and even those films dealing with Nazi Germany sidestepped the Jewish issue. Typical in its approach to German anti-Semitism is *Confessions of a Nazi Spy* (1939), directed by Anatole Litvak. A heavy-handed attack on Nazi activities in America, it was inspired by a series of articles by ex-FBI agent Leon G. Turrou. Like *Hitler's Reign of Terror* in its interweaving of newsreel footage (here of Nazi rallies in New York's Madison Square Garden) with a semi-fictional storyline, the film relies on a pseudo-documentary approach. Litvak later utilized the technique successfully in the *Why We Fight* segments such as *The Battle of Russia* (1943) he made under Frank Capra.

Confessions of a Nazi Spy proved extremely controversial. Pro-Nazi sympathizers burned a theater that showed the film in heavily German Milwaukee, and German diplomat Hans Thomsen denounced the film's "pernicious defamations" to Secretarty of State Cordell Hull. The head of the German-American Bund, Fritz Kuhn, even threatened Warners with a five-million-dollar libel suit. Jack Warner claimed "no picture ever aroused so much bigotry and hatred as this one." Later, in 1940, a shocked Hollywood learned that several Poles who showed the film were hanged in their own theaters. Such events forced the Warners to hire security guards for the film's New York premiere.

Though less violent, critics were hardly kinder to Warners' foray into political filmmaking. Otis Ferguson called it "a hate breeder if there ever was one...(that) overstresses the theme of a Nazi America." Frank Nugent's *New York Times* review begins:

> Hitler's pledge of non-aggression toward the Americas reached the Warners too late yesterday. They had formally declared war on the Nazis at 8:15 a.m. with the first showing of the *Confessions of a Nazi Spy* at the Strand. Hitler won't like it; neither will Goebbels.

Later in the article, he attacks the film's simplistic characterizations:

> We can endure just so much hissing, even when Der Fuehrer and the Gestapo are its victims....The editorial bias, however justified, has carried it to childish extremes. Membership in the National Socialist party

Dr. Felix Klauber (Ricardo Cortez) shares his concern about his future with his immigrant mother (Anna Appel) in SYMPHONY FOR SIX MILLION *(1932).*

cannot be restricted entirely to the rat-faced, the brute-browed, the sinister. We don't believe Nazi Propaganda ministers let their mouths twitch evilly whenever they mention our Constitution or Bill of Rights.

When, however, Warners re-released the film in 1940 after further government disclosures about Nazi activities in America, Nugent ruefully admits:

> If the film is less startling today than a year ago, it is because its exposure of Nazi "fifth column" preparation before the invasion is now common knowledge and because the scope of treachery has been immeasurably widened. The film overreaches its point in reducing all the Nazi henchmen to stock company villains, but it is a tribute to its prophetic accuracy that the newly inserted sequences that show havoc wreaked by international Nazi sympathizers in Norway, Holland, and Belgium become a logical climax to events whose shadows had been cast before them.

FBI Investigator Renard (Edward G. Robinson) searches a defense plant for German infiltrators in CONFESSIONS OF A NAZI SPY *(1939).*

In 1941 when Harry Warner defended his production before Senator Nye's hostile Subcommittee on Interstate Commerce, he boldly stated: "I abhor and detest every principle and practice of the Nazi movement. To me, Nazism typifies the very opposite of the kind of life every decent man, woman, and child wants to live." When specifically questioned about *Confessions of a Nazi Spy,* he justified it as a "factual portrayal of a Nazi spy ring that actually operated in New York City" and argued it was "carefully prepared on the basis of factual happenings and not twisted to serve any ulterior purpose."

Clearly the film does serve an "ulterior purpose." In fact, it represents the most determined anti-Nazi statement Hollywood produced prior to America's entry into World War II. Warner Brothers had been at war with the Nazis since at least 1936 when its chief salesman in Germany, Joe Kaufman, was murdered by Nazi thugs in an incident long remembered by Jack Warner: "Like many an outnumbered Jew he was trapped in an alley. They hit him with fists and clubs and then kicked the life out of him with their boots and left him dying there." Immediately afterward, Warner Brothers closed its German distribution unit, so it had little to lose financially from producing anti-Nazi films. By the middle and late forties when survivors finally revealed, in graphic details, the Nazi atrocities against Jews and others, the strutting hypocrites portrayed in *Confessions of a Nazi Spy* paled in comparison to their real-life counterparts.

Since Litvak sets the action in America, the film can be at least partially excused for saying little about the Nazis' anti-Semitic programs, although there remain many allusions to their attitudes. Near the beginning Dr. Kassel (Paul Lukas), head of the German-American Nazi activities, calls on all good German-Americans to "save America from the chaos that breeds in democracy and racial equality. Germans in the United States," he continues, "must be brought back to racial unity." Later, of course, we learn his speeches function as part of a concentrated Nazi attempt to disrupt American society, an attempt that "cloaks itself in the American flag and appears as a defense of Americanism." In this way, Nazi leaders encourage racial, religious, and class hatred and thus weaken America for eventual conquest. As one of his major undertakings, Kassel traces Americans back four generations and classifies them according to blood types and race. He feverishly warns Inspector Renard (Edward G. Robinson), head of the F.B.I. team set up to investigate his activities, that all Americans must become aware of the "insidious, international conspiracy of sub-human criminals greedy for world power." American audiences, we assume, understood who these "sub-human criminals" were, though Jews are never mentioned by name and the film has no Jewish characters.

In *Confessions of a Nazi Spy*—as in other films made about America's foes—political corruption is symbolized by moral corruption. For example, Dr. Kassel is shown as a womanizer callously rejecting his long-suffering wife, who has faithfully supported him through the years, for a far younger admirer. Later, when charged by the F.B.I. with criminal activities, Kassel first claims his rights as an American citizen are being violated and then quickly agrees to sell out his Nazi friends in exchange for his own freedom. Likewise, Kurt Schneider (Francis Lederer), a Nazi sympathizer, deserts from the U.S. Army and embezzles his company's funds. Litvak firmly juxtaposes these moral deficiencies with the ethical qualities displayed by those people who represent "the true voice of the American people." Unlike their Nazi counterparts, men like Inspector Renard support democracy, defend racial equality, and demand religious tolerance for all the country's citizens.

So events both abroad and at home combined to make the thirties a lost decade in the history of Jewish-American films. The silent films of the twenties had depicted a generation's miraculous rise in American society. The sound films of the thirties cloaked Jews in the invisiblity of neglect. As such, the cinema reflected the desire of many American Jews to maintain a low profile, to stress their similarities with other Americans rather than their differences. As one callous Jewish studio executive put it, "Jews are for killing, not for making movies about."

Chapter 4

The Forties

Greenbaum (Sam Levene) comforts Carnelli (Richard Conte) after his wrist is broken by brutal Japanese torture in THE PURPLE HEART (1944).

Greenbaum (Sam Levene) gives moral support to a frightened comrade (Farley Granger) about to undergo interrogation in THE PURPLE HEART (1944).

Greenbaum (Sam Levene) angrily responds to a question from one of his accusers (Richard Loo) in THE PURPLE HEART (1944).

Just as prewar films present a symbolic acceptance of the dominant, Gentile American culture through intermarriage, so wartime action films present self-sacrificing death as the Jew's symbolic replacement of religious parochialism with American democracy. The Jews in these movies usually act heroically to save their fellow soldiers and usually die as a result of their bravery. Since rabbis do not inhabit Hollywood trenches, the Jewish soldier's funeral is frequently conducted without benefit of clergy or, occasionally, by a religiously nondescript chaplain. In addition, as David Weinberg notes, the soldier-Jew never seems at all concerned with his fellow Jews perishing in Europe, and, with only a few exceptions, films having major Jewish characters are set in the Pacific theater rather than in Europe. The reason for this seems apparent now. Jewish moguls and filmmakers throughout the decade feared that even hinting at a possible connection between American Jews and those suffering in Europe would lead critics to conclude that Jews were fighting for personal rather than patriotic reasons.

A typical film in this category is director Lewis Milestone's *The Purple Heart* (1944), in which some fictionalized 1942 Doolittle raiders are shot down over Tokyo, tried as spies, and executed. Unlike the more "authentic" presentation of the Doolittle raids in Mervyn LeRoy's *Thirty Seconds Over Tokyo* (1944), Milestone's film (based on Darryl Zanuck's fictionalized conjecture) seems specifically designed as propaganda to help prejudice American audiences against their "sadistic" enemy. As such it was highly successful. *The New York Times* noted it was "so honest and thoroughly consistent with American character…so clearly in keeping with the nature of the enemy in its grim detail, that we are safe in accepting this picture…as general truth." In his book *On Visual Media Racism*, Eugene Wong characterizes *The Purple Heart* as "the most terrifying and incendiary product Hollywood ever would produce dealing with the Japanese" and feels it emphasizes "the assumed sub-human quality of the enemy." Further, he argues, it successfully fed "America's racist beliefs about the Japanese…misled the American

Lt. Wayne Greenbaum (Sam Levene) lectures the Japanese court on the illegality of the proceedings in THE PURPLE HEART *(1944).*

public and justified the government's anti-Japanese activities at home." The audiences' gut level reaction to the film was summed up by an exuberant Louella Parsons: "I defy anyone to see this picture and not want to go out and kill, singlehandedly, every Jap." Part of its force comes from Milestone's attempt to convey historical accuracy in his fictional tale. He even employed a technical advisor, a minister's daughter who lived in Tokyo during the early days of the war. Milestone's meticulous attention to the grim details of life behind bars, fluid-moving camera, pseudo-documentary approach, and decision not to show the physical torture on the screen but to let us imagine it, all combine to produce an extremely effective film.

The Purple Heart opens with eight confused American fliers being led into a courtroom de-clared off-limits to all but reporters from nations friendly to Japan. We quickly discover the Americans are on trial for bombing nonmilitary targets, although their leader, Captain Harvey Ross (Dana Andrews), vehemently denies the charges. Throughout the trial, fabricated evidence mounts against the hapless fliers: witnesses lie, films are doctored to support prosecution distortions, and the right of cross-examination is not allowed. A running battle between two Japanese military men, one an army general (Richard Loo) and the other a navy admiral (Peter Ching), over who is to blame for the raid's success, continues throughout the proceedings. This divisiveness of the enemy

Family and friends gather to celebrate Professor Roth's (Frank Morgan) birthday in THE MORTAL STORM *(1940).*

contrasts sharply with the harmony inside the American unit. As the trial drags on, the Japanese resort to a series of sadistic attempts to brutalize the Americans into admitting their guilt. In one particularly cruel scene, an Italian-American artist (Richard Conte) has his wrists broken, and in another, a young boy (Farley Granger) has his tongue cut off. All these atrocities occur off screen, so the film's most brutal moments are left to the individual's imagination. Finally, the stubborn survivors are led to their inevitable execution, the

swelling strains of "Wild Blue Yonder" accompanying their march to glory.

Throughout the film, Lt. Wayne Greenbaum (Sam Levene) articulates the fliers' positions. A navigator on the plane, he performs the same function in the courtroom: his eloquent speeches determine the path for others to follow. Milestone, himself a Russian immigrant from Odessa whose real name was Milstein, immediately establishes Greenbaum as the film's intellectual center. When the sneering Japanese lawyer arrogantly introduces himself and adds, "Princeton, '31," Greenbaum introduces himself and concludes, "CCNY, '39," citing his connection with the liberal, tuition-free school that was so much a part of the New York intellectual scene during the thirties. Greenbaum rises many times during the trial to elucidate an erudite point of law. Displaying both his wisdom and scholarship, Greenbaum convinces even those reporters from enemy countries who are sympathetic to the Japanese position as to the accuracy of his legal and moral objections to the proceedings.

Greenbaum's activities, however, are not only intellectual. At a particularly emotional moment in the trial, he actually spits on a lying witness, and later in the film's warmest gesture, puts his arm around a frightened soldier to support and calm him. Near the end, when the fliers vote whether or not to reveal military secrets and thus avoid death, Greenbaum casts the first ballot for a heroic death. He pierces through the sham of the charges to reveal the real reasons for the trial, "They want to stop us from sending more planes over Japan; that's the reason for this trial." This awareness helps the others see their duty more clearly.

The Purple Heart is an interesting example of Hollywood's attitude toward race issues during the war. The platoon is an ethnically mixed unit. Besides Ross, Greenbaum, and Carnelli, it includes characters named Clinton, Skoznik, Vincent, Bayforth, and Stoner. The impression of a united American ethnic front even including the Italian-American whose ancestral land is at war with the United States represents another in a series of democracy-in-action tales. The Greenbaum character shows he is an American first and a Jew second, an attitude emphasized by Milestone's treatment of him within the movie. In fact, much of the moral strength exhibited by the downed fliers comes from their ability to cast aside individual differences and unite behind a solid American stance, one symbolized by their vote to die rather than to reveal more than their names, ranks, and serial numbers.

While some screen Jews fought battles against America's enemies, others suffered the cruel persecution of Hitler's policies in Germany and the countries it occupied. Before the United States entered World War II, two films dealt with the situation: *Escape* (1940) and *The Mortal Storm* (1940). Far more interesting than *Escape* is Frank Borzage's *The Mortal Storm,* though today its contrived melodrama seems less powerful than in

Martin Breitner (James Stewart) and Fritz Marberg (Robert Young) dispute politics as Freya Roth (Margaret Sullavan) listens in THE MORTAL STORM *(1940).*

Political disputes turn to personal violence as Fritz Marberg (Robert Young) tries to separate Freya Roth (Margaret Sullavan) from Martin Breitner (James Stewart) in THE MORTAL STORM *(1940).*

1940. Historically, the film remains important because it represents Hollywood's first attempt to depict Nazi Germany. Though the persecuted Doctor Viktor Roth (Frank Morgan) is identified only as a non-Aryan, the film makes it clear he is a Jew, by having the Nazis force him to wear an armband with a "J" on it. *The Mortal Storm* stands as one of the few attempts made during the forties to confront Nazi anti-Semitism, a fact reviewer Bosley Crowther recognized by calling it "one of the most harrowing and inflammatory fictions ever placed on the screen, [it] strikes out powerfully, with both fists at the unmitigated brutality of a system which could turn a small university community into a hotbed of hatred and mortal vengeance."

Set in January, 1933, on the eve of Hitler's appointment as chancellor, *The Mortal Storm,* like many of Borzage's other films, involves two lovers separated by outside forces. The prologue, heard against a visual background of clouds that gather speed and move across the sky, speaks of "the mortal storm in which man finds himself today" and of the "evil elements" within man. After an establishing long-shot of the picturesque mountains surrounding the small German town, the story focuses on the beloved patriarch, Professor Roth, and his family: wife (Irene Rich), daughter Freya (Margaret Sullavan), and stepsons Otto (Robert Stack) and Erich (William Orr). At the school's celebration of the professor's birthday, his two favorite students clarify their concerns: Fritz Marberg (Robert Young) talks of love for the fatherland and Martin Breitner (James Stewart) about personal love and affection. The professor's own speech stresses honor and loyalty above either patriotism or love. At home in the midst of a private birthday celebration, a maid breaks up the party with an excited announcement of Hitler's appointment. Fritz and the stepsons rush off to hear details on the radio; Martin, Freya, the professor, and his wife remain at the half-deserted table, the scene symbolically portraying Hitler's destruction of German family life.

As the film progresses, Hitler's policies disrupt many other aspects of German life. For example, when an old school teacher (Thomas Ross) refuses to return the "Heil Hitler!" salute, he is attacked and only barely saved by Martin's spirited defense.

Moreover, Roth's once respectful students have now metamorphosed into vehement Nazis. When the professor claims chemical analysis shows no difference between the blood of Aryans and that of non-Aryans, Fritz and the others boycott his classes. Later, the old professor sadly watches the burning of books by Einstein and Heine, among others, in a ceremony that ironically contrasts to his own birthday celebration. Finally, the government bars Roth from teaching. Taken into custody, he is sent to a concentration camp, where he finally dies. His fleeing family is stopped at the border and accused of "blasphemy" for attempting to smuggle Roth's final book out of the country. Martin, however, bravely attempts to save Freya, only to see her shot and die in his arms as they escape to freedom across the mountains seen in the film's opening shots.

John Belton's solid visual analysis of *The Mortal Storm* in *The Hollywood Professionals* (vol. 3) provides ample evidence of why Borzage's film remains aesthetically interesting today. His discussion of intricate group placement for symbolic reinforcement of ideological positions, his notation of Borzage's repeated camera movements and their thematic significance, and his striking discussion of the power, beauty, and meaning of the film's final scenes that unite images of rebirth with spiritual forces all show the strength of the director's visual artistry even within the confines of melodramatic claptrap. In addition, an analysis of Fritz Marber's attitude to Freya as compared to his notion of politics yields some interesting cross-associations. Throughout the film Fritz treats her as if she has neither intelligence nor ideas of her own. "I'll do the thinking for both of us," he tells her, echoing Hitler's attitude toward the German people. His dictatorial attitude contrasts directly with that of the professor, who prizes "tolerance and a sense of humor," and with that of Martin whom Freya labels "the sanest person I know." Service to the Third Reich, the film implies, means blind dedication without the restraints of personal feeling or thought.

The Mortal Storm was Hollywood's fledgling attempt to confront the Nazi menace against "non-Aryans," even though modern audiences find it difficult to accept Jimmy Stewart as a German,

"Marcus Welby" as a cruel Nazi, or "Elliot Ness" as a German soldier. (Ward Bond and Dan Dailey also appear as Nazis.) The film's strong anti-Nazi tone symbolizes Hollywood's growing desire to alert the nation to the dangers abroad, even though severely hampered by fears of isolationist criticism and the loss of foreign markets. The interracial love symbolized by Freya and Martin, a truly American approach to practical political differences, dominates such films throughout the decade. Thus, *The Mortal Storm* represents Hollywood's earnest attempt to confront German anti-Semitism on a personal rather than a global scale. It assumes that all large-scale issues can ultimately be reduced to much smaller concerns.

Once America entered the war, the stronger sentiments somewhat held in check by fear of objections from isolationists exploded in a series of anti-Nazi films with Jewish characters. In William Cameron Menzies's *Address Unknown* (1944), Jews move from secondary to primary roles, as this sometimes bizarre film traces the relationship between two families caught up in the world of politics and war. The opening shots depict the friendship and respect between two partners in the art business. Martin Schultz (Paul Lukas) returns to Germany and sends back artifacts, while Max Einstein (Morris Carnovsky) stays in San Francisco and sells them. Martin's son, Heinrich (Peter Van Eyck), resides with Max, while Max's daughter, Grisella (K. T. Stevens), goes to Germany for an acting job before she is to marry Heinrich. Because of his need for personal aggrandizement, Martin gets swept into Nazi activities, forgetting his ties to Max and totally forsaking Grisella when she needs him the most.

Menzies' handling of the Jewish elements in the film is both intriguing and contrived. Early in the film Martin calls Jew-baiting a "minor activity" in a voice-over letter to Max, while the camera shows a German merchant gloating as his Jewish rival's store is burned to the ground. Later, Martin denies any connection whatsoever with Max, fearing that, as his new-found aristocratic friend Baron von Friesche (Carl Esmond) says, "There's always a taste of something foreign when something comes from across the ocean." The effects of Nazi persecution are even clearer when Martin's activities

Heinrich Schultz (Peter Van Eyck) and Grisella Einstein (K.T. Stevens), two lovers separated by geography and hatred in ADDRESS UNKNOWN *(1944)*

During her debut in Berlin, Grisella Einstein (K. T. Stevens), a Jewish actress, is hooted off the stage as her director (Erwin Kalser) watches helplessly in ADDRESS UNKNOWN *(1944).*

Martin Schultz (Paul Lukas), whose return to his native Germany leads him to betray his lifelong friends in ADDRESS UNKNOWN *(1944).*

A strange letter from Heinrich's father in Germany puzzles Heinrich Schultz (Peter Van Eyck) and Max Einstein (Morris Carnovsky) in ADDRESS UNKNOWN *(1944).*

culminate in Grisella's death. Though she changes her name to Stone to find work in Europe, the girl refuses to capitulate to Nazi tyranny. When the German censor orders her to remove some offensive lines from a play ("Blessed are the meek for they shall inherit the earth; blessed are the peasants for they shall be called the children of God"), she refuses and causes a riot. The audience hoots her off the stage with cries of "Jüdin! Jüdin!" After she asks if calling "a man a Jew robs him of his humanity," they storm the stage and chase her from the theater. Martin refuses her sanctuary, and Grisella is tracked down and shot. There are no havens for Jews in Nazi Germany, even with those who claim to be their friends.

Tomorrow the World (1944) reverses the premise of *Address Unknown:* a twelve-year-old German boy, Emil Bruckner (Skip Homeier), thoroughly indoctrinated in Nazi ideology, is brought to America by an uncle (Fredric March) after his parents die in a concentration camp. Emile loathes the memory of his parents, schemes to steal secret plans from his uncle who works in the U.S. War Department, bludgeons his cousin, and displays fanatical hatred and murderous intentions toward Leona Richards (Betty Field), his uncle's Jewish fiancée. When he is finally captured and jailed for the attack on his cousin, Emile learns how American democracy differs from Nazi despotism when he is given a fair trial for his crimes.

Tomorrow the World, along with *Address Unknown,* is one of the few significant American films about Nazi anti-Semitism. In her tolerance and understanding, Leona demonstrates the Jews' moral and ethical superiority over the system trying to destroy them. Yet the results of a study in 1946 by psychiatrists Mildred Wiese and Stewart Cole prove how "message" films like these sometime communicate information never intended by their creators: "Those seeing *Tomorrow the World* who were already pro-German or easy-going about Nazism did not notice the anti-Nazi message, but thought that on the whole the young boy's behavior was all right—if a bit extreme. He could not, they thought, be blamed for the tragedy that ensued." Be that as it may, *Tomorrow the World* represents an early attempt to deal with the legacy of Nazi hatred that would linger long after the war.

Not coincidentally, it recommends a "turn the other cheek" philosophy for America's Jews. Hollywood counseled toleration, acceptance, and forgiveness as the proper path toward ultimate reconciliation with the Germans, even for the people most threatened by them. In the person of Leona Richards, Hollywood provided American Jews with a prototype of the patience and sympathetic understanding they were expected to show their potential executioners.

The Holocaust had vividly confirmed the idea of the Jew as sufferer rather than a fighter. How could so many people allow themselves to be herded into cattlecars and taken to their deaths without rising in defiance? No details of sporadic resistance attempts, hopes for providential miracles, or claims that European Jews could not believe a disaster of these proportions was possible dispelled the nagging belief among many that Jews were cowards, perpetual victims who would prefer to be murdered rather than to defend themselves. Such a widely held view proved an embarassment to American Jews, who were unable to explain the passivity of European Jews. Everywhere the Jew was perceived as a weakling rather than a warrior.

The devastating shock of events abroad tended to intensify Jewish fellowship at home. German Jews, after all, were considered the most highly cultured and best assimilated in the world. If it could happen there, why not in the United States? For a while, therefore, Jews became less interested in participation in the Gentile world, and less eager to belong to exclusive clubs. Reversing a trend of past decades, they showed greater interest in synagogue-sponsored events, another development that increased participation in Judaism by those who had previously been satisfied with mere Jewishness. Even Jewish-American intellectuals who had previously espoused scientific objectivity and rationalism retreated from their positions. "To be a Jew," says literary critic Alfred Kazin, "means one's very right to existence is always in question." Many of the strongly anti-religious Jews of the prewar era recanted their positions and retreated to more traditional Judaism. With brutal clarity, Hitler had proved that no matter what one said, you were a Jew if the Gentile world considered you one.

Emil Bruckner (Skip Homeier) bludgeons his cousin in TOMORROW THE WORLD *(1944).*

Later events led American Jews to an even more terrible conclusion: general indifference to the postwar fate of those who managed to survive the Holocaust. In 1946 a national survey concluded that only five percent of the American people favored allowing refugees to enter the country in any large numbers; a majority of those polled wanted all immigration drastically reduced or even totally halted. When the United Nations asked Argentina's director of immigration to accept refugees from Europe, he responded: "Immigrants have to be strong, healthy, and unaffected by the war. The misery that is left in war-torn Europe must remain there. Argentina cannot put up with that useless human wreckage." Even the sup-

The Nazi infiltrator disguised as a Polish patriot (Carole Lombard and Stanley Ridges), TO BE OR NOT TO BE *(1942).*

Planning stage strategy in Nazi-occupied Warsaw (Robert Stack, Jack Benny, Carole Lombard)

posedly liberal 1948 Displaced Persons Act endorsed by President Truman allowed only 393,542 people to enter the United States before it expired in 1952. Of this figure, 63,000 were Jews. Thus, the Nazi slaughter tended to draw American Jews beyond their national and local concerns into a tighter bond with Jews throughout the world. "The spectre of the Holocaust," says Lucy Dawidowicz, "continues to haunt Jews everywhere and to define their priorities." Whether they desired it or not, American Jews became the bearers of Jewish destiny in the years immediately following the war; the very survival of Judaism depended on them.

While most Hollywood films dared not depict the Jewish plight in any but the most melodramatic terms, a few filmmakers resorted to what would later become known as black comedy or concentration-camp humor. Today we are accustomed to comedy as a valid means of commenting on serious topics. Movies such as *Dr. Strangelove* (1963), *Catch 22* (1970), and *M.A.S.H.* (1970) mix their laughter with moral outrage. The forties, however, had no history of this approach to tragedy, and films presenting such a world view were inevitably labeled "offensive" or "callous." In particular, two films attempted to walk the thin line between poor taste and political satire: Ernst Lubitsch's *To Be or Not to Be* (1942), and Charlie Chaplin's *The Great Dictator* (1940). In these films, comedy is the weapon used against Jewish adversity.

To Be or Not to Be is not so much poetic as it is potent, though its fast-moving, neo-Restoration plot almost defies recapitulation. (As astute a critic as Francois Truffaut once claimed no one could possibly recount the plot after seeing it, even for the sixth time.) Suffice it to say, the film is about a group of Polish actors led by Joseph (Jack Benny) and Maria (Carole Lombard) Tura, and including a bit part player named Greenberg (Felix Bressart), who go through a series of elaborate poses to foil the Nazi invaders under the command of a blustering Sig Rumann as "Concentration Camp" Ehrhardt ("I do the concentrating; they do the camping"). The whiz-bang action gives Lubitsch, himself a German Jew, an opportunity for some savage satire and caustic wit.

The action centering around Greenberg is most crucial. Three times the bit actor utters Shylock's famous "Hath Not a Jew" speech from Shakespeare's *The Merchant of Venice,* each time with more tragic resonance and greater meaning. First we see him repeating the words backstage as an extra, dreaming of the time he can strut and fret upon the stage in a major role. Next, he speaks them amid the bombed-out Warsaw streets, Shakespeare's eloquent plea for human understanding sharply contrasting to man's brutality. Finally, and most importantly, Greenberg performs his "dream part" before an unsuspecting audience of Nazi soldiers, duped by a false fuehrer into watching a stage performance that, unknown to them, constitutes a courageous act of survival through art. Greenberg's last Shakespearean lines "and if you wrong us, shall we not revenge?" offer a submerged threat on behalf of his people.

Jack Benny (Tura) masquerading as "Concentration Camp Erhardt."

As in the films set in America, Greenberg's motivation in performing such a heroic act is to save his country, not its Jews. He proves his worth by rescuing his non-Jewish countrymen. Lubitsch's brilliant black comedy merges illusion and reality on its highest levels, showing that art is a necessary part of life and life an intricate creation of art. His world is one in which all the players are actors in some form or another. When the gentle Greenberg tells us "a laugh is not to be sneezed at," he speaks for Lubitsch, who forces us to witness life's cruelty as we laugh uneasily.

To Be or Not to Be initially received unfavorable reviews. The Philadelphia *Inquirer,* for example, called it a "callous, tasteless effort to find fun in the bombing of Warsaw," while the National Board of Review warned "sensitive people won't like it." One critic even labeled the work a propaganda piece for Goebbels. The attacks were so vicious that Lubitsch felt it necessary to defend himself:

> When in *To Be or Not to Be* I have referred to the destruction of Warsaw, I have shown it in all seriousness. The commentation under the shots of the devastated Warsaw speaks for itself and cannot leave any doubt in the spectator's mind what my point of view and attitude are toward those acts of horror. What I have satirized in this picture are the Nazis and their ridiculous ideology.

The critics were particularly critical of Ehrhardt's reply to Tura that "what he did to Shakespeare, we

Maria Tura cajoling the real Colonel Erhardt (Sig Rumann).

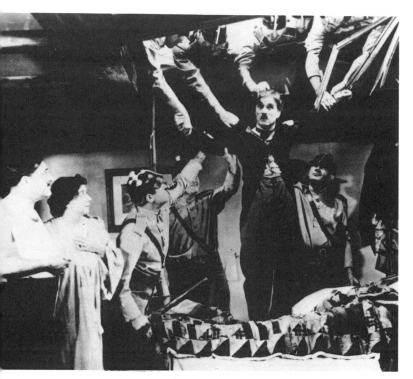

The troops of dictator Adenoid Hynkel finally capture the plucky little Jewish tailor in THE GREAT DICTATOR *(1940).*

Some lucky refugees (including Paulette Goddard) manage to escape the cruel rule of Adenoid Hynkel in THE GREAT DICTATOR *(1942).*

are now doing to Poland," though Lombard's appearance in a fancy dress she says she will wear "in the concentration camp scenes," seems far more appalling.

Finally, we come to Chaplin's early plea for tolerance in his first talking film, *The Great Dictator.* Made earlier than the Lubitsch movie, Chaplin's brilliant parody of Hitler and his satiric jabs at Mussolini (played by Jack Oakie) remains as fresh today as they were in 1940 when many still thought Hitler could be appeased. Chaplin himself bore an uncanny resemblance to Hitler, and it is a consummate irony that one of the world's best-loved men should so resemble one of its most hated. It seems natural, therefore, that his film would center around mistaken identities in which Chaplin plays two roles: a Jewish barber and the dictator Hynkel. Throughout the comedy, Chaplin discusses anti-Semitic activities more openly than is done in any of these more "realistic" melodramas that have worn so badly over the years. He shows, for example, how Hynkel's men paint "Jew" on the barbershop window, and how the little man wipes it off and battles his attackers. After Jewish bankers refuse Hynkel a loan which would enable him to invade Austerlich, he vents his rage on the hapless Jewish community in his own country, Tomania. Later, when Hynkel and the barber change places, the little man makes an impassioned speech for tolerance:

> We all want to help one another. Human beings are like that. We want to live by each other's happinesses—not by each other's misery. We don't want to hate and despise one another. In this world there is room for everyone. And the good earth is rich and can provide for everyone....The misery that has come upon us is but the passing of greed—the bitterness of men who fear the way of human progress. The hate of men will pass, and dictators die, and the power they took from people will return to the people. And so long as men die, liberty will never perish....The sun is breaking through! We are coming out of the darkness into the light! We are coming into a new world—a kinder world, where men will rise above their greed, their hate and their brutality. Look up, Hannah! The soul of man has been given wings and at last is beginning to fly.

The Dictator (Charlie Chaplin) between his Goebbels (Henry Daniel) and his Mussolini (Jack Oakie), in THE GREAT DICTATOR *(1942).*

Lee Diamond (Dane Clark) makes Al Schmidt (John Garfield) understand what he fought for in PRIDE OF THE MARINES *(1945).*

In this long, last speech, Chaplin seemed to speak for the desires of the free world. Yet it was already too late; there were to be years of darkness before the light would be seen again.

Pride of the Marines concludes the wartime action films and focuses on the ways that wounded servicemen responded to civilian life. When Al Schmidt (John Garfield), a foundry worker blinded in the war, returns home, it is to a San Diego hospital rather than to the waiting arms of his loyal girlfriend, Ruth Hartley (Eleanor Parker). His fellow patients constitute remnants of a platoon from the prototypical U.S. fighting unit: Lee Diamond (Dane Clark), Kebebian (Warren Douglas), and Irish (Don McGuire). Their problems range from bitterness about rehiring practices, to physical disabilities, to a feeling of having been exploited by a country that called them to war and now ignores them. While the combat films stressed racial harmony, ethnic animosities are allowed to surface in the post-war adjustment pictures. One soldier worries that when he returns home "some Mexican will probably have my job," while a Mexican serviceman slinks away in the face of such hostility.

Once again, it is the Jewish character, Lee Diamond, who articulates the film's liberal, humanitarian position. As Schmidt and Diamond become friends, we learn he is from Flatbush. His gentle concern for his lonely wife is manifested when, unmindful of his own pain, he reminds the nurse to send his wife a gift. "No guy killed or disabled in this war is a sucker," declares Diamond, and he goes on to lecture his dispirited comrades about why they fought the war:

> There's no free candy for anyone in this world. I know what I fought for. I fought for me, for the right to live in the U.S.A. When I get back into civilian life and I don't like the way things are going...I'll stand on my own two legs and holler. One happy afternoon when God was feeling good, he sat down and thought up a beautiful country and named it the U.S.A. Don't tell me we can't make it work in peacetime like we do in war.

On the way home with Al, Lee teaches him some

Lee Diamond (Dane Clark) consoles a blind Al Schmidt (John Garfield) in PRIDE OF THE MARINES *(1945).*

simple Hebrew words, "shalom aleichem" (Peace Unto You), along with a lesson in American democracy;

> Maybe some guys won't hire me because my name is Diamond and not Jones. 'Cause I celebrate Passover instead of Easter. We need the same kind of a world. We need a country to live in where no one gets booted around for any reason.

Thus, director Delmar Daves used Diamond as a spokesman for the film's sentiments. He epitomizes the reflective Jew who fights when necessary and understands why he and others were called upon to make such sacrifices. There is no bitterness in his words, no hint of ironic distance, as he forcefully speaks for the glory of his country and demands a role in its life.

American films set at home also adopted the strategy of the wartime action films, relegating religious preferences to minor importance and

Charlie Davis (John Garfield) watches anxiously as doctors examine Ben Chaplin (Canada Lee), an ex-champ he nearly kills in BODY AND SOUL *(1947).*

Charlie Davis (John Garfield) slips his ineffectual father (Art Smith) some money in BODY AND SOUL *(1947).*

stressing America's unity at home as well as on the battlefield. One of the more interesting films of the forties, though one that downplayed its hero's Jewishness, is director Robert Rossen's *Body and Soul* (1947). Its star John Garfield (born Julius Garfinkle) was not unlike the film's main character, Charlie Davis. Both were sons of poor Jewish immigrants who grew up on New York's tough Lower East Side, got into frequent brawls, and skirted with potential juvenile delinquency. Both escaped their surrounding: Garfield by winning a state debating contest and Davis an amateur boxing match. One of the top grossing films of 1947, *Body and Soul* got Garfield an Academy Award nomination for Best Actor, but he lost out to Ronald Colman in *A Double Life*. Its story of a hard, arrogant boxer who, with the help of his loyal girlfriend (Lilli Palmer), defeats the mob trying to fix his bout, seemed a natural role for the pugnacious and rebellious Garfield.

Charlie's father (Art Smith), an ineffectual Jewish merchant who slips his son money to buy boxing equipment over his mother's objections, is killed soon after his gift launches his son's career; he is never again mentioned. His mother (Anne Revere), however, is different from the stereotypical Jewish mothers seen in the silent films and later in the post-Portnoy era. She is a cold, slim, indifferent woman who drinks her tea in a glass, wants Charlie to go to school rather than to fight, and would rather go on welfare than allow him to box. When he brings home the obviously non-Jewish Peg, Mrs. Davis never objects to or questions the relationship.

Rossen's use of his characters' Jewishness is somewhat ambivalent. At one point in the film, a friend rooting for Charlie says: "In Europe Nazis are killing people like us just because of our religion, but here Charlie Davis is champ." Thus, Charlie clearly embodies the frustrated hopes of his people. He never, however, acknowledges this or even mentions his own Jewishness. We assume he wins the last fight, at least partially, so as not to betray those who put their faith in him—including the Jewish community that supports him—but Rossen's ethnic sensibilities fail to rise very far above other forties features.

One of the more intriguing aspects of *Body and*

Charlie Davis (John Garfield) con-templates whether or not to throw a fight in BODY AND SOUL (1947).

Police Detective Finley (Robert Young) questions some witnesses (Jaqualine White/Gloria Grahame) about the murder of a Jewish war veteran in CROSSFIRE *(1947).*

Joseph Samuels (Sam Levene) shares a drink with Sgt. Montgomery (Robert Ryan), the bigot who will eventually kill him in CROSSFIRE *(1947).*

Soul is Charlie's relationship with Ben Chaplin (Canada Lee), an ex-champ Charlie mauls, in fact nearly kills, on his way to the top. In a strange way, Ben becomes the father-figure to the young fighter, replacing the timorous storeowner killed and forgotten in the early scene. One of Rossen and scriptwriter Abraham Polonsky's points here is the union of the two minority group members against the vicious racketeers represented by Roberts (Lloyd Goff) and his bunch. Ben brings into focus the exploitation of ex-fighters, and by extension Blacks and other minority have-nots by the rulers of society, an indictment of an American system at odds with the united front presented in the decade's other films. Ben is seen as the moral and ethical center of the film. His death is a dynamic lesson in bravery and courage that inspires Charlie to save his "soul" at the end of the film. Rossen's sensitive treatment of this theme allows Ben to emerge as an articulate, proud, and dignified man, one of the most positive portrayals of a Black to come out of Hollywood during the forties. After Charlie rallies to win his last fight, even though he has bet all his money on his opponent, he spits out Ben's brave words to the frustrated Roberts: "What you gonna do, kill me? Everyone dies."

The shock of Nazi atrocities overseas motivated some American filmmakers to consider the problems of Jews in the United States. The decade's two most famous films about anti-Semitism are *Crossfire* (1947) and *Gentleman's Agreement* (1947). Though American history is not without examples of official anti-Semitism—one thinks particularly of the General Order issued by Ulysses S. Grant in December of 1862 and providing for the expulsion of "the Jew as a class" from Tennessee within twenty-four hours—these activities were never sanctioned by governmental authorities here as they were in most other countries. In fact, many American Jews and scholars concluded that the economic and social conditions which contributed to strong anti-Semitic attacks in other nations simply didn't exist in America. Particularly after World War II, there was little open anti-Semitism in this country, probably because the Holocaust still loomed so largely in the minds of most Americans. Films such as *Crossfire* and *Gentleman's Agreement* helped make anti-Semitism unrespectable by

Dave Goldman (John Garfield) explains about being Jewish to his friend Phil Green (Gregory Peck) in GENTLEMAN'S AGREEMENT *(1947).*

showing it as a Gentile problem, not a Jewish one. The fault was with those who insisted on perpetuating untrue stereotypes.

Director Edward Dmytryk's *Crossfire* was the first important film to confront American anti-Semitism. Through a series of flashbacks, the viewer learns how the confrontations between Joseph Samuels (Sam Levene), a decorated Jewish war hero, and Sgt. Montgomery (Robert Ryan), a bigoted, sadistic bully, culminated in the Jew's

death. "No Jew is going to tell me how to drink his stinking liquor," Montgomery tells Samuels in one scene. Later, he reveals his racial hatred to Sgt. Keeley (Robert Mitchum), a fellow soldier, saying: "I've seen a lot of guys like Samuels, guys who played it safe during the war, scrounged around

Phil Green (Gregory Peck) discovers Jews can be anti-Semitic in a conversation with his secretary (June Havoc) in GENTLEMAN'S AGREEMENT *(1947).*

Phil (Gregory Peck) and Kathy (Dorothy McGuire) hear Professor Lieberman (Sam Jaffe) give an intellectual Jew's view of his religion in GENTLEMAN'S AGREEMENT *(1947).*

keeping themselves in civvies, had swell apartments and swell dames. Some are named Samuels and some got funnier names." Viewing Montgomery's racism with disgust, Keeley responds, "There's a lot of funny names on the casualty list too." It is the cynical Keeley who, after helping police detective Finley (Robert Young) trap the vicious Montgomery into revealing how he murdered Samuels, adds: "My best friend, a Jew, is lying back in a foxhole at Guadalcanal. I'm gonna spit in your eye for him because we don't want people like you in the U.S.A. There's no place for racial discrimination now." The film's final message, however, comes not from Keeley but from detective Finley, who says:

> This business about hating Jews comes in a lot of different sizes. There's the "can't join our country club" kind. The "you can't live around here" kind. The "you can't work here" kind. Because we stand for all these, we get Monty's kind. He grows out of all the rest…Hating is always insane, always senseless.

In his autobiography, *It's a Hell of a Life but Not a Bad Living* (1978), Dmytryk calls *Crossfire* a "milestone" in his career, claiming that because he, Adrian Scott (the producer), and John Paxton (the script writer) were not Jewish, "no one could accuse us of selfish interest or religious bias." He was shocked to hear of one of his assistants complain after seeing the completed film: "There's no anti-Semitism in America. If there were, why is all the money in America controlled by Jewish bankers?" In the film, Dmytryk and cameraman J. Roy Hunt create a virtual *film noir* tour-de-force showing the seamy underbelly of American nightlife. Low-key lighting, low angles, alternative points of view, out-of-focus images, double exposures, and a multilevel soundtrack help get their point across. As a problem film *Crossfire* is perhaps a bit dated and simplistic, but as an aesthetic accomplishment it remains a captivating piece of filmmaking that ranks with the best films made during the forties.

Whereas *Crossfire* was a low-budget quickie made for $500,000 and shot in twenty days, *Gentleman's Agreement* had a big budget and was personally supervised by Darryl F. Zanuck (head of production at the 20th Century-Fox), written by Moss Hart (based on Laura Z. Hobson's novel), and directed by Elia Kazan. Zanuck, as the Gentile head of the town's only "goy studio," faced some stiff opposition within the industry before making the film:

> ...there was a terrific uproar from the rich Jews of the Hollywood community. And there was a meeting at Warner Brothers, called I think by Harry Warner. At that meeting...all the wealthy Jews said: "For Chrissake, why make that picture? We're getting along all right. Why raise the whole subject?" And Zanuck, in a polite way, told them to mind their own business.

Even after more than thirty years, *Gentleman's Agreement* remains the best known film about American anti-Semitism ever made in Hollywood. It won Academy Awards for Best Picture, Best Supporting Actress (Celeste Holm), and Best Director, though Peck, like John Garfield, lost that year's Oscar sweepstakes to Ronald Colman. The film also proved a financial success, became Fox's most profitable production of the year, placing eighth in *Variety's* annual tabulation of grosses. Critical acclaim further added to its luster. *Time* called it "an almost-overpowering polemic film," the *Hollywood Reporter* dubbed its premiere "a profound occurrence in the history of the motion picture industry," and *The New York Times* lauded its "dramatic forcefulness."

The plot of *Gentleman's Agreement* revolves around the story of a reporter, Phil Green (Gregory Peck), assigned to do a story on anti-Semitism for *Smith's Weekly*. To add drama to his piece, Green pretends to be a Jew, a choice that almost wrecks his romance with Kathy (Dorothy McGuire), though it gives him a greater understanding of his Jewish friend, Dave Goldman (John Garfield). After several humiliating and frustrating encounters with prejudice, Green writes his article, patches things up with his girlfriend, and receives due praise for his all-American stand.

Early in the film, Phil and his son Tommy (Dean Stockwell) sit at a breakfast table, and the ensuing conversation reveals the film's position:

Tommy: What's anti-Semitism?
Phil: Some people don't like other people just because they're Jews.
Tommy: Why? Are some bad?
Phil: Some are, some aren't. Just like everybody else.
Tommy: What are Jews?
Phil: There are lots of different churches. Some people who go to them are Catholics. People who go to other churches are called Protestants. Then there are others who go to still different ones, and they're called Jews, only they call their churches synagogues and temples....You can be an American and a Protestant or a Catholic or a Jew. Religion is different from nationality.

This notion that underneath it all, Jews, Catholics, and Protestants are all alike permeates the entire film. In fact, even the overt physical differences between various ethnic minorities are downplayed, as in a later scene when Phil finally hits on his personal angle for the journalistic series:

> I'll be Jewish. All I've got to do is say it. I've even got a title, "I was Jewish for six months." (Peck looks in a mirror.) Hmm. Dark hair, dark eyes, just like Dave. No accent, no mannerisms, neither has Dave. I'll just call myself Phil Greenberg. Ha! It's a cinch.

The ruse, of course, is spectacularly successful, as Green discovers anti-Semitism lurking around every corner. When he announces he's Jewish at a magazine luncheon, all heads turn toward him and the conversation ends abruptly. A society doctor called to attend his sick mother (Anne Revere) won't recommend a Jewish physician because he fears some of the "chosen people" overcharge and string out visits. Even though Phil has a two-year lease on his apartment, the janitor warns him the building's owner will try to force him out once he sees the name Greenberg on the mailbox. A man in a bar assumes Green was in the army's Public Relations Division because he "seems like a clever

Phil Green (Gregory Peck) tries to explain anti-Semitism to his son Tommy (Dean Stockwell) in GENTLEMAN'S AGREEMENT *(1947).*

sort of guy" and then defends himself by claiming "some of my best friends are Jewish." Green is refused admittance to a swanky hotel, and Tommy is called a "dirty Jew" and a "stinking kike." Finally, even Kathy releases some of her pent-up prejudice: "They [Jews] always make trouble for everyone, even for their friends. They force people to take sides against them."

The film also takes a minor swipe against Jewish anti-Semitism in the character of Miss Wales (June Havoc), Green's secretary, who is passing as a Gentile. To get her job at the magazine, she changes her name from Walofsky, telling Green how she was rejected when she used it in her first application. Later, after Green encourages his boss, John Minify (Albert Dekker), to hire more Jews, Miss Wales complains: "They'll get the wrong kind, the kikey ones who'll give all of us a bad name." When he finally reveals that he is not Jewish and sees her shock, Green accuses Wales of not "believing anyone would give up the glory of being a Christian even for eight weeks."

A second Jew in the film is the world-famous physicist Professor Lieberman (Sam Jaffe), who represents the evasions of Jewish intellectuals. At a party, he tells Phil and Kathy:

> I have no religion, so I am not Jewish by religion. I am a scientist, so I must rely on science which tells me I am not Jewish by race, since there's no such thing as a Jewish type....I remain a Jew because the world makes it an advantage not to be one. So, for many of us, it becomes a matter of pride to call ourselves Jews.

Here Jewishness is somehow equated with simple stubbornness, a kind of cantankerousness that passes for pride. Given what Lieberman says, he would not call himself a Jew if the world did not make it so difficult to be one. Are there no other reasons for maintaining a Jewish identity? Apparently, with Lieberman's world view, one would have to answer "no." Thus the film's most intellectual Jew provides no rational reason for remaining a Jew.

In spite of their laudable intentions, both *Crossfire* and *Gentleman's Agreement* do little more than skirt the issue of American anti-Semitism. Neither sees the problem as a deep, pervasive issue of religious, psychological, and cultural indoctrination. Jews play relatively minor roles in the films. Samuels is barely seen in the first one, and in the second, Dave informs Phil, "I'm on the sidelines. It's your problem not ours." How can anti-Semitism not be a problem for the Jews of America? Don't they have a stake in this issue? Remaining "on the sidelines," as Dave suggests, is akin to closing one's eyes and hoping the problem will disappear. If it proves nothing else, the history of the Jews clearly documents that this is one problem that will not just vanish.

The Jews in both films are Americanized to the point where little of their heritage remains. They have, in David Weinberg's terms, become "a socially acceptable minority." Both Samuels and Goldman function quite well in Gentile society. Total assimilation is their major preoccupation, and they are more concerned with melting into American society than they are with maintaining any religious or ethnic identity. The very fact that Peck assumes a Jewish persona so easily bespeaks volumes for Hollywood's vision of what it means to be Jewish. It takes no more than dark hair and eyes to fit right in.

Issues raised in these two films provide insight into Hollywood's approach to making any sort of problem picture: the basic problems of all minority groups are seen as identical. *Home of the Brave* (1949), for example, was based on a play written by Arthur Laurents about a Jew, yet the protagonist became a Black in the movie version. *Crossfire* was originally about a homosexual. It is questionable whether the problems of Jews are interchangeable with those of Blacks, Indians, homosexuals and other minority group members. Often, as Howard Suber concludes, "ethnicity is little more than a gimmick…no more significant than if they just happen to be 5′4″ in their stocking feet or happen to be just a little bit cross-eyed."

The naïveté runs even deeper, and is, in fact, at the heart of why most Hollywood problem pictures fail to deal effectively with the complex nature of the issues they claim to examine. Put simply, the confusion results from an inability to present the issues squarely, or for that matter, even to follow the sentiments expressed within films to their logical conclusions. Inevitably, Hollywood stacks the deck. The victim in *Crossfire,* for example, is a gentle compassionate war hero, and in *Gentleman's Agreement,* not even Jewish. The films persuade the audience of their message by making their victims such certifiable white knights that we feel outraged at the circumstances they are forced to endure. The outrage, however, is for the wrong reasons. We strongly identify with targets of anti-Semitism, warmly congratulate ourselves on our good taste, and feel smugly superior to the film's villainous bigots. The anti-Semitism does not disturb us, but rather the fact that it is directed against such worthy figures who have a claim on our admiration and respect. Performing this sleight-of-hand trick, Hollywood blunts its own propaganda. The film's focus changes from persecution to personality. A story told by Moss Hart, scriptwriter on *Gentleman's Agreement,* drives home the point. When told by a stagehand on the film that he loved working on the picture because it had such a "wonderful moral," Hart asked him what was the moral as he saw it. The man responded, "I'll never be rude to a Jew again because he might turn out to be a Gentile."

Mike Dillion (Dana Andrews) listens as Vogel (Stephen McNally) pleads with him to join the Jewish battle for a homeland in SWORD IN THE DESERT *(1949).*

Only one film of the forties acknowledges the question of a Jewish homeland that was so much in the news: director/writer George Sherman's *Sword in the Desert* (1949). The first film to deal with the issue of a Jewish homeland, *Sword in the Desert* sets its action before the establishment of Israel. Starring Dana Andrews as Mike Dillion, the American captain of a merchant ship who lands illegal immigrants, the film presents a very positive portrait of the valiant Jews battling the stiff-necked British who deny them a homeland. The movie follows a shipload of illegals protected by the Jewish underground as they desperately try to avoid the British soldiers sent to deport them. At one point, they are captured, only to be freed by some daring Jewish commmandos on Christmas Eve. Director Sherman uses the American as the audience's point of identification, as will be done later in *Exodus* (1960), *Cast a Giant Shadow* (1966) and *The Little Drummer Girl* (1984). At first, Dillion resists becoming involved in the cause, wary of joining people determined to use violence if necessary. Impressed by the courage of Jews such as Sabra (Marta Toren), a radio operator who

Fighting for statehood (Marta Toren) in
SWORD IN THE DESERT *(1949).*

Jeno (Paul Marion) and Vogel (Stephen McNally) supervise the landing of illegal refugees to Palestine in SWORD IN THE DESERT *(1949).*

hoodwinks the British, and Kurta (Jeff Chandler), leader of the underground, he eventually joins the freedom fighters. The film leaves little doubt as to how the director feels about Jewish independence: the British are inept bumblers or merciless killers, while the Arabs are not even an issue.

Sword in the Desert casts its conflict into basic Hollywood war imagery, and the film's Jewish characters are very much like their American counterparts in typical World War II movies. The emphasis is on bravery and courage above all else, and there is little time for reflection or for political and ethical questions about Jewish statehood. All the complex problems boil down to a war mentality. *Sword in the Desert* thus is little more than an American war movie, but this time the Jews are the good guys and the British the enemy. Once again, Hollywood uses old formats for new situations, squeezing the Israeli question into the traditional war genre.

After an absence during the thirties, screen Jews reappeared during the forties—their muddied faces part of the wartime buddy films, their exuberant talent part of entertainment biographies, and their placid Americanism part of problem pictures following the war. To scratch the surface of these films, however, is to plummet to their depths, for nothing has really changed very much since the silent days. Jewishness is still seen only as a tangential afterthought. To fit in, to be "respectable," is the goal of these screen Jews and anything that makes them different or unique is discarded as dangerous and avoided as detrimental. When they fight and die it is not for God but for the bland vision of American Democracy hawked by the studio heads and their army of employees. Screen Jews of the forties seek to creep into the cocoon of American society and to remain as inconspicuous as possible.

Uncle David (Eli Mintz), Molly (Gertrude Berg), Jake (Phillip Loeb) Alenander (Larry Robinson), and Rosalie (Arlene McQuade) Goldberg sit down to sabbath dinner in MOLLY *(1950).*

Chapter 5

The Fifties

The American films of the fifties function as a shield rather than a mirror for the country's Jews. Hollywood was running scared. Trapped between sagging profits, governmental attacks on their industry, and the fierce competition of television, moviemakers retreated to safe topics and simple answers. Thus, war films with black-and-white situations, Biblical epics protected by the centuries, and sunny biographies of well-known personalities proliferated, dominating the Jewish-American cinema. So in terms of Jewish character development, thematic complexity, and story diversity, the fifties remain a lost period in the evolution of the Jewish-American movie.

Almost all the films with Jewish characters discussed in this book have one thing in common: men act and women react to them. Even in earlier periods of the American cinema when performers like Bette Davis, Joan Crawford, and Katharine Hepburn demanded and received starring roles, Jewish-American films contained few complex, strong roles for Jewish women. The major Jewish

Molly Goldberg (Gertrude Berg), the archetypal Jewish mama, takes charge as Uncle David (Eli Mintz) looks on in MOLLY *(1950).*

female role passed on from decade to decade was that of the long-suffering Jewish mother, a role that quickly degenerated into a comic cliché. In most films, the Jewish mother responds to events; she does not initiate them. She has little control over her own fate but merely responds to a diverse series of problems. Celluloid Jewish mothers worry most of the time; they sigh and cry a lot. They protect their children. The 1950s began with a continuation of this traditional figure in the portly form of Gertrude Berg's Molly Goldberg, but ended with the arrival of a new Jewish prototype: Marjorie Morningstar, the budding Jewish-American Princess.

Gertrude Berg's character, Molly Goldberg, was no stranger to the American public when she made her film debut in *Molly* (1951). Her radio program of fifteen years had attracted a legion of devoted listeners, and she had capitalized on her character's popularity with an equally successful stage play, *Me and Molly* (1948). In *Molly,* the Bronx home of Molly and Jake (Philip Loeb) Goldberg is a virtual compendium of good-natured Jewish stereotypes, from kindly Uncle David (Eli Mintz) to friendly neighbor Mrs. Kramer (Betty Walker) across the airshaft. But Molly reigns at its center, and through her, Berg perpetuates the *Yiddishe Mama* image so dominant in Jewish-American films from the silent era to the present day. Dark, plump, and full-breasted, Molly maneuvers the various members of the family through good-hearted cajolery, not the threats and recriminations Sophie Portnoy will resort to in the next decade. There is never any doubt that her common-sense wisdom and open generosity unite head and heart into an irresistable combination.

The Goldbergs, for American Jews, become what Amos 'n' Andy are for American Blacks: even-tempered minority types who exaggerate their ethnicity to the point of caricature. Gentiles perceive them as "good Jews" who give them no reason to worry; they just make them laugh. Their exaggerated mannerisms and quaint customs encourage a patronizing attitude toward American Jews, one hard to overcome in the more serious films on Jewish topics. Like court jesters, the Goldbergs gambol for the delight of their masters, the dominant Gentile society in America. Such a presentation is common for all ethnic groups who fear reprisals from the alien world surrounding them. It counteracts any ill will that may emerge from the inevitable conflicts between minority and majority group members in a heterogeneous society. It is important to realize, however, that such comic portrayals may do harm as well as good. Stepin Fetchit did little to help the cause of Blacks in America. All those westerns with dumb, drunken Indians helped engender an attitude of contempt toward that American minority group. It is hard to hate a people you laugh at, but it may be equally difficult to respect them or to address their grievances.

Jewish grievances were addressed in Edward Dmytryk's *The Juggler* (1953), the first film to approach Israel as a homeland rather than as a battlefield. Kirk Douglas plays Hans Muller, once the finest juggler in Germany, who has spent ten years in a concentration camp. Once liberated, Hans goes to begin a new life in Israel, and immediately runs into trouble. Terrified of confinement and distrusting all men in uniforms, Hans bolts from the Israeli relocation center, accidentally wounding a sympathetic policeman. His odyssey across Israel to avoid capture brings Hans into contact with a young orphan (Joey Walsh), and the two eventually end up in a small farming village near Nazareth. There, befriended by an Israeli woman, Ya'El (Milly Vitale), Hans finally faces his fears and asks for help.

The Juggler, actually filmed on location in Israel, represents a radical departure from previous Hollywood movies about the Jewish state in that it explores the role of the new land in the lives of the the tortured survivors of Hitler's reign. Scarred by the past, in his plea to be healed of his psychological wounds, Hans draws attention to Israel's promise of regeneration of the Jewish victims of persecution. Hans and others like him go to Israel not only to forget their pain but to surmount their grief and become "human beings" once again. Israel, for them, functions not only as a refuge, but as something far more important: a place where pain and suffering are transformed into productivity, where human hearts desensitized by cruelty can once more be taught to feel. The union of Hans, the old, with Ya'El, the new, symbolically reaffirms the triumph of love over fear and of understanding over savagery.

Another Edward Dmytryk film, *The Caine Mutiny,* (1954) deals with equally serious and complex problems. The central Jewish character, Lt. Barney Greenwald (Jose Ferrer), is a smart "Jew-lawyer" who decides to defend the film's Gentile hero, Lt. Steve Maryk (Van Johnson), against charges of mutiny when no one else will take the case. Greenwald does so because he realizes that Maryk, a naïve idealist, is innocent. He has been egged on to forcibly relieving the *Caine's* commander, Capt. Queeg (Humphrey Bogart), of his post by the fast-talking Lt. Tom Keefer (Fred MacMurray), an unethical writer more interested in gaining material for his war novel than in worrying about the consequences of his actions. To defend Maryk, Greenwald must totally discredit Queeg, dubbed "Old Yellowstain" by his mocking junior officers. He mercilessly hounds the captain until the beleaguered old sailor breaks down on the witness stand in a fit of nervous twitching, flustered stutter-

A sympathetic Israeli, Ya'El (Milly Vitale), restrains a disturbed Hans Muller (Kirk Douglas) in THE JUGGLER *(1953).*

ing, and mental confusion, thus demonstrating to the members of the court martial why Maryk took over the ship in a moment of crisis.

In one sense, *The Caine Mutiny* is classically representative of the film industry's paranoid reluctance to deal candidly with Jewish themes and characters. Herman Wouk's novel, which provides the film's basic plot, is concerned with the issue of gentlemanly anti-Semitism, and Greenwald represents the precarious position of Jewish-Americans even in safe periods of apparent acceptance. Hollywood, however, ignores the subject almost entirely. Take Greenwald's dramatic, post-trial speech near the end of the novel:

Lt. Barney Greenwald (Jose Ferrer) asks Lt. Steve Maryk (Van Johnson) to explain his shipboard actions in THE CAINE MUTINY *(1954).*

Capt. Queeg (Humphrey Bogart) breaks down under the relentless questioning of Lt. Barney Greenwald (Jose Ferrer).

If I wrote a war novel I'd try to make a hero out of Old Yellowstain....I'm a Jew, guess most of you know that. Name's Greenwald, kind of look like one, and I sure am one, from way back. Jack Challee said I used smart Jew-lawyer tactics....The reason I'd make Old Yellowstain a hero is on account of my mother, little gray-headed Old Jewish lady, fat....See the Germans aren't kidding about the Jews. They're cooking us down to soap over there....I just can't cotton to the idea of my mom melted down into a bar soap. I had an uncle and an aunt in Cracow, who are soap now....So when all hell broke loose and the Germans started running out of soap and figured it's time to come over and melt down old Mrs. Greenwald, who's gonna stop them? It took a year and a half before I was any good. So who was keeping Mama out of the soap dish? Captain Queeg...Queeg deserved better at my hands. I owed him a favor, don't you see? He stopped Hermann Göring from washing his fat behind with my mother.

In the movie version of this scene, the emphasis of Greenwald's post-trial defense of Queeg shifts away from his Jewish consciousness to his sense of debt to the old-time navy men.

Greenwald enters drunk, and when Maryk asks him if he is "kinda tight," he answers:

Sure. I got a guilty conscience....I torpedoed Queeg for you. I had to torpedo him, and I feel sick about it. You know something. When I was studying law, and Mr. Keefer here was writing his stories, and Willy was tearing up the playing fields of dear old Princeton, who was standing guard over this fat, dumb, happy country of ours? Not us. We knew you couldn't make any money in the service. So who did the dirty work for us? Queeg did. And lots of other guys. Tough, sharp guys who didn't crack up like Queeg....You don't work with a captain because you like the way he parts his hair. You work with him because he's got the job. The case is over. You're all safe. It was like shooting fish in a barrel.

Shortly after this speech, Greenwald throws his drink in Keefer's face, adding contemptuously: "If you want to do anything about it, I'll be outside. I'm a lot drunker than you are so it'll be a fair fight." The effect of this transformation is totally to divorce the Jewish issue from the political context of the argument, thus rendering the ethnic identification of little importance and even less dramatic interest. In Wouk's version, Queeg's presence and activity make him valuable above and beyond what may now have become his faults. The film blunts this side of Greenwald's ethnically motivated position and replaces it with a more general discussion of mental fitness, loyalty, and conduct under stress.

Another good example of Jews as secondary characters in Hollywood films of the fifties occurs in *Good Morning, Miss Dove* (1955). Set in Liberty Hill, a typical American small town, the film examines the career of Miss Dove (Jennifer Jones), a revered school teacher whose "gray, calm, neutral eyes" have watched over several generations of students. One of these is Maurice Levin (Jerry

Capt. Alfred Dreyfus (Jose Ferrer) responds with shock as the judges pronounce him guilty of treason in I ACCUSE! *(1958).*

Mr. Levin (Than Wyenn) and his family welcomes Miss Dove's (Jennifer Jones) class to their sabbath meal in GOOD MORNING, MISS DOVE *(1955).*

Paris), an eleven-year-old Polish immigrant nick-named Rab because he is Jewish. Because of his limited command of English, Maurice finds himself placed in a class of younger students, and a target for the school's bullies. Miss Dove, however, befriends the confused newcomer, even tutoring him after class to speed his progress toward becoming an American. In class, she teaches the children about Palestine, thereby initiating the topic of Jews and explaining about their religion. Later, she takes her students to Levin's home for a traditional Jewish feast. Such actions make acclimation to his new world easier for Maurice. The more he is accepted by his peers, the more confidence he gains. Eventually, he leaves Liberty Hill and becomes a famous playwright in New York City.

Good Morning, Miss Dove uses Rab as the embodiment of the American Dream, showing the United States as the land of opportunity and promise it had been in many silent films that featured Jewish characters. But the film goes further than its predecessors. Director Henry Koster and scriptwriter Eleanor Griffith make the film one of the few in the fifties to acknowledge differences between Jews and Christians, as well as the similarities. Rab prospers in school because Miss Dove shows the other children how his traditions are as valuable as theirs. At one point, Rab even informs his startled schoolmates that Jesus was a rabbi, a fairly radical piece of information for the fifties. Allowed a Jewish identity, Rab obtains respect for the uniqueness of his heritage as well as for his ability to fit into American society. In the world of *Miss Dove*, one's differences are something of value, not something to be disguised or shared only by a small congregation of like-minded believers. Everything different adds to the tapestry of American life.

The decade's film biography that pays most attention to its subject's Jewishness is director/actor Jose Ferrer's uneven retelling of the Dreyfus Affair, *I Accuse* (1958). As the first Jew on the general staff, Captain Alfred Dreyfus (Ferrer) realizes he must do everything twice as well as his fellow officers. His patriotism, however, remains vibrant and strong. "I'd rather be a captain in the army," he tells his brother, "than President of France." Soon after these remarks, Dreyfus is falsely accused of treason, and the real traitor, Major Esterhazy (Anton Walbrook), stirs up public opinion against him by egging on a bigoted newspaperman whose walls are decorated with anti-Semitic headlines. Dreyfus's courtmartial is a farce: all positive questions and answers are perverted into negative statements, his accusers are never named, the evidence against him is totally circumstantial. He and his family are even treated as Germans because their homeland, which was once French, has now been annexed by Germany. Ferrer even manages a sly visual joke. Above the courtmartial board hangs a picture of Christ's mutilated body on the cross—another martyred Jew betrayed for a handful of silver.

Following his sentence of life imprisonment on Devil's Island, Dreyfus is dishonored in public, his sword broken and his uniform torn into shreds. The mocking crowd's cries of "Jew!" and "Traitor!" wring from the humiliated Dreyfus his most emotional outburst: "An innocent man has been degraded! Long live France!" Five years of solitude (even the other criminals on Devil's Island shun him) pass before Emile Zola's incendiary "J'Accuse" ignites public opinion and gets Dreyfus a new trial. A weary and beaten man, Dreyfus finally accepts a government pardon that also affirms his guilt. He wants to be a man once again, not a cause. Meanwhile, safe in England, Esterhazy at last admits his guilt and clears Dreyfus's name forever.

While fifties film critics like Bosley Crowther attacked Ferrer for making an undramatic, tedious film, he does at least call attention to Dreyfus's Jewishness, a fact the more critically praised *The Life of Emile Zola* (1937) failed to stress. Perhaps the film failed because Ferrer purposely distances us from Dreyfus, making him a cold, almost passive victim of racism and bureaucratic bungling. For example, when he is finally freed after five lonely years on Devil's Island, Dreyfus never even embraces his wife. So in *I Accuse*, Ferrer does precisely what more highly acclaimed movies like *Gentleman's Agreement* and *Crossfire* do not: he focuses attention on issues rather than personalities. We feel Dreyfus should be exonerated not because we like him, for we really are not encouraged to empathize with the character, but because he is innocent. Ferrer's story of a man railroaded by false charges, unnamed accusers, circumstantial evidence, and racism is too similar to typical Communist witch hunts, particularly the HUAC hearings, to be accidental. It is something of a political allegory that uses historical events to comment on contemporary activities. In this way, Ferrer could attack fifties scare tactics without running the risk of controversy or blacklisting.

A Communist witchhunt without the disguise of historical events becomes the focus of director/ writer Philip Dunne's *Three Brave Men* (1957). Based on a series of Pulitzer Prize-winning articles by Anthony Lewis about an actual incident, the Abraham Chasanow case, the film becomes an American version of the Dreyfus affair. In terms of its obvious parallels with the Dreyfus case, *Three Brave Men* resembles *The Life of Emile Zola* more than it does *I Accuse*. The film's central figure, Bernie Goldsmith (Ernest Borgnine), is Jewish, but this fact is barely mentioned and Dunne never even hints it might be the reason for this character's problems with the government. Goldsmith's overwhelming patriotism in the face of governmental harassment resembles Dreyfus's steadfast faith in France, as does his insistence that, right or wrong, he owes his country his allegiance. In the face of all his problems, Bernie maintains his stoic patriotism. "You can't blame people for hating Communists," he lectures his children, oblivious to the fact that the blind hatred he so readily excuses almost destroys his life.

Memorial Day, 1953, finds Helen (Virginia Christine) and Bernie Goldsmith proudly watching their daughter (Diane Jergens) receive the American Legion Prize for her essay, "What Memorial Day Means to Me." Appropriately, part of her essay details how her "poor, immigrant ancestors came to this country in search of precious freedom." Freedom, and how it is limited in the paranoid America of the 1950's, will become the film's focus, as Bernie Goldsmith and his family discover how quickly such a blessing can disappear in a society obsessed with fear. Hard at work in his naval office job the next day, Bernie is called into his boss's office, charged with treason, and abruptly suspended. Later we discover that some unsigned accusations about Bernie's involvement with the Communist Party have motivated these actions.

Bernie Goldsmith's daughter (Diane Jergens) reads her prizewinning essay on American values in THREE BRAVE MEN *(1957).*

Bernie Goldsmith (Ernest Borgnine) warns his family not to answer the phone after he is accused of espionage in THREE BRAVE MEN *(1957).*

Bernie Goldsmith (Ernest Borgnine) and his wife Helen (Virginia Christine) ponder their future in THREE BRAVE MEN *(1957).*

Lawyer Joe Dimarco (Ray Milland) encourages Bernie Goldsmith (Ernest Borgnine) to fight the espionage charges in THREE BRAVE MEN *(1957).*

Throughout these and subsequent events, Bernie, like Alfred Dreyfus, expresses no anger toward government officials who accuse him of disloyalty on the basis of undocumented charges. Instead, he feels like a failure, acting as if he were guilty even though he has committed no crime: he cries, declares he would rather be accused of murder than disloyalty, goes home, draws the curtains in his house, and contemplates moving away. As with the Dreyfus family, life for the Goldsmiths changes radically after the charges become known. Friends shun Bernie, convinced of his guilt without knowing the facts of the case. Crank calls clog their telephone line, and the Goldsmith children are ostracized at school. Even Mrs. Goldsmith expresses nagging doubts about her husband's loyalty.

The first person to come to Bernie's aid is a Presbyterian minister, Reverend Browning (Andrew Duggan), who visits the family because their rabbi, Dr. Josephson, is ill. (Apparently, he never recovers, for he does not appear in the movie.) Browning encourages the Goldsmiths to face their neighbors, even accompanying them on walks and defying hostile glares, and he advises Bernie to get a good lawyer. Bernie subsequently enlists the services of Joe Dimarco (Ray Milland), an Italian lawyer who takes the case because it intrigues him. Eventually, after a bitterly disappointing series of trials and retrials, Goldsmith is exonerated when the evidence against him is dismissed as malicious gossip and unsubstantiated hearsay.

In terms of its Jewish elements, *Three Brave Men* never bothers to discuss Bernie's religion or its possible place in his persecution. His relationship with Reverend Browning shows ministers as interchangeable with rabbis; in Hollywood, religion is no barrier to understanding. The film, however, depicts some frightening aspects of fifties cold war mentality. The opening voice-over speaks about problems with Communist infiltration into various aspects of American life and justifies governmental actions as "drastic steps necessary to combat it." The Secretary of the Navy (Dean Jagger) argues that America needs strong security programs like the one that almost ruins Bernie, confidently assuring us that such measures are never harmful when properly used. By juxtaposing the secretary's words with the film's actions, director Dunne proves how hollow such assurances are when nameless government officials are allowed to wield enormous power over the lives of American citizens. *Three Brave Men* thus shows how extremism in the defense of patriotism is indeed a vice.

The fifties gave rise to a new Jewish male in the movies: the sensitive, often alienated, protagonist to whom the girl is drawn precisely because he is different, emotionally not socially, from her Gentile boyfriends. In *The Young Lions,* (1958), for example, Hope Plowman (Hope Lange), a blond Christian from a small Vermont town, falls in love with the dark, urban Noah Ackerman (Montgomery Clift) because his delicate vulnerability and decent honesty strike her as preferable to the glittering, superficial insincerity she finds in most of her non-Jewish beaus. When he journeys to visit Hope at home in Vermont, Noah confronts her father who lectures him about the family's deep American roots. He points out seven generations of Plowmans in the family plot, and director Edward Dmytryk's camera lingers on the crosses marking the graves, a silent indication of Mr. Plowman's unspoken meaning. Later, Hope's father tells Noah, "I never knew a Jew before." Hope's and eventually her father's acceptance of Noah makes him a part of that long American tradition of Plowmans, albeit with an urban flavor somewhat removed from their Vermont roots.

Edward Dmytryk, who confronted anti-Semitism in his earlier film *Crossfire* (1947), again raises the issue within the war-time segments of *The Young Lions.* Though never the central focus, its presence contradicts the image of peaceful minority co-existence so prevalent in forties combat pictures, and provides a more realistic portrait of the racial tensions in World War II platoons. During basic training, the gentle Noah Ackerman is subjected to a number of harsh lessons. First, he's accused of reading a "filthy, dirty book" —Joyce's *Ulysses*—and the work is confiscated. Then a bigoted sergeant (Lee Van Cleef) warns him against turning the barracks into a "crummy tenement in the Bronx." His fellow soldiers provide little com-

Hope Plowman (Hope Lange) introduces Noah Ackerman (Montgomery Clift) to her father, who has never met a Jew, in THE YOUNG LIONS *(1958).*

Friendship turns to love for Jacob Diamond (Efrem Zimbalist, Jr.) and Charlotte Brown (Jean Simmons) in HOME BEFORE DARK *(1958).*

Jacob Diamond (Efrem Zimbalist, Jr.) discovers he is an outsider in the house of Arnold (Dan O'Herlihy) and Charlotte (Jean Simmons) Brown in HOME BEFORE DARK *(1958).*

fort. Talking about New York City as though it were a foreign country, one asks, "Who's our ambassador there?" and another responds, "We don't recognize it." Finally, after twenty dollars he is saving for his girl's birthday present is stolen, Noah challenges the platoon's four toughest guys. His valiant fight wins their respect, and eventually Noah is welcomed by his former enemies, gets his book back, and finds the missing money inside it.

Even more intriguing in this respect than *The Young Lions* is director Mervyn LeRoy's perceptive 1958 film, *Home Before Dark* (1958), a movie unjustly ignored both by fifties and contemporary commentators. Bosley Crowther's review in *The New York Times* typifies those of earlier critics who attacked the picture. Crowther takes LeRoy to task for wasting his time with "over-elaborated sets" and "under-elaborated characters" and accuses LeRoy of making the move just so Jean Simmons could have "a chance to emote." Modern critics like Clive Denton and Kingsley Canaham simply ignore the film. LeRoy's sensitive treatment of the

pressures of small-town life deserves better. His handling of the film's Jewish character, Jacob Diamond (Efrem Zimbalist, Jr.), and the mentally unstable woman he befriends, Charlotte Brown (Jean Simmons), plunges beneath the stuffy surface of fifties life to reveal much of the hypocrisy and racism that lurks beneath its placid exterior.

LeRoy opens the film at Maraneck State Mental Hospital, where Arnold Brown (Dan O'Herlihy), a teacher at a small New England college, has gone to collect his wife, Charlotte, who has been confined there for a year following a nervous breakdown. "We'll be home before dark," he assures Charlotte as they drive off together. But the island of safety and security represented by "home" becomes the film's shattered ideal. Once back in the isolated town, Charlotte finds her stepsister Joan (Rhonda Fleming) and her stepmother (Mabel Albertson) have usurped her roles in the home. She also discovers a mysterious stranger living there: Jacob Diamond, the first Jew on the tiny school's faculty. When Charlotte asks Arnold if there are any problems with Jacob being Jewish, he tells her "no," but adds: "Of course, nobody wants an influx of them."

After her return, the situation between Charlotte and her husband rapidly deteriorates. Arnold lies to her, saying doctors at the hospital advised him not to sleep with her, when in fact they told him just the opposite. He avoids Charlotte whenever possible. During the first month after her return home, Charlotte complains to her husband that she has not "had a moment alone with him." Most disturbing to Charlotte is how much Joan has assumed the role of Arnold's surrogate wife, going on long walks with him, talking over intimate problems, typing his notes, planning menus for his dinner parties, and accompanying him to social functions. Charlotte has become an alienated outsider in her own home, an intrusion on the relationship between her husband and her stepsister.

Slowly, Charlotte and Jacob begin to draw closer together for mutual comfort and support. Both, as Jacob puts it, are "tourists in the town," two outsiders characterized by the town gossips as the mad woman and her "Jewish" friend. Symbolically, the two find themselves together on New Year's

Eve, and both resolve to begin new lives. Charlotte forces Arnold to admit his relationship with Joan and then orders the adulterous pair out of her house. Jacob rejects the faculty's pettiness and thinly disguised racism by quitting his position. He and Charlotte go off to Boston together, not to marry but to get away from the stifling New England hypocrisy represented by Arnold and Joan.

Looking merely at the surface of *Home Before Dark* reduces it to a simple Hollywood melodrama and ignores the film's far deeper significance. Charlotte's eventual realization of her own self-worth represents nothing less than a fifties feminist revolt, though a tame one by contemporary standards. At her lowest emotional point, she dresses up in Joan's evening gown, dyes her hair blonde, and introduces herself as her stepsister. Charlotte strives so desperately to become what her husband obviously desires (but will not openly admit) that she submerges her own personality, an act of emotional suicide guaranteed to lead her back to the brink of madness. The painful recognition that Arnold purposely sent her to a public rather than a private hospital, where she had to have eight gruesome shock treatments, becomes almost unbearable anguish when she also realizes he wanted her away permanently so he could go on living with Joan. Ultimately, Charlotte comes to understand her breakdown as the inevitable result of sacrificing her own personality to the wishes of another. In Charlotte's epiphany, LeRoy pinpoints the plight of some women in the fifties driven to breakdowns in a futile attempt to squeeze themselves into stereotypes demanded by men.

Significantly, only the Jewish character in the film recognizes Charlotte's personal worth. Their growing, nonsexual attachment nourishes Charlotte with the understanding and support necessary for her to recognize her own strength, to declare her independence from Arnold and all he represents, and to begin living her life as an independent individual. Jacob's masculine, yet gentle, sensitivity makes the Jew the film's emotional center, particularly when LeRoy juxtaposes him with Arnold's cruel indifference and intellectual hypocrisy. Jacob accepts Charlotte for what she is instead of attempting to turn her into what he

Dr. Samuel Abelman (Paul Muni) returns home weary after late-night medical rounds in THE LAST ANGRY MAN *(1959).*

wants. In using Jacob as a foil to Arnold, LeRoy foreshadows the qualities of the American film hero who surmounts his own vulnerability by providing emotional support for others. In this way, the Jewish protagonist helps himself as well as others. His positive qualities differ from the rough-and-tumble appeal of the taciturn Gentile heroes so common in the American cinema. His is a characterization that reaches its acme in the more involved, vulnerable, and sensitive movie males portrayed by Dustin Hoffman, Gene Wilder, Richard Benjamin and George Segal. By uniting the emerging demand of American women for acceptance on their own terms with the Jewish man

Dr. Samuel Abelman (Paul Muni) becomes the subject of a television documentary produced by Woody Thrasher (David Wayne) in THE LAST ANGRY MAN *(1959).*

emotionally secure enough to do just that, LeRoy sets the stage for new screen relationships. Such unions are healthy outgrowths of relationships between strong men and women who demand mutual respect rather than rigid subservience.

The better-educated Jews of the fifties far surpassed the economic achievements of their parents. Many entered the fields of medicine, law, and teaching. Endowed with an acceptable middle-class background equal to that of their Gentile counterparts, these fifties Jews felt their Jewishness was no impediment to attaining economic, social, and educational goals. For example, director Daniel Mann's *The Last Angry Man* (1959), based on Gerald Green's popular novel, has a Jewish doctor

as a major figure: Dr. Samuel Abelman (Paul Muni). It seems fitting that Muni, who began his career with the Yiddish Art Theater, should end it as Dr. Abelman, a dedicated, old-world physician lost in the impersonality of new-world medicine. An aging anachronism, Abelman becomes the focus of a television documentary put together by a harried, cynical TV producer, Woody Thrasher (David Wayne). When Abelman forfeits his chance at video immortality by dashing out to treat a mistrusting Black youth (Billy Dee Williams) before the program begins, Thrasher reevaluates his own priorities in light of the doctor's unselfish idealism. Here, at last, is a well-rounded Jewish character. Abelman is no plaster saint. He is argumentative and stubborn, alternately annoying and endearing. He is, however, a man with decent instincts, impeccable integrity, a profound sense of duty, and pride in his personal worth. Though one might wish for a deeper insight into how his heritage helped shape

such a man, Muni's admirable blend of pathos and dignity raises *The Last Angry Man* far above the level of common Hollywood melodramas.

If *Molly* represents a link with the past, then *Marjorie Morningstar* (1958) foreshadows a future of Brenda Patimkins and Judy Benjamins. The film follows the rite of passage of its eponymous Jewish heroine (Natalie Wood) from naïve college girl to sophisticated woman of the world. While at South Wind, a plush summer resort, young Marjorie becomes infatuated with Noel Airman (Gene Kelly), a handsome composer who stages the hotel's shows. Noel, however, rejects her when she insists on remaining a "respectable" girl. Such is not the case with Wally (Martin Milner), Noel's assistant and an aspiring playwright, who declares his love for Marjorie. Blinded by her feelings for Noel, Marjorie rejects the young writer's offer of marriage.

Finally, Noel gets his big Broadway break. His meager talents, however, fail to sustain him beyond South Wind. A dejected Noel retreats to his limited hotel productions in his refuge, the grand illusion of his superior talent forever destroyed. Marjorie constantly supports Noel through his defeats, despite his often harsh rejections of her attention. But when he returns to South Wind and resumes his affairs with a succession of impressionable young girls, she finally accepts the futility of their relationship and turns to Wally. At long last, Marjorie Morningstar recognizes that the playwright's mature stability gives her the comfort and support that Noel's adolescent volatility renders him incapable of providing.

Based on Herman Wouk's best-selling novel, the film takes some liberties with the original story. Most specifically, Marjorie ends up with Wally, rather than as the wife of a young Jewish lawyer, Milton Schwartz. Her brief fling with bohemia behind her, the novel's heroine slips rather easily into middle-class life as:

> a regular synagogue-goer, active in the Jewish organization of the town....The only thing remarkable about Mrs. Milton Schwartz is that she hoped to be remarkable, that she ever dreamed of being Marjorie Morningstar.

A more mature Marjorie Morningstar (Natalie Wood) confronts Noel Airman (Gene Kelly) about his numerous infidelities in MARJORIE MORNINGSTAR *(1958).*

The film never goes quite this far as it follows Marjorie's upwardly mobile journey from the Bronx to Hunter College to Central Park West.

One laudable thing about *Marjorie Morningstar* is director Irving Rapper's and scriptwriter Everett Freeman's decision to leave Wouk's characters Jewish, rather than turning them into Italians, Irishmen, or simply token Jews. One could not hope for the rather extensive examination of the characters' Jewishness that the book provides, but the film preserves its characters' ethnic integrity. Importance, for example, is placed on Jewish customs, like a bar mitzvah scene in a synagogue and a seder in a plush Central Park West apartment. At the very least, the decision to make a film with a Jewish heroine as its focus, not just as part of its environment, signals the greater interest that will be paid to Jewish female protagonists in the sixties, the seventies, and the eighties.

Safe Jews, like the Goldbergs and Bernie Goldsmith, or admirable Jews, like Dr. Samuel Abelman, dominate Jewish-American films through the era. Only in *Marjorie Morningstar* and *Home Before Dark* could one catch glimpses of the celluloid future of American Jews. Though the sixties would develop, refine, and sometimes castigate the Jewish-American Princess and her sensitive Jewish male counterpart, it would be a time when Jews would appear on the screen in ever-increasing numbers and in even more diverse roles. With the death and replacement of Hollywood's immigrant Jewish moguls, a new generation of Jewish filmmakers would ascend to power in the Hollywood community, men less afraid of confronting their own heritage.

159

The widowed American nurse becomes involved with Haganah fighter (Eva Marie Saint and Paul Newman) in EXODUS *(1960).*

Two refugees attempting a new life in the new land (Jill Haworth and Sal Mineo) in EXODUS *(1960).*

Chapter 6

The Sixties

The movies of the sixties offer a more diverse series of Jewish portraits than seen in any previous era. These films attest to the Jews' growing stature in American society and to the centrality of the Jewish experience within the American experience of the sixties. Whatever esthetic criticism may be leveled against pictures like *Bye Bye Braverman,* (1968), *Funny Girl* (1968), *The Pawnbroker* (1965), *No Way to Treat a Lady* (1968), and *Goodbye, Columbus* (1969), one must still recognize them as movies in which clearly identifiable Jews appear and wrestle with very human, and specifically Jewish, problems. Jews still function as the butts of humor in many of these pictures, but as the decade

The British general sympathizes to the creation of the new state (Ralph Richardson with Eva Marie Saint), in EXODUS *(1960).*

Ari disguises himself as a British officer (Newman with Peter Lawford) in EXODUS *(1960).*

progresses even the comedy films confront very serious issues. Jews are no longer an "invisible" minority. They have moved into the heart of American culture, and this move disturbed those who longed for the comfortably safe anonymity that characterized earlier times. In presenting a fuller portrait of Jews, many of the decade's films seemed to emphasize the unpleasant elements of Jewish-American life, and many feared that such movies would fuel the fires of anti-Semitism.

Hollywood during this decade responded to the Holocaust not only by dealing with the Jewish victims of the past but also by portraying the Jewish heirs of the future. In particular, the decade's filmmakers paid increasing attention to the Jewish battle to create and then to maintain the state of Israel, a psychological and geographical safety valve for survivors of Nazi atrocities. The most famous Hollywood film about the founding of Israel made during the sixties is director Otto Preminger's *Exodus* (1960). It is not generally known that MGM actually commissioned author Leon Uris to write a novel about the creation of the Jewish state because they felt it would make a good film. However, the way Preminger finally obtained the property, or at least how he recounts the story in his autobiography, *Preminger* (1977), tells something about the role of economics and fear in Hollywood. Preminger frightened the studio into selling him the film rights to *Exodus* by raising the specter of Arab boycotts of MGM theaters and movies. It worked. The studio sold the film rights for $75,000, a ridiculously low figure for a novel that was the biggest bestseller in the United States since *Gone With the Wind*. Preminger insisted on hiring then-blacklisted writer Dalton Trumbo and using his real name in the screen credits. The film thus played a part in finally breaking the blacklist of Hollywood writers begun with the HUAC hearings.

The focus of the most popular Hollywood film ever made about the founding of Israel is not an Israeli, or for that matter, even a Jew. Instead, Kitty Fremont (Eva Marie Saint), an American widow who finds her life entangled with some Palestinian refugees, emerges as the film's central character. Early in the movie, Fremont seems desolate and alone. Her husband's recent death in Palestine

Ari (Paul Newman) prepares to lead the young pioneers away from the danger zone, in EXODUS *(1960).*

Kitty prepares to aid Ari in a mass break-out of Jewish prisoners in the stockade at Acre (Eva Marie Saint and Paul Newman) in EXODUS *(1960).*

Mickey Marcus (Kirk Douglas) leads his Israeli troops to victory in CAST A GIANT SHADOW *(1966).*

where he went to tend the country's poor leaves Kitty a detached cynic. "Is there anything worth dying for?" she asks early in the picture. By the movie's end, she has an answer. Dressed in an army uniform, a gun slung over her shoulder, Kitty marches off with the Jewish freedom fighters, a part of something far larger than her personal grief. Through Fremont's educational journey toward understanding the importance of a Jewish homeland, Preminger shows there are causes worth sacrificing one's life for.

In the figure of Ari Ben Canaan (Paul Newman), American audiences met a character far different from Hollywood's earlier portraits of weak, ineffectual, and passive Jews that had dominated America's movie screens since the silent days. Ari is a fighter who resembles John Wayne more than he does George Sidney. But in doing this, Preminger robs Ari of much that might be considered Jewish. He quotes the Bible but has no apparent religious feelings. His participation in ceremonial tradition is limited to his parent's home. And, of course, he falls in love with a non-Jew—the blond, Presbyterian American Kitty Fremont. What Preminger presents, therefore, is one type of Jew found in Palestine, a nonreligious type with whom American audiences can easily identify because he reminds us of our own conceptions of military daring, battlefield valor, and bland ethnicity. "The image of the Jew as patriot, warrior, and battle-scarred belligerent is rather satisfying to a large segment of the American public," observes Philip Roth, who adds: "It fills any number of Jewish readers with pride…and Gentile readers less perhaps with pride than with relief." The glory of the Jewish military man wipes away the shame of the Jew as victim, implying that what happened in Germany will never occur again because now, at long last, the Jew can defend himself.

Ari's union with Kitty, however, is certainly not the total assimilation witnessed in earlier films about mixed romances. "People are the same no matter what they're called," Kitty lectures Ari, speaking the beliefs that underpin the majority of the mixed-marriage films of the past. "Don't believe it," he responds forcefully. "People have a right to be different." But in the union itself, even with Ari's steadfast refusal to be swept up in Kitty's romantic universalism, eventually does echo the old silent film victory of democratic love over religious duty. For Preminger, Palestine functions as a kind of mini-America, the Jewish struggle for a homeland becoming suspiciously like our own western history. Ari and his compatriots are the explorers and settlers of a new land, the Arabs represent the heathens who seek to destroy them, the British become the cattle barons who refuse to share their land with the newcomers, and Kitty symbolizes the typical "Easterner" who comes West to civilize the wilderness. It's a Hollywood Western played out in the desert instead of on a prairie, a tale of brave men overcoming the dangers of a wild frontier to bring law, order, and civilization to a new land.

Another image of the Jew as fighter appears in *Cast a Giant Shadow* (1966), directed by Melville Shavelson. This screen biography of Colonel Mickey Marcus (Kirk Douglas)—a West Point graduate, lawyer, and World War II hero who became the first commander of the Israeli Army since Joshua—traces his growing commitment to the cause of Jewish freedom fighters in Palestine. Like Kitty Fremont early in *Exodus,* Marcus at first feels quite removed from the Jews' problems. "I don't feel like one of them" he tells his wife Emma (Angie Dickinson) after refusing the offer of some representatives to fight alongside them. Eventually, he changes his mind, more because of what Emma calls his "love of war" than because of any deep religious, or even moral, concerns. Dramatically this alteration in Marcus's feelings is conveyed via the rejection of his American wife for the charms of Magda (Senta Berger), a Jew in Palestine. Though he comes to feel comfortable with his comrades in arms, Marcus never makes a personal commitment to a Jewish state. The film even hints he may return to Emma, or at least to the United States, but is accidentally shot by one of his own men before he can make this decision.

The decade's most lavish attempt to confront the question of German guilt during the war years is director Stanley Kramer's *Judgment at Nuremberg* (1961), about the famous postwar trials held in Germany; the film won an Academy Award nomination for Best Picture. The defense attorney, Herr Rolf (Maximilian Schell), sees the case

Mickey Marcus (Kirk Douglas) must decide whether or not to assume command of the Israeli army in CAST A GIANT SHADOW *(1966).*

against his client, Justice Ernst Janning (Burt Lancaster), as one in which all the German people are accused of complicity with the Nazis. "The brutality was brought about by a few extremists, the criminals, and very few Germans knew about what was going on," Rolf assures American Judge Dan Haywood (Spencer Tracy). "Men like Janning stayed in power to prevent worse things from happening." Rolf argues that "a judge does not make the laws. He carries out the laws of his country. To refuse to carry out laws would make him a traitor." Thus, the defense's position rests on two familiar excuses: "My country right or wrong" and "We didn't know." "Responsibility," declares another of the defendants on trial, "is not a cut and dried thing."

In order to support his charges of criminal brutality, U.S. Army prosecutor Colonel Lawson (Richard Widmark) draws on the infamous Feldenstein case, argued years ago before Judge Janning, in which a Jew was executed for having allegedly had sexual relations with an Aryan, Irene Hoffman (Judy Garland). He puts a pathetic victim of involuntary sterilization (Montgomery Clift) on the stand. He shows documentaries of the libera-

Irene Hoffman (Judy Garland) relives the horrors of Nazi imprisonment on the witness stand in JUDGMENT AT NUREMBERG *(1961).*

Rudolf Petersen (Montgomery Clift), a pathetic victim of involuntary sterilization, tells his story in JUDGMENT AT NUREMBERG *(1961).*

tion of Buchenwald and of the living dead housed there. The cruelty of these events is highlighted by the words of a jailed bureaucrat who calmly explains to a fellow prisoner that "It wasn't the killing that was a problem. We could kill them a thousand an hour. It was the disposing of the bodies that was the problem."

Finally, Haywood and the other judges arrive at a split decision: the majority finds all the defendants guilty of war crimes and sentences them to life imprisonment. Through Haywood, director Kramer and screenwriter Abby Mann sum up the complicated ethical issues at the core of this decision. The significance of the defendants' actions, as Haywood sees it, is that "under a natural crisis men can delude themselves into vast and heinous crimes." Janning, too, finally admits his own guilt, thus adding credence and support to Haywood's decision, as he explains to the American how the movement of events got beyond his control:

> What difference does it make if a few political extremists lost their rights? What difference does it make if a few racial minorities lose their rights? It's only a passing phase. It's only a stage we are going through. It will be discarded sooner or later. Hitler will be discarded sooner or later. The country is in danger....What was going to be a passing phase became a way of life.

As Haywood is leaving, Janning gives him a written record of his judicial decisions for safekeeping because he admires the American judge's honesty and ethical integrity. The film, however, ends on a bitterly ironic note. The decisions arrived at so thoughtfully at Nuremberg are quickly reversed by a higher court, all the defendants pardoned, and then freed.

The Jew as victim in such films as *Judgment at Nuremberg* becomes an image expanded to almost archetypal proportions in director John Frankenheimer's 1968 adaptation of Bernard Malamud's book *The Fixer.* Malamud's novel, which won both the National Book Award and the Pulitzer Prize in 1967, tells the story of Yokov Bok, a Jew in Czarist

Russia accused of murdering a young boy and then forced to undergo a series of excruciating tortures when he will not confess to the crime he has not committed. Malamud based his tale on the story of Mendel Beiliss that became the subject of earlier films like *Accused by Darkest Russia* (1913). On one level, Frankenheimer simply tells Bok's story. On another level, however, his film raises some provocative questions about how American directors perceive anti-Semitism and its victims.

In an interview, Frankenheimer claimed that the movie "has nothing to do with the fact that Yokov Bok (Alan Bates) is a Jew. It could be any man, any time, anywhere." Apparently he missed the basic irony of Malamud's book" Yokov: Bok is persecuted for a ritual murder he could not possibly have committed because his religion forbids it. Bok, whose name means "goat" in Russian, becomes a scapegoat, a victim, because of the environment of hate that limits his opportunities for advancement and makes him an outsider. He is different not only in terms of his religion, a voluntary matter, but in terms of the social, political, and economic life he is forced to live because of his religious choice. Thus, his case has everything to do with being a Jew, with being trapped by forces that create an environment of prejudice which makes him a second-class citizen.

To concentrate, as Frankenheimer does, totally on the universal implications of Bok's situation is to see Bok's suffering as a kind of Jungian archetype and to ignore the specific elements that foster anti-Semitism. The potential for anti-Semitism is present in most societies at all times, but it takes a specific moment in history to bring it to the surface, a moment usually created by a public crisis, the need for a scapegoat to explain a country's ills, an economic imbalance, or an upsurge in religious fervor. Such hatred, therefore, is very different from simple racial prejudice or political persecution. Acts against Jews are not the same as those against Blacks or Communists, for anti-Semi-

Yakov (Alan Bates) and Raisl (Carol White) happily join the village dance in THE FIXER *(1968).*

Yakov (Alan Bates) denies the charge of ritual murder and becomes a victim of Russian anti-Semitism in THE FIXER *(1968).*

Sol Nazerman (Rod Steiger), one of the "living dead" in THE PAWNBROKER *(1965).*

Sol Nazerman (Rod Steiger) enjoys an idyllic family picnic before the Nazis murder his wife and children in THE PAWN-BROKER *(1965)*

tism is usually the result of a unique fusion of religion, politics, and economics. Malamud understands that Bok is a Jewish Everyman, not an Everyman, and uses him as a metaphor for suffering, alienation, and loneliness within this particular context. Frankenheimer does not see this. His emphasis is on the suffering itself, not on why that suffering took place. The film confuses the symptom with the disease, allowing Bok's ordeal to be equated with the universal suffering endured by victims of persecution.

Bok's triumph, like his suffering, is Jewish. It cannot be equated with that of other passive resisters like Mahatma Ghandi, who protested specific civil issues, because Bok does not seek out a cause; it is thrust upon him. It resembles the quiet victory of the Jews who persevered in the concentration camps of Germany and the prisons of Russia. Unlike the soldiers in *Exodus* and *Cast a Giant Shadow,* Bok does not physically fight for Jewish freedom. Unlike the financial shrewdness that allows Nathan and his brothers to secure Jewish rights in *House of Rothschild* (1934), Bok possesses no economic power to bend society to his wishes. His victory comes from waiting and enduring. Such patience, itself, becomes an eloquent statement of the morality that defeats prejudice by holding it up to the light of ethical behavior. The ability to act like a human being in a world in which people are treated like animals is, in and of itself, an act of humanity, an ethical form of resistance which mocks a world of obscene cruelty. To say, as Frankenheimer does, that Bok's situation has nothing to do with his being Jewish is to be naïve; to say that his triumph is not the triumph of a Jew is to misunderstand the very reason for his persecution and thereby to disassociate his Jewishness from his victory.

Two films, *The Pawnbroker* (1965) and *The Producers* (1968), also show Hollywood's interest in Nazis, though they present this subject in very dissimilar ways. Directed by Sidney Lumet, the earlier movie remains the American cinema's most successful attempt to confront the pain and trauma of concentration camp survivors. In some ways, *The Pawnbroker* updates *Vengeance of the Oppressed* (1916), the powerful silent picture about the tragedy of allowing the past to dominate the

present. Lumet, however, handles the delicate interplay between past and present in the life of Sol Nazerman (Rod Steiger) with a highly refined series of modern techniques. The twenty-fifth anniversary of his wife's death forces Nazerman to confront the painful feelings about concentration camp experiences he has long suppressed. To indicate Nazerman's state of mind, Lumet employs so-called "shock cuts" that feed us tiny bits of information, almost frame by progressive frame, in a highly disjointed manner. Finally, the director brings these moments together to form an entire sequence. This technique functions like the memory itself, blocking out unpleasant information, injecting small moments of remembrance into our consciousness, and finally forcing a confrontation with the previously sublimated event. Also, Lumet juxtaposes sounds from Nazerman's present with visuals from his past: a memory will be seen while a present action is heard. This, in effect, allows the viewer to participate in the confused mingling of past and present experienced by Nazerman.

In the present segments of the movie, Lumet often shoots Nazerman behind bars of one kind or another, emphasizing his emotional entrapment in the past. Ultimately, the past cannot be ignored. It intrudes on the present. For example, when several boys corner a youngster against a fence and beat him up, Nazerman flashes back to one of his most vivid concentration camp memories: a friend attempting to escape the camp is caught on the barbed wire fence surrounding it, and his legs are chewed off by vicious guard dogs. Later, on a subway ride home, Nazerman finds himself catapulted back to a cattle car on its way to the death camp. In this manner, Lumet demonstrates how Nazerman's refusal to deal with his past destroys his present. When the past finally forces its way to the surface, it erupts and totally disintegrates the life of a man intent on ignoring it. Slowly, the roles of past and present are reversed; memories control present actions.

Nazerman refuses to have his approach to life softened despite the social worker's efforts (Geraldine Fitzgerald and Rod Steiger), in THE PAWNBROKER *(1965).*

It is a vicious cycle from which Sol Nazerman is powerless to escape: the present sparks memories of the past, the past memories force him to act in a specific manner in the present, which, of course, forces him to think even more about the past. For instance, Nazerman ultimately refuses to deal with a black gangster (Brock Peters) when he realizes how heavily the criminal is involved in a prostitution ring. This realization, along with an incident when a Black whore tempts him to trade money for sex, reminds Nazerman of his wife and her sexual humiliation at the hands of the sadistic Nazis; he can no longer close his eyes to his own part in the oppressive exploitation of other human beings.

Nazerman, as his name implies, has a bit of the Nazi within him. As a pawnbroker, he decides which of the desperate people who seek him out to trade their goods for money will receive funds and how much they will get. They curry favor with the pawnbroker the way camp inmates sought to ingratiate themselves with their guards. Nazerman can destroy people in less overt but equally deadly ways as the Germans. His realization of this fact brings Nazerman's latent guilt over having survived the horrors of the camp into the present. To purge himself of his pain, he forces a confrontation with the Black gangster that he is sure will result in his own death. When it doesn't, Nazerman is left with even more guilt and greater humiliation. In a moment of agony, he plunges his hand down on a sharp spindle, an eloquent and complex physical action that functions as penance, a recognition of his need to feel once again, and an acceptance of his pain.

Nazerman's relationship with his young, Puerto Rican assistant, Jesus Ortiz (Jaime Sanchez), further seals his spiritual doom. In the person of Jesus, as the name implies, Nazerman has a final chance for redemption, an opportunity to reach out and rescue something of value for the future out of the pain of the past. He is, however, too much a part of the "walking dead," too much concerned with his own tragedies, to recognize the humanity of others. Nazerman retreats from his responsibilities to Ortiz, hiding behind an unfeeling cynicism and a series of enigmatic responses. When Ortiz asks him if the numbers on his arm represent membership in some "secret society" and how he can

Max Bialystock (Zero Mostel) and Leo Bloom (Gene Wilder) try to convince a Nazi (Kenneth Mars) to sell them his play in THE PRODUCERS *(1968).*

A scene from the Nazi musical "Springtime for Hitler" in THE PRODUCERS *(1968).*

join, Nazerman responds, "You learn to walk on water." Later, when Ortiz wants to know why "you people come to business so naturally," Nazerman plunges into a lengthy explanation of the wandering Jew and his transformation into a merchant that totally confuses the young man. Only when it is too late does Nazerman realize what Ortiz can mean for him: a possible son substitute who can bring about his redemption via love.

At the end of the film, Ortiz dies from a bullet meant for Nazerman. The distraught pawnbroker cradles the dead boy in his arms, rocks him like a father would a son, and mouths an agonizingly silent cry. There is no solace for Sol Nazerman, no spiritual victory to compensate for his pain. He is condemned to life, forced to remember the suffering of his wife and his friends in the camp, and now sentenced to absorb the death of Ortiz. For Nazerman, life is a fate worse than death. Lumet sees no triumph in simple survival. It is how one lives that remains important, not just the fact that one continues to live.

At first it may seem silly, or even sacreligious, to lump *The Pawnbroker's* serious treatment of Nazi horrors together with *The Producer's* broad, farcical humor. A closer examination, however, reveals that both films are responding to the Holocaust's bitter legacy of pain and guilt. Because most of director/writer Mel Brooks's humor emanates from his Jewish roots, it would be surprising to find him totally ignoring the Holocaust. "He's urban, New York City Jewish," says James Monaco, "He has vaudeville in his blood and chicken fat in his head." Brooks, himself, seems to concur and locates the roots of his own comedy in Jewish pain:

> Look at Jewish history. Unrelieved, lamenting would be intolerable. So, for every ten Jews beating their breasts, God designated one to be crazy and amuse the breast-

171

Max Bialystock (Zero Mostel) and Leo Bloom (Gene Wilder) admire the charms of their new secretary in THE PRODUCERS *(1968).*

beaters. By the time I was five I knew I was that one....You want to know where my comedy comes from? It comes from not being kissed by a girl until you're sixteen. It comes from the feeling that, as a Jew and as a person, you don't fit into the mainstream of American society. It comes from the realization that even though you're better and smarter, you'll never belong.

Brooks' revealing remarks provide further evidence of the mixture of pain and pleasure that characterizes much Jewish comedy, including his own and Woody Allen's.

Jewish laughter is usually bitter, often the only means available for a weak and impotent people to protest their oppression. As such, it inevitably springs from some sort of misfortune and follows the advice of the old Jewish sage: "When you're hungry, sing; when you're hurt, laugh." Jewish humor, more than any other type of ethnic comedy, often becomes self-aggression: the target of the joke is usually the Jew himself. Obviously, this tactic functions as a defense mechanism to make the Jew seem innocuous, and therefore not threatening to the alien world that surrounds him. But another element in such a method cannot be ignored. Many observers note that oppressed people often come to see themselves through the eyes of their oppressors; they accept the attitudes of their oppressor as being at least partially true, thus incorporating a negative view of themselves as an integral part of their own self-image, i.e., Blacks who call themselves "niggers" and Jews who refer to each other as "kikes."

This tendency is clearly evident in *The Producers.* The protagonist, Max Bialystock (Zero Mostel), is a fat, vulgar, boisterous conniver anxious to seduce rich old ladies to obtain funds for his rotten plays. Leo Bloom (Gene Wilder), his reluctant partner, is a timid accountant given to fits of nervous hysteria that can be calmed only by caressing a fragment of his old baby blanket. Together, the two decide to find the worst possible play, finance it far beyond production costs, close the play to disastrous first-night reviews after one performance, and keep the extra money as a profit. Unfortunately for them, the play they chose, *Springtime for Hitler,* is a smashing success.

Brooks's characters are a compendium of ethnic clichés that, in the past, might well have been attacked as blatantly anti-Semitic: the cunning Jew who unscrupulously fleeces others, the money-hungry Jew who sacrifices all morality in his quest for riches, the manipulating Jew who trades on the finer emotions of others for his own gain, the garish Jew who flaunts his wealth at the least opportunity, the parasitic Jew who lives off the talent of others, the mild-mannered Jew who is easily bullied by more powerful personalities, the unethical Jew who cheats in business, the neurotic Jew who is unbalanced but brilliant, the sexually insecure Jew who exploits women, the ostentatious Jew who lavishly spends more than he earns, the smart Jew who becomes the victim of his own cleverness.

So why is all this so funny? What Brooks does in *The Producers* is to create a film in which the Jewish characters, however unappealing they may be, are far more attractive and loveable than the people they exploit. In particular, Brooks's merciless parodies of a talentless, homosexual director

(Christopher Hewett), a spacy rock star (Dick Shawn), and a sentimental Nazi playwright (Kenneth Mars) renders his two Jewish characters harmless by comparison. The Nazi, Franz Liebkind, receives the brunt of Brooks's satire, a bitter but hilarious diatribe against those who insist on perpetuating the Fuehrer's memory. Liebkind describes his play, *Springtime for Hitler,* as a "gay romp with Adolph and Eva in Berchtesgaden." He frequently longs for Hitler's resurrection, forcing Bialystock and Bloom to sing German war songs with him, and agrees to sell them his play only because he thinks it will be a "way to clear the Fuehrer's name" and to show once and for all that Hitler "was a nice guy who could dance the pants off Churchill."

Surely there is something going on here beyond the surface content of this absurd situation. Indeed, Brooks's comic intentions resemble Chaplin's in *The Great Dictator* (1940). Both filmmakers confront the Nazi menace and expose it the best way they can: they make people laugh at the obscene absurdity of the Master Race by turning its leaders into dumb stumblebums. Without arguing that *The Producers* reaches the level of *The Pawnbroker,* it is still possible to see both movies as arising from the same feelings of pain and as expressing similar senses of outrage. One may cry about the Holocaust but may also be reduced to bitter laughter when faced with a tragedy so enormous that it defies rational understanding. Truly, Brooks's tears mingle with his laughter. The sheer audacity to present a musical called *Springtime for Hitler,* and then have it become a hit, satirizes an American public willing to find humor, however grotesque, in the Third Reich. Bialystock and Bloom fail to find their flop because they underestimate their audience's deadened sensibilities.

Two of the decade's other films favor the black comedy so evident in *The Producers,* injecting it into a venerable old genre: the horror film. *The Fearless Vampire Killers* (1967), a film eventually disowned by its director, Roman Polanski, after disputes with MGM, contains a strange Jewish vampire, Yoine Shagal (Alfie Bass). After he is bitten by Count von Krolock (Perdy Mayne) and turned into a vampire, the lusty Shagal heads straight for the voluptuous blonde, Magda (Fiona Lewis), who has rejected him in life. When Magda

Yoine Shagal (Alfie Bass), the Jewish vampire in THE FEARLESS VAMPIRE KILLERS *(1967).*

tries to defend herself with a crucifix, Shagal gleefully exclaims, "Oy! Have you got the wrong vampire!" Though the character of the licentious Jewish vampire provides much of the film's humor, Polanski injects a few social comments on the class hierarchy present among the undead. For example, Shagal remains an outsider even in vampire society, much as he was in his former life. The Count and his ghoulish aristocracy ostracize him, and his coarse, wooden coffin is dragged out to the barn, segregated from the other vampires' resting places. The cleverness of the Jew, however, apparently extends into the world of the living dead, as Shagal whittles his way into the coffin of the count's son and sleeps obediently at his feet.

The Little Shop of Horrors (1960) provides an even stranger mixture of Jewish comedy and horror. Like its predecessor, *A Bucket of Blood* (1959)—which was also directed by Roger Corman and written by Charles B. Griffith—it focuses on the conflict between a Jewish schnook and the Gentile world that oppresses him. The film's protagonist is Seymour Krelboin (Jonathan Haze), a

Seymour Krelboin (Jonathon Haze), Mushnik (Mel Welles), and Audrey (Jackie Joseph) admire what they later discover is a maneating plant in THE LITTLE SHOP OF HORRORS *(1960).*

put-upon lackey for the greedy Mushnik (Mel Welles), a Lower East Side florist. Seymour loves Muchnik's dizzy daughter, Audrey (Jackie Joseph), who pays no attention to him. Early in the picture, Seymour becomes very disturbed over the droopy condition of a strange plant in Mushnik's shop. When he accidentally cuts his hand and some blood drips onto the plant's leaves, Seymour makes the startling discovery that the plant's natural food is human blood. The more blood it receives, the more the plant blooms—and the more blood it needs to keep it growing. "Feeeeed Me! I'm hunnnnngry!" it screams at Seymour, who dutifully goes out to locate new sources of nourishment for his newfound dependent. He finds it in the veins of his oppressive Gentile neighbors, whom he feeds to the demanding plant. As the plant grows larger and larger, a horticulture magazine decides to do a feature story on the exotic specimen and the man who has made it thrive. But when its gigantic petals open during the interview, they reveal the faces of Seymour's hapless victims. Finally, after a wild chase, Seymour tumbles into the plant and becomes the last scrap of food for its carnivorous appetite.

Corman shot *The Little Shop of Horrors* in two days on an unused backlot set, and it looks it. Certainly, it scares no one over three. Horror is not Corman's point, and any fears quickly disappear beneath the film's dominant one of Jewish humor. But some social commentary remains. Seymour, the modern descendant of generations of Jewish schlemiels, becomes a coarse precursor of the persona Woody Allen will adopt in the next decade, though Allen uses the role with far greater effectiveness and meaning. In *The Little Shop of Horrors,* the schlemiel takes out his frustrations in a deadly manner, resorting to murder in order to attain and then to keep his social status, as well as to capture the affections of the girl he desires. Obviously, these themes must strike a responsive chord in contemporary audiences, since the picture has been turned into a long-running off-Broadway musical and 1986 movie.

Chris Morris's essay in Todd McCarthy and Charles Flynn's *Kings of the B's* (1975), suggests that Corman's film is "a satire of Jewish social climbing of the most ruthless sort," an observation supported by the film. But Morris's argument that the plant becomes a "surrogate Jewish mother" misses the point completely. It is Seymour who becomes the mother-figure in the film; the plant is the whining, parasitic, spoiled child. Seymour basks in the reflected glory of his "offspring," much as does Mrs. Kolowitz in David's theatrical debut (in Carl Reiner's *Enter Laughing*). But, of course, Seymour goes further than Mrs. Kolowitz: he kills to fulfill his "child's" demands. As such, the film becomes a parable of black humor that emphasizes the disastrousness of giving all to a child, of defining oneself by the achievements of others, and of losing any sense of moral values in a blindly desperate attempt to provide for a child's wishes. Such a course of action can lead only to one end: destruction by the very thing the parent has created, a monstrous dependent whose appetite remains forever unsatiated.

Another film using black comedy as a vehicle for social satire is director Sidney Lumet's *Bye Bye Braverman* (1968), based on Wallace Markfield's first novel, *To an Early Grave* (1964). Lumet claims that this movie is "the most personal picture I've ever made....The four post-Depression Jewish intellectuals are everyone I grew up with. Me, in fact....I knew all those neighborhoods like the back of my hand. It must have taken me about five minutes to scout locations for the whole works." The film depicts the comic odyssey of four friends seeking the funeral of their recently departed companion, Leslie Braverman, whose untimely death is likened to "leaving before the end of a Hitchcock movie." After a series of humorous mishaps, the four wind up at the wrong funeral. The focus is on the New York cultural scene, but these are second-rank intellectuals: reviewers and critics—poets and novelists *manqués*. Braverman, himself, was a limited writer and renowned

Barnet Weiner (Jack Warden), Holly Levine (Sorrell Brooks), Felix Ottensteen (Joseph Wiseman), and Monroe Reiff (George Segal) make peace with a black cab driver (Godfrey Cambridge) in BYE BYE BRAVERMAN *(1968).*

The Rabbi (Alan King) tries to comfort Monroe Reiff (George Segal) about his friend's death in a dream sequence from BYE BYE BRAVERMAN *(1968).*

Harold Fine (Peter Sellers) and Joyce Miller (Joyce Van Patten) set the date, once again, in I LOVE YOU, ALICE B. TOKLAS *(1968).*

Harold Fine (Peter Sellers) searches for peace and contentment as a hippie in I LOVE YOU, ALICE B. TOKLAS *(1968).*

whoremonger described by one of his surviving friends as "a second-rate talent of the highest order."

At its thematic center, *Bye Bye Braverman* speaks of the modern, wandering Jew condemned to alienation more by his psyche than by his heritage. The four central figures are victims of personal, not religious, problems, as they engage in a series of endless disputes with each other and with people they claim to love. Monroe Reiff (George Segal) fights with his wife about all things great and small, from why she won't attend Braverman's funeral to why she refuses to make him orange juice in the morning. Holly Levine (Sorrell Brooks), a fussy reviewer and pop-culture writer unable to complete his own monograph on John Ford, savages the work of better authors. Barnet Weiner (Jack Warden) argues constantly with his mistress, Myra Mandelbaum (Phyllis Newman), over whether or not to visit his nagging mother. Felix Ottensteen (Joseph Wiseman), an arrogant yet vibrant socialist, has such vicious battles with his son that he wishes the child dead.

Throughout their trip to find Braverman's funeral, all four friends alternately attack and embrace each other, never willing to forsake an opportunity for a sarcastic remark but not wishing to alienate each other permanently. For example, one moment Felix berates Holly for driving a Volkswagen ("This legacy from Hitler!"), and the next he is striving for something to rekindle their former closeness. Lumet juxtaposes the silly bickering of these lost, modern Jews with the peacefulness of their contemporary Hasidic counterparts. Neither Holly's writing, nor Felix's politics, nor Barnet's sexual exploits, nor Monroe's marriage provides any of the four with the security, contentment, and serenity of the Orthodox Jews. The film, in fact, attacks those American Jews who have forsaken traditional beliefs and have nothing with which to replace them. For the four friends, life is simply an extended argument.

Disturbing as is Lumet's portrait of contemporary Jews without meaning in their lives, his vision of the modern American rabbi, played by comic Alan King, is even more disquieting. The rabbi bears little resemblance to the revered figure so prominent in Jewish-American films of previous decades. In the sixties, the rabbi has become, in effect, a standup performer. His speech of condolence turns into a comic vision of Jewish fate. "Have a little pleasure from the grandchildren," he lectures the mourners, "Get a coronary." In this manner, Lumet undercuts the authority and usefulness of the rabbi in America. His new role is to provide entertainment rather than comfort and enlightenment. Lumet's clean-shaven contemporary rabbi wears buttondown shirts and shiny silk suits; he is more of a businessman than a spiritual leader. His traditional roles have been usurped by therapists, psychiatrists, doctors, and self-help textbooks. The loss of this figure's authority and guidance becomes the bleakest element in the picture. "What can I tell you," mumbles Monroe to an attentive row of headstones in the cemetery that houses the remains of his friend, Braverman, "things have changed." These four friends share only memories and a vague attachment to a shared religious heritage they seem not to understand. In a world of shifting values and displaced traditions, Reiff finds only one thing to do when faced with his grief: he returns home and cries alone, not only for Braverman but for himself and his lost contemporaries as well.

Director Hy Averback's *I Love You, Alice B. Toklas* (1968), written by Paul Mazursky and Larry Tucker, is another film that deals with how "things have changed." Harold Fine (Peter Sellers), a successful lawyer, succumbs to the nubile charms of Nancy (Leigh Taylor-Young), a lovely hippie. This infatuation turns the uptight conservative Harold into a free-living hippie. Harold's journey from lawyer to hippie allows Averback to take several pot shots at various Jewish characters and institutions. Harold's brother, Herbie (David Arkin), a California beach bum, represents young Jews who search endlessly for meaning in their lives, totally ignoring the significance their own religion might play in their quest. Herbie, for example, attends a funeral dressed in the burial outfit of the Hopi Indians, but is completely unaware of the burial rituals associated with his own heritage. Harold's girlfriend, Joyce Miller (Joyce Van Patten), has one main goal in life: to marry Harold. As such, she is used by Averback to embody the Jewish girl whose life revolves around trapping a successful profes-

David Kolowitz (Reni Santoni) must somehow deal with his histrionic mother (Shelley Winters) and ineffectual father (David Opatoshu) in ENTER LAUGHING *(1967).*

sional, no matter how unsuited he may be as a mate. Harold's mother (Jo Van Fleet) is a typical Hollywood version of the Jewish mother, who uses guilt to manipulate Harold and stocks his cupboards with Manischewitz products. Finally, Averback includes a stinging parody of the Jewish wedding ceremony, here performed by two cantors, and the lavish Jewish reception that follows, complete with a gigantic Jewish star atop a large mound of green jello.

The focus of the film, however, remains on Harold's inability to find peace and meaning either in the straight world or the hippie commune. Like the four modern wanderers in *Bye Bye Braverman,* Harold loses his way in a world devoid of traditions and ethical morality. Harold finds the straight world too confining, for he has the heart of a hippie, and the hippie culture too loose, for he has the head of a corporate lawyer. *I Love You, Alice B. Toklas* thus filters the marginal man syndrome through a comic Jewish perspective. When he is with Joyce, Harold longs for the freedom associ-

Natalie Miller (Patty Duke) and her mother (Nancy Marchand) attempt to overcome the generation barrier between them in ME, NATALIE *(1969).*

Natalie Miller (Patty Duke) the troubled teenager in ME, NATALIE *(1969).*

ated with Nancy. When he is with Nancy, Harold tries to lock her into a confining relationship more rigid that that Joyce demanded of him. Harold searches in vain for an alternative that will provide some independence and some repsonsibility, but at the movie's conclusion he is alone, able neither to marry Joyce nor to sustain his relationship with Nancy.

Enter Laughing (1967) follows the humorous misadventures of David Kolowitz (Reni Santoni), a star-struck Bronx adolescent who tries to break into show business despite the objections of his nagging, overly-protective Jewish mother (Shelley Winters) and his kind but ineffectual father (David Opatoshu). Carl Reiner, who directed the movie, draws on his own early experiences to endow the film with a personal, gentle touch. But it is not Reiner's alter ego, David Kolowitz, who dominates the film. This distinction goes to Shelly Winters's overbearing Jewish mama, one of the decade's most overacted embodiments of that much maligned figure. Unlike sarcastic Mrs. Brummel of *No Way to Treat a Lady,* Mrs. Kolowitz does not constantly berate her son; instead, she just *"noodges"* him to the point of exasperation, unable to understand why David wants to be an actor, a job she feels certain will end in starvation and homelessness. She is, however, eventually won over by David's persistence. Attending her son's stage debut, a bit part in an off-off-off Broadway theater, Mrs. Kolowitz loudly shushes the inattentive audience when David appears for his brief moment on stage. When the play continues, she interrupts the performance by proudly proclaiming to those around her, "That's my son. That's my son."

Mrs. Kolowitz's uneasy blend of caring and controlling, of fear for David's future and pride in his every accomplishment, shows the Jewish mother as part nurturer and part obstacle. Reiner never turns Mrs. Kolowitz into Mrs. Portnoy; his humor keeps Mrs. Kolowitz more human than harpie. In fact, her better qualities shine through in David's personality, making him a caring, sympathetic character. The important point here is that David does persist in doing what he thinks is right. He realizes his dream of theatrical involvement, though on an appropriately small scale.

Me, Natalie (1969), a more painful and serious

film than *Enter Laughing,* presents the identity crisis from the perspective of another adolescent—the Jewish-American female. "Little girls with sweet faces like yours always grow up pretty." These words spoken by her mother remain indelibly etched in the mind of Natalie Miller (Patty Duke), a plain-looking eighteen-year-old living in Brooklyn with her parents (Phil Sterling and Nancy Marchand). "Mother lied," observes Natalie early in the film as she studies her face in the mirror, preparing for another blind date arranged by her popular friend, Betty Simon (Deborah Winters). Indeed, Natalie cannot even scrounge up her own date for the senior prom. She makes up a story about having to go down to the ferry landing to pick up her escort, an imaginary pre-med student from Staten Island, and actually begins to believe her lie: she journeys to the landing and scans the faces of those leaving the boat for her "date." When he fails to arrive and she is faced with the reality of her loneliness, Natalie visits her only confidant, Uncle Harold (Martin Balsam), a sympathetic pharmacist who tells her it is the contents of a bottle that are important, not its attractive packaging.

Desperate to find her niche in life, Natalie leaves her parents' home soon after high school and heads for Greenwich Village, where her life takes on several new dimensions. She secures a job as waitress in a topless-bottomless nightclub, buys a motorcycle, and most important of all, becomes romantically involved with a handsome architect-artist, David Harris (James Farentino). Her new-found confidence, however, is shattered after Natalie unexpectedly bursts into David's apartment and finds a woman there—a woman he introduces as his wife. Depressed, Natalie ponders suicide. She goes to the East River pier and jumps off, but since the tide is out, her suicide attempt is unsuccessful. Returning to her apartment, Natalie finds a distraught David who tells her how much he loves her and vows to obtain a divorce. She rejects his offer because he has lied to her. The last scene shows Natalie returning to Brooklyn on her motorcycle, not in defeat but with a surer sense of her own self-worth and a confidence in her ability to survive.

Me, Natalie, based on an original story of Stanley Shapiro and a script by A. Martin Zweiback,

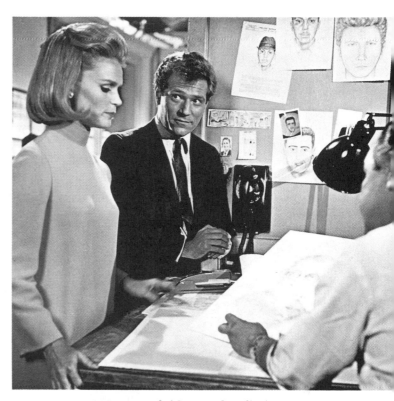

Morris Brummel (George Segal) sizes up Kate Palmer (Lee Remick) in NO WAY TO TREAT A LADY *(1968).*

was directed by Fred Coe and has some very intriguing elements. Its emphasis on the problems of a plain girl makes it a kind of *Funny Girl* sans music and allows the movie's creators to make some insightful comments about an American value system that stresses physical appearance above inner values. From her contact with Betty Simon, a popular girl who eventually marries out of desperation because she is pregnant, and Uncle Harold, who preaches inner values but marries for beauty, Natalie comes to understand the hypocrisy of a system that claims to admire integrity and brains but is really obsessed with looks and clothes. Natalie is an outsider in this world. Her rejection of Betty Simon's marriage-at-any-cost philosophy, represents her triumph over these superficial concerns as she searches for a love based on honesty, mutual respect, and affection.

No Way to Treat a Lady (1968) also deals with a Jewish/Gentile romance, but in a far more complicated and interesting way. It has, however, excited little critical attention since its release. Most critics simply dismiss the film as an excessive ego trip for Rod Steiger, claiming that the actor overplays all six of his roles using overdone accents for each. Such comments ignore the film's intricacies and insights. On the surface, *No Way to Treat a Lady* offers a witty, sardonic murder story featuring a

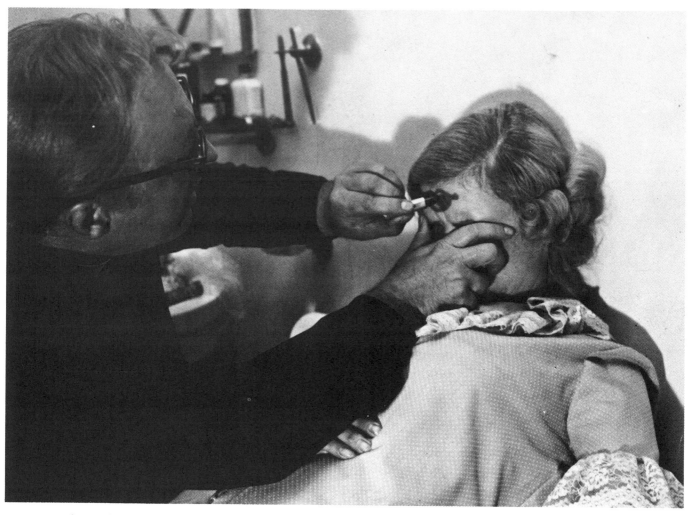

Christopher Gill (Rod Steiger) leaves his gruesome trademark on one of his victims in NO WAY TO TREAT A LADY *(1968).*

Jewish detective, Morris Brummel (George Segal); a psychotic theater owner, Christopher Gill (Rod Steiger); and a flippant working girl, Kate Palmer (Lee Remick). The three are drawn into a dangerous triangle when Kate observes the disguised killer before he commits a gruesome murder and Morris becomes the homicide officer assigned to investigate the case. But director Jack Smight is not concerned with creating a typical murder mystery. He even robs the film of any "whodunit" suspense by unmasking the killer in the opening scene.

A look beneath the film's crime elements reveals Smight's real concern: a study of American momism. He develops his theme through a complex series of image patterns, visual motifs, and dialogues, and he mixes these elements together within the alternating Jewish and Gentile perspectives of Brummel and Gill. Through a carefully developed pattern of images and incidents, Smight relates the murderer to his pursuer, a Doppelgänger structure that centers on the relationship between the killer, the cop, and their respective mothers.

Christopher Gill (Rod Steiger) delivers his dramatic dying speech in NO WAY TO TREAT A LADY *(1968).*

The film opens with Gill's first murder. Disguised as a Barry Fitzgerald-like priest, and calling out "top of the morning" to everyone he meets, Gill makes his way to the cramped apartment of Mrs. Molloy, a middle-aged widow and lapsed Catholic. After talking a bit, Mrs. Molloy offers the priest a glass of port. Gill stares at the red liquid and remarks to the widow how its color is "like the blood He shed for you and me." He then walks behind the unsuspecting Mrs. Molloy and chokes her to death. After dragging her lifeless body into the bathroom and depositing it on the toilet seat, Gill takes her lipstick and paints a garish red kiss on her forehead. This mark becomes part of Gill's murder ritual, a grotesque signature that eventually helps Brummel capture him.

Smight's initial scene immediately unites religion and murder, two of the film's most important elements, in the first of many moments when the two are fused. For example, as Gill lies dying in the film's final scene, he ironically begs Morris to forgive him, to give him "Christian charity." The Jewish policeman refuses. Rebuffed, Gill grasps the bloody wound on his side and loudly cries out, "Sweet Jesus, save me. O my beloved Savior, please save me." On a metaphoric level, the murderer's every name ties him to Christian symbology: his first name, Christopher, contains Christ within it, and the entire name recalls the patron saint of travelers; his last name, Gill, evokes the image of fish, commonly associated with Christian symbolism. Smight firmly establishes Gill as one part of his delicate balance between Judaism and Christianity, an association that becomes even more evident in the relationships between Gill, Brummel, and their mothers.

Throughout the film, Smight slowly reveals Gill's total obsession with his deceased mother, Amanda Gill, a famous actress who had little time for her son. Often, he integrates Christopher's mother fixation with the film's religious imagery. The walls of Gill's theater, which is named in honor of his mother, contain large portraits of Mrs. Gill in various madonna-like poses. At other times, Smight associates Amanda with sexuality. The theater contains various busts and portraits of Mrs. Gill in her most famous role: Cleopatra, the Egyptian queen who seduced men to her will. All the

women Gill murders are his mother's age, and all are left half-naked on their toilet seats, a symbol of Gill's disgust for them once they have been "violated." Before he murders the kindly Mrs. Molloy, Gill talks with her about his mother using a combination of religious and sexual references. He calls her his "sainted mother" who had such a "voluptuous figure" that when she walked down the street "like a queen, men would pursue her with their eyes." Notice his choice of words to describe how men related to his mother. He uses "pursue" rather than "follow" or even "stare," implying a hunted, violent quality to the male/female relationship. Later in the film, Morris infuriates Gill by telling a reporter that the murderer is clearly a mother-hater. Enraged, the killer calls Morris and, for once, drops his phony accent, an extreme reaction that provides Morris with another clue he will use to trap Gill.

The kiss Christopher leaves on his victims' foreheads shows the combination of repressed sexual longing and murderous disgust he feels toward his mother. In a perverted manner, Gill's killing of these women is an act of revenge on a mother he claims to revere but whom he secretly hates because she neglected him. Symbolically, the lipstick kiss he paints on the dead women's foreheads shows Gill's sublimated desire to have a physical relationship with his mother. He murders his "partners" partially to assuage his guilt over these feelings and particularly to act out his hatred for his mother.

The policeman's side of the story, the Jewish side, emphasizes comedy as Smight juxtaposes Gill's obsession with his mother to Morris's problems with Mrs. Brummel (Eileen Heckart). Initially, Mrs. Brummel epitomizes the castrating Jewish mother so common in sixties literature and culminating in Philip Roth's vitriolic portrait of Sophie Portnoy. Mrs. Brummel berates her son for eating too little, for not finishing college, and for not marrying so she can have grandchildren. In particular, she holds up the accomplishments of her other son, Franklin, the doctor, who earns "a thousand dollars a day." Even Morris's profession is not safe from her constant attacks. "Who ever heard of a Jewish cop?" scolds Mrs. Brummel derisively. "Everyone knows you gotta be Irish to

181

Gambler Arnold Rothstein (David Janssen) taken to task by his respectable father (Joseph Schildkraut) in KING OF THE ROARING TWENTIES: THE STORY OF ARNOLD ROTHSTEIN *(1961).*

get ahead on the force."

Given Mrs. Brummel's overbearing attitude and sarcastic badgering, it seems strange to find Morris dating Kate, a girl with similar traits. When they first meet, Kate pokes gentle fun at Morris's nose and makes humorous comments about how little resemblance the plainly dressed cop bears to his namesake. Moe Brummel is certainly no Beau Brummell. Kate takes almost total control of their relationship throughout the film. She is the aggressor who pursues Morris. On the police tug where the two first declare their feelings for each other, it is Kate who tells Morris he can kiss her. Later, Morris is overjoyed because Kate warns him "to be careful," much as a mother might warn her son to wear his overshoes in case of rain. For the Jewish male, warnings and prohibitions denote caring and love. Though he yearns to free himself of his mother's smothering attention and sarcastic manner, Morris is attracted to a woman with many of the same qualities.

The best example of Kate's ability to manipulate others successfully occurs when she visits Morris's apartment, which—naturally—he shares with his mother. Initially Kate enters the flat and stands on the upper steps leading down to the living room, dominating Mrs. Brummel who has come to greet her. She then steps down to Mrs. Brummel's level, a physical gesture that foreshadows her future assumption of that role in Morris's life. As the evening progresses, Kate wins over the skeptical Mrs. Brummel, who has fretted about the relationship because Kate is not Jewish. She does this by agreeing with, indeed participating in, Mrs. Brummel's attacks on Morris. "Morris is only good for two things," Kate tells her: "Yelling at and ordering around. Oh, I only wish I had met Franklin first." She proves her point by telling Morris to get his feet off the living room table, by ordering him to light her cigarette, and by demanding that he fetch her things throughout the entire evening. In fact, Kate metamorphoses into a younger version of Mrs. Brummel, though she does so with a sly wink to Morris, implying it is a game the two are playing on his mother. Game or not, the implication of Kate's actions are that Morris is trading one mother for another. "She's a gem," declares Mrs. Brummel at the end of the evening, "and she's very much like me." Indeed she is. Thus, Smight slyly comments on the Jewish male's emotional masochism: he fights to overcome the suffocating attention of his mother and then marries a girl just like her.

Smight overtly unites Morris and Christopher throughout the film. Gill calls Brummel after each murder and discusses his crime with the distraught policeman, hanging up before the call can be traced. He even forces the police department to put Morris back on the case, after he has been dismissed for not finding the killer, by threatening to murder another woman if Morris is not reinstated. In the last scene, after Morris shoots Gill and mortally wounds him, the killer summons up one last burst of strength to knock the cop unconscious. Dying, the murderer crawls upon the breast of the policeman, which is how Morris's partner finds the two men. In its own sometimes confusing manner, therefore, *No Way to Treat a Lady* endoreses the cloying, hovering Mrs. Brummel over the detached, distant Mrs. Gill. One motivates neurosis, the other psychosis. The film searches for a middle ground between the two mother images it presents, but finds none. Even the strongest female character, Kate, is reduced simply to imitating one model, Mrs. Brummel. So while the picture presents two negative portraits of mothers and their children, it fails to offer anything resembling a wholesome mother/son relationship.

The differences between the films created by new sixties producers and those of their predecessors is apparent in all movie categories. Most earlier film biographies, for example, spotlighted popular Jewish entertainers (Al Jolson, Benny Goodman, Eddie Cantor), role models of decency and courage (Alfred Dreyfus) or success stories (the Rothschilds, Benjamin Disraeli). The sixties, however, widened the area of Jewish screen biographies to include some far less savory characters. In *King of the Roaring Twenties: The Story of Arnold Rothstein* (1961), the Jewish gangster makes his first screen appearance. David Singer, in his essay "The Jewish Gangster," observes, "The American Jewish establishment—the defense agencies, the scholars, the historical societies—have systematically denied any awareness of this important aspect of Jewish history whose major figures constitute a veritable *Who's Who* in the annals of American crime." Hollywood, prior to this film, had tacitly cooperated in this effort by denying the existence of Jewish thugs, but after the Rothstein picture other Jewish gangsters—Lepke Buchalter, Bugsy Siegel, Meyer Lansky—appeared on the screen.

Director Joseph M. Newman traces Rothstein's (David Janssen) early criminal tendencies back to his childhood rivalry with his brother, Harry. Many of Arnold's boyhood crimes result from his desire to make himself look superior to Harry. Arnold's father (Joseph Schildkraut) intensifies the family tension by continually asking Arnold why he "can't be more like his brother." When he finally curses his brother and wishes him dead, after which Harry suddenly dies, Arnold spends the rest of his life feeling guilty for having caused his brother's death.

Arnold's family problems only partially account for his life of crime. His desire to attain the riches

Arnold Rothstein (David Janssen) plays his last hand in KING OF THE ROARING TWENTIES: THE STORY OF ARNOLD ROTHSTEIN *(1961)*.

and power promised in the American Dream of success motivates many of his actions. "You have no faith in anything but money" his father lectures Arnold, and the story bears out his observation. Arnold's lifelong dream is to have a royal flush in a no-limit game. He leaves his wife on their honeymoon to fix a horse race. He turns on his boyhood friend, Johnny Burke (Mickey Rooney), humiliates him, has him framed, and arranges his murder so

Nicky Arnstein (Omar Sharif) tells Fanny Brice (Barbra Streisand) how much he loves her in FUNNY GIRL *(1968).*

he cannot squeal on him. He even goes so far as to fix the world series, an act which disgusts his fellow criminals. Only a Jewish gangster, so it seems, would desecrate the national pastime.

Though not a major part of the story, Arnold's Jewishness does become important in several crucial scenes. When he first brings home his girlfriend, Carolyn (Diane Foster), to meet his parents, Arnold's father asks the girl if she is "of their faith." She answers "no" and then explains she will not convert because she believes strongly in her own religion. "It does you honor" replies Mr. Rothstein, ending the entire issue of intermarriage on a conciliatory note. Arnold's religion also figures in his criminal career, since his main rivals are Irishmen Phil Bulter (Dan O'Herlihy) and Tim O'Brien (Jack Carson). In this way, the film contains remnants of the old Irish versus Jewish competition so prevalent in silent and early sound movies. Rothstein must make his fortune in a business dominated by Irishmen, so he remains an

outsider even in this world of outsiders.

The most lavish biography of the decade, and the one that finally puts Jews into the musical, is director William Wyler's *Funny Girl* (1968), the story of Fanny Brice. Barbra Streisand's name and nose in their unaltered state represents a turning point in the cinematic protrayal of Jews, one that shows Jewishness as something to be proud of, to exploit, and to celebrate. Streisand revels in the role of the Henry Street comedienne, making her face and body a constantly changing collage of characteristic ethnic expressions and movements. Her phrasing and accent highlight her actions. Here, for once, is the Jewish performer being Jewish, instead of hiding behind a neutral name or twisting his/her features out of shape to conform to a standard of WASP beauty. Unlike gross caricatures such as in the "Cohens and the Kellys" series, the Jewishness of *Funny Girl* becomes a source of strength as well as of humor. It is, indeed; not only limited to a particular character but forms the emotional, and often the thematic, core of the picture. With the predominance of Jewish writers, the growing ethnic pride heightened by the 1967 Israeli War, the new Hollywood filmmakers' feelings of confidence, and the lessening fears about American anti-Semitism in the Jewish community, it was "in" to be Jewish, and Streisand was as "in" as one could get.

The concern of the Jewish-American community about its own self-image surfaced in regard to *Funny Girl* in a rather unexpected way, one that had nothing to do with Streisand. The casting of Omar Sharif, an Egyptian, as Brice's gambler-husband Nicky Arnstein aroused some heated debate, not unlike that occasioned by the casting of Vanessa Redgrave, a PLO sympathizer, as a concentration camp survivor in the television production "Playing for Time" (1980). Photos of Sharif in what appeared to be an Egyptian Air Force uniform, later discovered to be stills from a film in which he played an airline pilot, added fuel to Jewish demands for Sharif's dismissal from the picture. Wyler labeled such demands as "ridiculous" and refused to be intimidated. Streisand, too, was angered by the protests. "Because he is Egyptian," she asked, "are we supposed to fire him—or hang him?" The furor died down with Israel's victory in the 1967 war, but it proved at least

A klutzy Fanny Brice (Barbra Streisand) skates out of control in FUNNY GIRL (1968).

one thing: Hollywood filmmakers finally recognized that how they wrote, played, and directed a Jewish role would have offscreen repercussions. The protest over Sharif's part demonstrated the growing concern of Jews around the country about how they were portrayed on the screen.

"Hi, gorgeous." Those are Barbra Streisand's first words on film, and they give a good indication of the mixture of self-consciousness and self-conceit that dominates *Funny Girl,* and to some extent the rest of her career. Because Streisand usually plays opposite handsome but not specifically ethnic-looking leading men, such as Robert Redford,

James Caan, Ryan O'Neal, Michael Sarrazin, and Kris Kristofferson, her own nontraditional beauty becomes quite evident. In a society where Farrah Fawcett and Suzanne Somers set beauty standards, Nefertiti has to strike out on her own. Streisand does just that, making an issue of her looks while simultaneously eliminating any "problem" because of them. Any audience reservations about her as a romantic lead opposite such standard handsome men vanish when it becomes obvious that they

Neil Klugman (Richard Benjamin) and Brenda Patimkin (Ali McGraw) converse at poolside in GOODBYE, COLUMBUS *(1969).*

find her overwhelmingly attractive, often because her looks are so original.

Streisand's talent, perserverance, agggressiveness, and humor more than compensate for any lack of the traditional idea of beauty that has long dominated America's movie screens. Even the semi-satirical song in *Funny Girl,* "When a Girl Isn't Pretty," answers the unspoken question with its rhetorical line: "Is a nose with a deviation a crime against the nation?" The film encourages us to accept the belief that talent is what counts, and with enough of it anyone can succeed. The careful mixture of self-mockery and self-confidence established just the right tone, easing the path for other performers whose offbeat appearances might have denied them leading roles, such as Richard Benjamin, Richard Dreyfuss, Bette Midler, and Walter Matthau.

Funny Girl treats Fanny Brice's Jewish roots kindly and gently, seeing them as partially responsible for her remarkable resilience and zestful approach to life. A sanitized Lower East Side houses a happy collection of immigrant Irish, Poles, Italians, and Jews all enjoying a marginal life on Henry Street and all joining Mrs. Brice as she celebrates Fanny's theatrical successes. Brice gets her big break in *The Ziegfield Follies* early in her career. However, her Jewish sensibilities rebel. "It's too easy," she moans looking up at her name in lights on the theater marquee. "Where's all the suffering?" Too easy or not, Brice cleverly capitalizes on the unconventional looks that make her an outsider in the glamorous world of show business. Costuming herself as a pregnant bride, she counteracts the silly, syrupy lyrics she's forced to sing and which seem ridiculous given her physical appearance. Later, she gets laughs as she skates, quite disastrously, through the midst of a chorus line of typically attractive showgirls, playing on her own klutziness to win over the audience.

Throughout the film, Brice keeps in touch with the commonsense training she received in a loving, immigrant Jewish household, never abandoning her Jewish sensibilities or her Jewish pride. In one of the film's most famous musical numbers, "Don't Rain on My Parade," she sings as her tugboat steams past the Statue of Liberty, a symbol of her own immigrant roots, in search of the totally assimilated Nicky, a symbol of her future. But, unlike Nicky, Fanny never stops being Jewish. She dissolves into Yiddish expressions in Arnstein's suave arms. When he introduces her to first-class life aboard a luxury cruise ship, she notes that the fancy paté is just chopped liver. She marries the worldly Arnstein and, as she exuberantly notes, becomes "Sadie, Sadie, married lady." In fact, the picture hints that one reason Nicky is so attracted to Fanny is precisely because she is so natural, so unpretentious, and so real. Arnstein falls for exactly the kind of girl who reminds him of his own roots now carefully hidden beneath expensive clothes and sophisticated manners.

Neil Klugman in *Goodbye, Columbus* (1969) also searches unsuccessfully for the midpoint between two mutually exclusive worlds, a position that incorporates the most positive values of each environment. Philip Roth's 1959 novella, upon which director Larry Peerce based his film, ignited a stormy controversy about the so-called self-hatred and anti-Semitism many claim dominates the book. In defense of this and subsequent works, Roth argues that his fiction, unlike that of other Jewish authors such as Bernard Malamud and Saul Bellow, rejects the simplistic equation of Jews with "restraint and righteousness" so common in American literature. Instead, Roth says he deals with the "libidinous and aggressive actions that border on the socially acceptable.... The solution to prejudice and persecution," he continues, "is not to convince people to like Jews so as not to want to kill them; it is to know that they cannot kill them even if they despise them." Be that as it may, Roth remains something of a pariah within conventional Jewish circles, a man accused of transgressing the unspoken covenant between all American Jews: never admit to the Gentile world that there are greedy, dishonest, despicable Jews. When the film *Goodbye, Columbus* reached American movie screens ten years after the novella's publication, Roth had just completed *Portnoy's Complaint,* a novel (and ultimately a film in 1972) destined to receive even more vitriolic criticism than his earlier books. Neil Klugman's observations seem rather tame when compared with Alex Portnoy's disturbed memories

A pensive Mr. Patimkin (Jack Klugman) ponders the future of his beloved children in GOODBYE, COLUMBUS *(1969).*

and outlandish sexual fantasies, but *Goodbye, Columbus* remains one of the most important films in the Jewish-American cinema of the sixties.

The movie's relatively simply plotline revolves around the summertime love affair between Neil Klugman (Richard Benjamin), a discontented Bronx librarian, and Brenda Patimkin (Ali MacGraw), a beautiful college girl home on vacation. Director Larry Peerce opens the picture with an extreme close-up of a jiggling, slippery navel. The camera then pulls slowly back to reveal a lush suburban country club filled with bronzed girls, athletic boys, heavily made-up women, and pot-bellied men. Throughout the film, Peerce juxtaposes these denizens of the spacious houses and luxurious country clubs of suburbia with the people who live in the crowded streets and cramped houses of Neil's Bronx neighborhood. The congested apartment Neil shares with his Aunt Gladys (Sylvie Straus), seems to shrink even more when compared with the abundant openness of the Patimkin estate. But what have the Jews lost in their journey from ghetto to country club? What has been the cost of obtaining "refrigerators that grow fruit" and "trees that drop sporting goods?"

These questions rest at the center of Roth's novella, and Peerce admirably captures their spirit in his film. Though disgusted by the parochial crudeness he feels in the Bronx, Neil is equally repelled by the materialistic tastelessness he finds at the Patimkins. "I can't go all the way on either side," he admits to Brenda, "they both seem so ridiculous to me." In that statement lies the complex ambiguity of the movie, and one may assume, of Roth himself. Missing in the Bronx is the fulfillment of the American Dream of economic success. Missing at the Patimkins is a sense of tradition to fill life's hollow spots. Leaving a place at the table for Mickey Mantle, as does Brenda's brother Ron (Michael Meyers), is no substitute for leaving a place for Elijah at the Passover Seder. The Bronx reeks of failure, the Patimkins of spiritual emptiness.

The inability of American Jews to avoid spiritual failure as they attain economic success is at the heart of the relationship between Neil and Brenda. While most commentators center their attention on Brenda, accusing her of being a spoiled little Jewish-American Princess unable to see through the sham and pretentiousness of her life, it seems equally important to analyze Neil. In reality, he is nothing but a wishy-washy wimp without a moral center of his own. He condemns and criticizes but never creates. Obtaining Brenda is a triumph for Neil, a sign that he, too, has grasped a piece of the American Dream through securing Brenda's affections. But he always views their affair as a contest. When he makes love to Brenda for the first time, Neil equates it to winning the elusive twenty-first point against her bratty little sister, Julie (Lori Shelle), who always quits the ping-pong game when it appears she will lose. Sex with Brenda is aggression for Neil, symbolic compensation for his dull life at home and at the library. Neil not only wants to have Brenda; he wants to dominate her, to take out his various frustrations on her.

The issue which brings these elements to a climax is Neil's demand that Brenda obtain a diaphragm, a symbolic admission of her sexual activity. The diaphragm becomes an obsession with Neil, part of a complicated power struggle in which he strives to prove his superiority over her, and all she represents, by engaging in domineering sexual politics. When Mrs. Patimkin later discovers the diaphragm Brenda has reluctantly purchased, she bans Neil from the house. He angrily accuses Brenda of betraying him to her parents and using his banishment as an easy way to end their relationship. But is it entirely her fault? Most critics say it is, and, indeed, Brenda is not one for confrontations or unpleasantness. But Neil, too, cannot escape culpability for the demise of their love affair. He must have Brenda on his own terms or not at all. His drive for dominance over her to compensate for his own failures in life forces Brenda to reject him. Neil's inability to integrate moral values into the suburban world of vulgar materialism or to find any ethical significance in his gloomy Bronx environment dooms him to exist unhappily in both settings; he remains part of the Bronx while envying, and simultaneously despising, the Patimkins.

The only figure in the film who successfully blends ethical values and material success is Mr. Patimkin (Jack Klugman), Brenda's good-hearted father. Unlike his brother Leo, a pathetic light-bulb salesman trapped in the past, Mr. Patimkin has been financially successful, and unlike his crass wife (Nan Martin), he has kept his humanity, expressed chiefly through his genuine concern for family. Though proud of his bumpy nose, he is equally happy to fix Brenda's. Displaying his own sense of moral priorities, he lectures Neil on the smugness of the new generation that looks down on their parents because they earn a good living and provide for their families. Willingly, Mr. Patimkin finds a place "in the business" for the dumb but kindly Ron, and he even offers Neil a job if things work out with Brenda. Unlike Mrs. Patimkin, who feels Neil's status makes him unworthy of her daughter, he is unconcerned with Neil's low financial and social status.

Mr. Patimkin's concern for his family manifests itself most clearly at his son Ron's elaborate wedding, a scene of gross gluttony and conspicuous consumption that many in the Jewish-American community found particularly offensive. Such criticism, however, totally ignores the sense of joy and caring expressed by Mr. Patimkin throughout this sequence. At one point, he sits crying with Brenda, spinning out his hopes and his love for her. His offer to buy her a new fur coat is not a bribe, not a form of manipulation, but rather a concrete demonstration of his love and protection. Commentators have argued that such gestures and the sentimental nurturing they symbolize are precisely what have turned the Patimkin children into pampered complainers who expect the world to provide them with whatever they desire. Such is not totally the case. Mr. Patimkin never loses sight of his children's faults and never rejects them because of their failings. His material success is used to support his ethical concerns. Family, not finances, are paramount for Mr. Patimkin, and as such he functions as the moral center of the film.

Goodbye, Columbus shows American Jews struggling to find ways of uniting past values and present demands. Roth offers no solution to this problem. Neither do the films of the sixties. What they do offer, however, is a growing ethnic sophistication and cultural consciousness. No picture containing minorities will ever be the same after the scrutiny provided by sixties filmmakers. It will be up to the seventies and eighties to develop and deepen the way America's filmmakers portray the country's Jews.

Young Lovers with problems, Neil Klugman (Richard Benjamin) and Brenda Patimkin (Ali McGraw) in GOODBYE, COLUMBUS *(1969).*

Sophie Portnoy (Lee Grant) gives her son Alexander (Richard Benjamin) another of her many lectures in PORTNOY'S COMPLAINT *(1972).*

Chapter 7

The Seventies

Continuing the diversification in Jewish screen roles begun during the sixties, the films of the seventies present Jewish characters in an even wider variety of parts. The decade's genre films, in particular, demonstrate how seventies filmmakers fit Jewish figures—sometimes in central roles—into conventional characterizations, positions rarely occupied by screen Jews in earlier decades. Previously, for example, relatively few identifiable Jewish characters appeared in Hollywood Western, musical, detective, horror, or gangster films. When they did crop up in such traditional stories, Jews mainly cavorted comically, beat their breasts histrionically, or fought heroically. Occasionally, specific "Jewish issues" such as anti-Semitism and the founding of Israel engaged filmmakers.

The complex currents of love and hate, of praise and guilt, that characterize many Jewish families became the source of much speculation and dissection during the seventies. One of the hallmarks of Jewish-American life, of course, is the emphasis on family, highlighted by large, noisy rites of passage like bar mitzvahs, weddings, and religious holidays. Children have important roles in such celebrations, and the Jewish home has always been child-centered. As much as he is babied and protected, however, the Jewish child is expected, encouraged, nagged, and chastised to excel. The guilt inherent in the child's failure to meet his parents' expectations—not to measure up to what the Goldbergs' son achieved or what the Cohens' daughter accomplished—is such stuff as Jewish jokes are made of. Yet it has a serious side. It creates a sustained tension between children and their well-intentioned parents who smother them with gifts and love, while they drive them onward with guilt and cajolery. Eventually, many children come to resent such mixed messages, rebelling against those who "only want the best" for them.

The archetypal cajoler, smotherer, guiltlayer, and castrater is Philip Roth's immortal Sophie Portnoy, who arrived on the screen in director/writer Ernest Lehman's *Portnoy's Complaint* in 1972. Its protagonist, Alexander Portnoy (Richard Benjamin),

presents himself to the world as an urbane, competent city administrator. However, his personal life is in shambles. His suffocating mother, Sophie (Lee Grant), loads him with so much guilt, fear, and frustration that it drives him to a psychiatrist's couch. In desperation, and partly because he knows it will horrify his mother, Alexander takes up with The Monkey (Karen Black), a sexy, Gentile fashion model who fulfills his bizarre sexual fantasies. Like Roth's book, Lehman's movie stirred up a storm of controversy. Fred Hechinger called it "a truly anti-Semitic film…also an unforgivably vulgar one." The film, however, is barely worth the effort to attack it. Lehman totally fails to catch the comic flavor of Roth's novel, and Lee Grant's Sophie Portnoy never comes close to capturing her literary counterpart's complexity.

A frustrated Gordon Hocheiser (George Segal) reproaches his unsavory mother (Ruth Gordon) in WHERE'S POPPA? *(1970).*

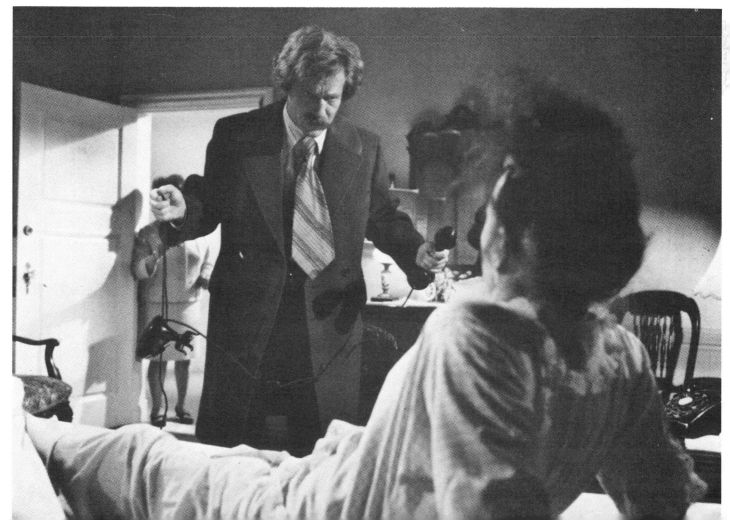

The decade's most vicious screen portrait of a Jewish mother is not Lehman's Sophie Portnoy; rather, it is senile old Mrs. Hocheiser (Ruth Gordon) in director Carl Reiner's *Where's Poppa?* (1970). In notes that accompanied a 1976 screening of the film at the Museum of Modern Art, Leonard Maltin called *Where's Poppa?* "one of the most controversial comedies of the 1970s" and told how the film's initial showing occasioned "violent reactions" from the assembled press and industry members. Such hostility caused Reiner to change the movie's ending, to give it a more upbeat, romantic conclusion, but his alterations failed to stem the heated critical debate that followed the picture's general release. *The New Yorker*'s film critic, Pauline Kael, called the movie "full of talent" but then went on to decry that "it all goes down the drain....The trouble with this sort of unlimited, omni-destructive humor is that there's nothing for our laughs to bounce off, nothing to hold on to—not even an idea behind the movie, or a dedication to the craft of comedy." Vincent Canby of *The New York Times* argued that "the movie works beautifully....When you come down to it, *Where's Poppa?* is, at its slyly cheerful heart, optimistic." Stanley Kauffmann's review in *The New Republic* offered still another point of view: "The vein is farce-comedy, vaguely surrealistic, in the newly liberated areas of sex and social reference and vocabulary. But Reiner and Klane [the scriptwriter] are drunk on the new freedom and think the mere use of it self-justifying."

At its center, *Where's Poppa?* is about Jewish son/Jewish mother problems cast in a particularly ugly light. Thirty-five-year-old Gordon Hocheiser (George Segal) promises his dying father to keep his mother out of a nursing home. This pledge results in a series of mother/son clashes that render Lehman's *Portnoy* tame by comparison. Gordon grows to hate his mother so violently that he dreams of throwing her out a window, all the while acceding to her dietary whims (she likes her orange sliced six ways and her cereal soaked in Pepsi) and her domineering orders. At every turn, Mrs. Hocheiser humiliates Gordon: she falls asleep during dinner with her face buried in mashed potatoes; she pulls off his pants and bites his buttocks when he brings home a girl to dinner; she watches television and ignores him when he tries

to talk to her. Reiner's Mrs. Hocheiser possesses none of the saving graces his earlier Jewish mother, Mrs. Kolowitz (Shelley Winters), displayed in *Enter Laughing* (1967). Finally, in desperation, Gordon lugs his mother off to a nursing home, deposits her there, and runs away with his girl friend (Trish Van Devere). The nastiness of this film's Jewish parent/Jewish child relationship is unmatched throughout the decade. It insensitively finds humor in senility and fun in the plight of America's aged. With absolutely nothing to balance her negative qualities, Reiner's Mrs. Hocheiser becomes the most unsavory portrait of a Jewish mother in the history of the Jewish-American cinema.

The most interesting film made during the seventies about mother/son relationships is director/writer Paul Mazursky's *Next Step, Greenwich Village* (1976). Film critic Richard Corliss calls Mazursky "the Horace with the heart of gold," and goes on to note:

> Paul Mazursky is likely to be remembered as *the* filmmaker of the seventies. No screenwriter has probed so deep under the pampered skin of this fascinating, maligned decade; no director has so successfully mined it for home-truth humor and quirky human revelations....Mazurksy has created a body of work unmatched in contemporary American cinema for its originality and cohesiveness.

Mazursky's probings come through a distinctly Jewish perception of the world, and one senses that many characters in his films, even some not identified as such, are Jewish. *Alex in Wonderland* (1970) contains a secondary character who, after searching for an identity in hippiedom and drugs, finally accepts his own heritage and becomes an Orthodox Jew. *Blume in Love* (1973) features a Jewish lawyer (George Segal) who does not discover how much he loves his wife until they are divorced. In *Harry and Tonto* (1974), Art Carney portrays a Jewish old man on the road to discovery and independence. Erica's (Jill Clayburgh) lover in *An Unmarried Woman* (1978) is a Jewish painter Saul Kaplan (Alan Bates). A bearded sensitive artist, Kaplan discovers abstract art when his mother "throws a jar of pickled herring at his father and it

Saul Kaplan (Alan Bates), a sensitive Jewish painter, becomes Erica's (Jill Clayburgh) lover in AN UNMARRIED WOMAN *(1978).*

splatters on the wall." Mazursky, himself, has said about his work: "I'm Jewish. I was brought up in a Jewish neighborhood. So, it's natural that my films show that part of my personality."

Mazursky's most explicitly Jewish film, as well as his most autobiographical, is *Next Stop, Greenwich Village.* It's the story of Larry Lapinsky's (Lenny Baker) move away from a suffocating homelife with his parents toward independence in his own Greenwich Village apartment. Mazursky opens the picture with Larry packing his suitcase, the final step in leaving his parents' Brooklyn home. He takes a yarmulke out of his dresser drawer, contemplates it for a moment, and then throws it back in the dresser. Later, on the subway ride to the Village, Larry puts a beret on his head.

The new has replaced the old, and Greenwich Village is no place for religion. His parting, however, is made difficult by his overbearing mother (Shelley Winters), who forces Larry to feel intensely guilty over "deserting" his parents. When she refuses to kiss him goodbye, Larry erupts in anger: he swears, storms out of the house, and makes his way to "fame and fortune" in a new environment. But he can't leave his mother totally behind; a bit of her still clings to him like unwelcome lint. "Oh boy, am I guilty" mutters Larry in front of his new apartment house, admitting to himself what he won't tell his mother.

Larry Lapinsky (Lenny Baker) journies from his Brooklyn home to his Greenwich Village apartment in NEXT STOP, GREENWICH VILLAGE *(1976).*

A Jewish mother in full cry. Lenny Baker and Shelley Winters in NEXT STOP, GREENWICH VILLAGE *(1976).*

Once in Greenwich Village, Larry collects an odd assortment of bohemian friends, but he remains faithful to his girl friend in Queens, Sarah (Ellen Green). Now that he has an apartment, the two are free to make love any time they want, but Sarah seems more interested in washing her hair and keeping her makeup fresh. "Don't you love me?" asks the confused Larry after she rebuffs his advances. "I'm getting a diaphragm aren't I," responds Sarah, as though in answer to his question. When they finally do make love, Sarah tells him "You were fine," as if commenting on a new play. Later when Sarah becomes pregnant, Larry offers to marry her. She says she will think about it, but instead has an abortion without first informing Larry. At the film's conclusion, Sarah still lives at home and continues lying to her parents about where she spends her nights. She, unlike Larry, is unable to break free from her restrictive environment, preferring hypocrisy to direct confrontation with her parents. Indeed, as the picture progresses she seems more and more an unlikely match for Larry's expanding sensibilities: "I think about suicide once or twice a day," he tells her. "That's natural," she responds calmly, "thinking about suicide makes you feel talented."

Larry also has problems with his friend Robert (Christopher Walken), a self-styled poet and intellectual. Mazursky constantly compares and contrasts the dark, very Jewish Larry with the blond, very Gentile Robert, whose intellectual brilliance, good looks, and introspective sensitivity clashes with Larry's ebullient, and far coarser, personality. But Robert is eventually revealed as a superficial, egotistical, and weak character who preys on the feelings of lonely older women to obtain a living. His intelligence, so admired in the earlier segments of the movie, is seen as a weapon that allows him to destroy other people. He even seduces Sarah with no thoughts about his "friend" Larry or about the girl's feelings for him. Robert becomes the most negative character in *Next Stop, Greenwich Village*. His intellectual affectations are simply a disguise for his cruelty: he draws people to him, exploits them, and then refuses to take responsibility for the damage he has caused. He is all show and no substance.

Larry's conflicts with Robert and with Sarah, however, are far less heated than his clashes with his mother. Though he leaves his parents' home for the free, bohemian life of Greenwich Village, Larry never fully leaves his mother behind. Indeed, the film becomes a virtual compendium of Jewish son/Jewish mother conflicts, with enough pop Freudian psychology thrown in to delight any armchair psychiatrist. The weekly visits paid by Larry's parents to his new apartment betray the lack of communication which plagues this family. The three sit silently: the father (Mike Kellin) reads his newspaper, the mother listens to her opera records, and the son stares out the window wishing he were somewhere else. When his uninvited parents show up at his rent party, Larry seethes in quiet embarrassment. His fears that his mother will make a fool of herself—and therefore of him—give way to anger when his friends readily accept Mrs. Lapinsky and she becomes the life of the party. In particular, her semi-seductive dance with Berstein, the homosexual Black man whose mother named him after her Jewish employers, infuriates Larry, perhaps because he harbors a hidden resentment at seeing her with another "child."

Larry's fantasies about his mother contain these elements of suppressed sexuality and anger. In one, he is reciting Shakespeare before a hostile audience that pelts him with pies. His mother joins them, shouting, "Be a doctor!" In another dream, Mrs. Lapinsky actually takes over Larry's acting class, reciting Shylock's famous "Hath not a Jew" speech to the enthusiastic applause of his classmates. Larry's most clearly Oedipal fantasy has him playing a romantic scene with his mother. At one particularly passionate moment, he grabs her, bends her over backward, and kisses her on the lips. All these dreams speak of Larry's love/hate relationship with this powerful figure whom Mazursky describes as "my own mother [whose] energy was not used, not plugged in. So it fizzled all over the joint. The silver cord tremendously overdone is bad. But no cord is worse."

To Mazursky's credit, he never turns Mrs. Lapinsky into a raging Sophie Portnoy. She is no crass castrater. Her sensitivity reveals itself as she weeps while listening to her opera records, tearfully telling Larry how her one desire is to go to the

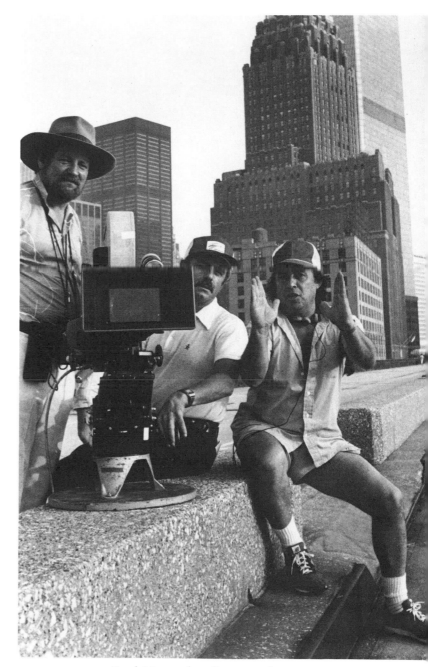

Paul Mazursky, director of ALEX IN WONDERLAND *(1970),* BLUME IN LOVE *(1973),* HARRY AND TONTO *(1974),* NEXT STOP, GREENWICH VILLAGE *(1976), and* AN UNMARRIED WOMAN *(1978), frames a shot for his cameraman.*

195

Duddy Kravitz (Richard Dreyfuss) talks with his surrogate father figure Mr. Farber (Joe Silver) in THE APPRENTICESHIP OF DUDDY KRAVITZ *(1974).*

Metropolitan Opera House and actually see her favorite opera singers. When Larry prepares to leave New York for Hollywood, where he has been offered an acting job, Mrs. Lapinsky tells him about his roots, although in serio-comic form: "You come from good stock. Your grandmother snuck across the Polish border buried under sacks of potatoes. The guards put bayonets into the sacks, but she never cried out. That's where you came from." She then hands Larry some apple strudel to eat on the plane to California. By the film's conclusion, Larry, unlike the still resentful Alexander Portnoy, has learned to accept his mother's foibles. "I'm not angry any more," he tells his long-suffering father, "I'm crazy, not angry." Larry recognizes what his mother has done to him, but he also understands her actions were misguided expressions of her love.

Mazursky's loving remembrance of his own past in *Next Stop, Greenwich Village* is much like Fellini's gentle *Amarcord* (1974). In the Village, Larry finds the intellectual and emotional fellowship missing at home. His sojourn allows him to accept his mother more readily, opening him to a very real humanism that converts his anger to mature compassion. Unlike Portnoy, Larry is not crippled by his life within a "Jewish joke." Though it creates problems, such a life also strengthens Larry and provides him with confidence in his own talents, whereas Robert is driven to cruelty to "prove" his superiority.

Mazursky never loses sight of the feelings of insecurity, guilt, and frustration that are part of his background. But he never becomes either a totally assimilated Groucho Marx or a bitter, cynical Lenny Bruce. He turns his aggressions and frustrations into warm comedy. Because his films present us with portraits drawn from his Jewish roots and lessons learned from his Jewish perspective of the world, they are high points in the history of the Jewish-American cinema.

Director Ted Kotcheff's *The Apprenticeship of Duddy Kravitz* (1974) also focuses on family tensions, but this time on son/father relationships. Throughout the picture, Duddy (Richard Dreyfuss) obsessively searches for a father figure he can admire. Ambitious, he quickly outgrows his biological father, Max (Jack Warden), a taxicab driver part-time pimp, and replaces him with the "Boy Wonder," Jerry Dingleman (Henry Ramer). At first Dingleman's apparent financial success dazzles the young Kravitz, but he soon sees Dingleman for what he is: a relatively small-time wheeler-dealer who exploits Duddy by having him smuggle heroin across the border into New York. Duddy eventually gains his revenge on Dingleman. In one of the film's most brutal scenes, Duddy savagely humiliates the severely crippled Dingleman, mocking his now-defeated rival. In so doing, Duddy ignores his own spiritual paralysis. He has become the new boy wonder, but at what price? Along the way, he has abandoned those characters who represent the film's ethical center, his girl friend Yvette (Micheline Lanctot), his best friend Virgil (Randy Quaid), and his grandfather. The gross materialism of Dingleman's world has overwhelmed Duddy Kravitz. He, too, has become a cripple by destroying the people and things that could have made him whole.

The second father substitute Duddy finds is Mr.

Tevye (Topol) holds one of his frequent conversations with God in FIDDLER ON THE ROOF *(1971).*

Farber (Joe Silver), a wealthy junk dealer. A nouveauriche Jew who stages a lavish bar mitzvah for his son, Farber takes Duddy into the steam bath—a traditional place where Jewish fathers held man-to-man talks with their sons—to teach him the realities of the business world. Amid the hellish environment of heat and steam, Duddy confesses to Farber his guilt about an accident in which the epileptic Virgil, whom he has un-scrupulously employed as a driver, is crippled for life. Farber warns Duddy that he must get the paralyzed Virgil to release him from all liability, noting that he himself had let his own partner go to jail rather than take responsibility for a death in his junkyard. "It's war Duddy; it's war," Farber lectures Duddy. "If you want to be a saint, go to Israel and plant orange trees." Farber's ruthless pragmatism becomes Kravitz's credo, his way of dealing with all business and personal rela-tionships. Later, Duddy heeds Farber's advice by forging Virgil's name on a check and taking his friend's last scrap of money to purchase a valuable piece of property.

Duddy also seeks masculine guidance from his revered grandfather, his beloved *zaida*. "A man without land is a nobody," the patriarch tells his grandson. But Duddy understands the old man's statement simply on a literal level; he totally misses the moral implications of his *zaida's* words, the emphasis on family and on roots. In a sense, Duddy attempts to unite the old world values of his grandfather with the new world economics of Mr. Farber via the purchase of beautiful Laurentian farmlands that he will develop in Kravitzville. But the grandson loses his *zaida's* respect by forging Virgil's name to obtain the land. Ultimately, the

Golde (Norma Crane) consults Yente (Molly Picon), the village matchmaker, about her daughter's chance for a good marriage in FIDDLER ON THE ROOF *(1971).*

"Do you Love Me?" asks Golde (Norma Crane) of Tevye (Topol) in FIDDLER ON THE ROOF *(1971).*

zaida refuses Duddy's offer of a home on his property because he despises his grandson's shady dealings. To the old man the process of achieving a goal is as important as the goal itself, a moral consciousness totally ignored by the rapacious Kravitz. For Duddy, the land is not important for its pristine beauty or for the center it can provide his disjointed life. Instead, it becomes just another way of making money, an investment devoid of human values or ethical meanings.

So Duddy's search for a surrogate father figure fails. At one point in the movie, Duddy himself assumes the role of father in a strange family setup with Yvette as mother and the crippled Virgil as their helpless child. But the peace and comfort inherent in this lifestyle fails to satisfy the money-hungry Kravitz. As the film concludes, we are aware of Duddy's hollow victory. The itch so much a part of his physical demeanor becomes an objective correlative for the constant yearning for money that no amount of scratching will ever relieve. His head convinces his heart that he has become a success, even though the film's most positive figures—Yvette, Virgil, his *zaida*—reject him. There is no one but the dumb, admiring Max to share Duddy's land with him. We last glimpse Duddy running to the left of the screen, and then back again to the right, and then to the left once again. Devoid of moral or ethical guidance, he lacks any direction. We have no doubt that Duddy Kravitz will "make it" in the world of business, but we mourn what he has left behind rather than envy what lies before him.

The most popular Jewish musical of the seventies was *Fiddler on the Roof* (1971), an idealized and nostalgic version of *shtetl* life that received an Academy Award nomination for Best Film of the Year. The picture's plotline follows the trials and tribulations of an old-world patriarch, Tevye, forced to confront a changing world: his three daughters marry against his wishes, his poverty condemns him to a life of want, and his fear of the alien, Gentile world surrounding him affects his every act. Despite his troubles, Tevye maintains his dignity, humanity, sense of humor, and ethical strength. But he is trapped in a time of shifting values, a man of tradition assailed by a world of rapid changes. In this figure of the put-upon dairyman, director Norman Jewison offers his audience a strong vision of Jewish family life, community involvement, and religious devotion.

Beneath this nostalgic surface, *Fiddler on the Roof* presents a rather conservative message, probably more as a result of Sholem Aleichem's tale, upon which it's based, than of Jewison's direction or Joseph Stein's script from his stageplay. On this subtextual level, the movie becomes a series of warnings about the price one pays for abandoning his heritage. It opens with Tevye's lusty rendition of "Tradition," a song about his people who, perched like a fiddler on the roof, have been able to survive for centuries because of a strong sense of tradition inherent in their religious and cultural prohibitions. Ironically, the rest of the film deals with a breakdown of these traditions and the disasters that result. All three of Tevye's daughters marry against his wishes, and the wedding of each is coupled with tragedy. Tzeitel (Rosalind Harris) marries a struggling tailor (Leonard Frey) instead of agreeing to an arranged match with a wealthy butcher (Paul Mann); her wedding is interrupted by a pogrom. Hodel (Michele March), Tevye's second daugher, weds a penniless student (Michael Glaser); he is soon jailed for his revolutionary activities and sent to Siberia. Chava (Neva Small) marries a non-Jew (Raymond Lovelock); shortly after, the entire Jewish community is evicted from Anatevka. In varying degrees, Tevye comes to accept all three marriages, all three deviations from tradition, even forgiving his supposedly "dead" daughter by muttering "God be with you," as she and her Gentile husband leave Russia with the departing Jews.

Clearly *Fiddler on the Roof* sides with love rather than tradition, a foreshadowing of what values await the immigrants in the new world to which they are forced to move. Because he ultimately accepts love over principle, Tevye resents the assimilationist ethos so common in Hollywood's Jewish-American films from the silent days onward. But by juxtaposing negative events with these triumphs of love over tradition, the film creates an implicit cause and effect relationship between the breakdown of religious prohibitions and the arrival of destructive events. Tevye's acceptance of new ways over traditional customs topples

Lila Kalodny (Jeannie Berlin) and Lenny Cantrow (Charles Grodin) embark on a disastrous Miami honeymoon in THE HEARTBREAK KID *(1972).*

Kelly Corcoran (Cybil Shepherd) flirts with Lenny Cantrow (Charles Grodin) during his honeymoon in THE HEARTBREAK KID *(1972).*

Katie (Barbra Streisand) and Hubbell (Robert Redford) share a tender moment during their marriage in THE WAY WE WERE *(1973).*

the fiddler from his perch; he is seen walking alone at the film's conclusion, following Tevye to a new land. Whether or not Jewison consciously intended his film's subtextual message is debatable, but perhaps not finally important. Underneath its assimilationist exterior *Fiddler on the Roof* shows a real concern for traditions, an element which adds an oblique criticism to the film's apparent acceptance of new-world, democratic choices. To miss this level of the film is to ignore its insistent, though understated, message: a place for tradition must be found in contemporary life.

Another film about the dangers of ignoring "tradition" is director Elaine May and screenwriter Neil Simon's *The Heartbreak Kid* (1972), one of the most interesting and unjustly overlooked screen versions of the Jewish/Gentile romance. May opens the movie with a shot of Len Cantrow (Charles Grodin) in a jaunty sports car—the Jew playing WASP playboy right down to his unlit pipe, nifty hat, and driving gloves. Nevertheless, Len marries Lila Kalodny (Jeannie Berlin) in a traditional Jewish wedding. Throughout this marriage sequence, May emphasizes family ties and Jewish traditions. The wedding takes place in Lila's home, not a huge rented hall. In the scene's warmest moment, Len and Lila, safely buffered from the outside world by a protective circle of relatives and friends, dance an enthusiastic hora.

Len and Lila are hardly out of New York and on their way to a honeymoon in Miami Beach when trouble develops. Their sexual relations range from horrible to boring, as Len's fantasy of married life clashes with the very real woman in rollers and face cream asleep beside him. Lila keeps repeating how nice life will be together "for forty or fifty years," pointing out old couples who totter by arm in arm. Such a thought fills Len with dread, as does the distasteful vision of Lila with egg salad dripping from the corners of her mouth as she drones on and on in a seemingly endless monologue of trivia.

Once in Miami Beach things get worse, particularly after Len meets Kelly Corcoran (Cybill Shepherd), the spoiled little rich daughter of a wealthy Minnesota businessman (Eddie Albert). May emphasizes the differences between the cool WASP and the unhappy Jewish bride in a series of crosscuts that juxtapose Kelly frolicking in the surf with Lila lying in bed covered with cream to soothe her outrageous sunburn. At first, Kelly flirts with Len just to annoy her bigoted father who moves his family out of the plush Miami Beach hotel because he doesn't like the "element" there. As the relationship between Kelly and Len develops, he begins talking with her about being together for "forty or fifty years," symbolically assuming Lila's subservient role in this new union with Kelly. Finally, Len can stand no more of Lila. He tells her he wants out of the marriage, and in an orgy of guilt, gives her everything but nine hundred dollars which he uses to pursue Kelly back to Minnesota.

Once there, Len's "otherness" becomes evident. The cold whiteness of the Minnesota landscape contrasts with the hot sun of Miami and the colorful warmth of New York City. Dressed in a skimpy overcoat, one fine for New York but woefully inadequate for Minnesota's bone-chilling winters, the desolate Len shivers and freezes in his lonely motel room. All he has left is his Jewish cleverness. After outsmarting the blond, Nordic footballers who hover around Kelly, Len convinces her to take him to her father's mountain retreat. Once there, Kelly remains a tease. She says they can undress and look at each other, but cannot touch. Kelly firmly controls their sexual contact; she determines whether, when, and where they will make love.

After several trying incidents, Len finally convinces Mr. Corcoran that he is serious about Kelly, even refusing a hefty bribe offered by the exasperated father who feels this is not a suitable match for his daughter. The second wedding stands in sharp contrast to the first. May ties the two celebrations together by inserting strains from "Close to You" and "I'd Like to Teach the World to Sing" within each segment. This time, however, the marriage couple take their vows in a large Christian church, not in the intimate surroundings of a private home. Len's best man is someone he barely knows and doesn't like, one of the dumb jocks he outsmarted to win Kelly. The wedding ceremony is as cold as the Minnesota winter and as formal as the uncomfortable outfits worn by the participants. At the reception that follows, the wedding guests talk and mingle politely. There is no dancing, no

A distraught Katie (Barbra Streisand) tries to convince an unbelieving Hubbell (Robert Redford) that their marriage can be saved in THE WAY WE WERE *(1973).*

joyous outpouring of love and tenderness. Len is left almost completely alone at the reception. A few guests talk to him now and then, but he is soon abandoned to some children, who eventually find him as boring as do the rest of Mr. Corcoran's friends.

Finally, Len sits by himself on a large, overstuffed sofa, an outsider at his own wedding left to contemplate what life will be like in this new world he cannot possibly ever fully enter. He has won the Irish sweepstakes. He has captured the heart of the Irish princess, the golden *shiksa* goddess deemed the ultimate prize in previous intermarriage movies. But *The Heartbreak Kid's* final, silent moments force us to examine what Len has lost. Kelly represents the romanticized American dream made flesh. To capture this dream, Len gives up his family, friends, and heritage, a poor bargain in the eyes of May and Simon.

In *The Way We Were* (1973), director Sidney Pollack also explores Jewish/Gentile romance, but from a different perspective. On its simplest level, *The Way We Were* represents another Streisand reversal of the typical inter-ethnic romance, this time the prize being the archetypal golden boy, Hubbell Gardiner (Robert Redford). The first meeting between Katie Moroski (Streisand) and the perfectly groomed Hubbell reveals how different from each other the two really are. He is the typical college fraternity boy with his snazzy convertible, crewcut, and v-neck tennis sweater. She is already the dedicated political activist, passing out leaflets against Fascist Spain. When Hubbell questions Katie about her cause, she dismisses him as another callous hypocrite, telling him contemptuously: "Go eat your goldfish. I won't try to make a Jew out of Hitler." While Katie addresses a rally, the rebuffed Hubbell lounges with his head in the lap of a more cordial partner: a blond sorority girl who cares nothing for Katie's "innocent women and children being blown to pieces in Spain at this very moment."

As time passes, however, Katie and Hubbell draw closer together. She admires his autobiographical short story, "The All-American Smile," in which Hubbell's protagonist admits that "everything came easy for him." Later, he asks if she is angry all the time because she's Jewish, or poor, or first-generation. "All three," she replies. Though they have little in common, Hubbell and Katie grudgingly start to respect each other. For her, he represents all she claims to despise: "impossibly handsome, impossibly invulnerable, impossible." For him, she becomes the only glimmer of truth in a world of "long American legs" and cashmere sweaters. Katie is the belligerent outsider embarrassed by her fleeting desire to be part of the "in" crowd, while Hubbell is the insider who longs for something more. Each possesses an intriguing spark of "otherness" that sets them apart.

Years after they graduate from college, during World War II, Katie and Hubbell accidentally meet again, this time in a New York City nightclub. Hubbell, resplendent in his snow-white summer uniform, dozes drunkenly on a barstool, a beautiful blonde caressing him. When the blonde abandons Hubbell, Katie takes her place on the barstool. But it is not the same Katie Hubbell remembers from college. Her hair is now straightened and she is smartly dressed. Eventually, Katie takes Hubbell home and into her bed, though their

sexual activity is less than memorable as Hubbell passes out in the middle of it. The next morning, he tries to tell her why she attracts him:

> You hold on and I don't know how. And I wish I did....Maybe you were born committed...I can't be negative enough. I can't get angry enough. And I can't be positive enough.

To keep Hubbell, Katie must give up precisely what attracts him the most: her commitment. In effect, she becomes what she has always hated, one of those giggling airheads for whom "the war and the world are largely a frame of reference for jokes and quips and funny stories." She trades in her Jewish conscience for WASP blandness. Even Hubbell recognizes the futility of her gesture:

> You're unhappy unless you do something. Because of me you've been trying to lay out, but that's wrong. Wrong for you. I'm wrong for you....Commitment is part of you. Part of what makes you attractive, part of what attracted me to you.

Katie, however, will not admit this.

Ultimately, they marry and move to the lotusland of dreams and illusions, Hollywood, where Hubbell becomes a successful screenwriter and Katie dedicates herself to looking "as though she has always driven in convertibles with the top down." They finally part over the HUAC hearings. Hubbell wants to "sit it out," but Katie cannot. She fights back with all the tools at her command, eventually alienating Hubbell. Commitment in the abstract is fine for him; but when it threatens to have consequences in the very real world he inhabits, Hubbell backs away, frightened about his job and his reputation. The strain proves too much for both of them. She loses respect for him; he can't tolerate her activism. In the film's last scene, Katie has become Mrs. David Cohen, has allowed her hair to return to its natural frizziness, and is handing out anti-bomb leaflets for SANE in New York City. They meet for a moment by chance on a city street. Katie touches Hubbell's hair in a loving gesture, but they realize their life together is past history. Hubbell cannot even summon up the courage to see their daughter, leaving her to grow up as Cohen and not Gardiner.

In his perceptive discussion of this film, critic Barry Gross argues that Streisand's Katie Moroski becomes a new type in the American cinema, "a Jewish American Princess that is not the usual spoiled rich bitch Ali McGraw plays in *Goodbye, Columbus.*" Even more, he notes, *The Way We Were* is one of only a handful of Jewish-American pictures that opposes assimilation. Katie overcomes the lures of a blond, glittering Gentile world to emerge as her own person. In so doing, she rejects the price of success paid by so many Jewish characters from Jakie Rabinowitz *(The Jazz Singer)* to Len Cantrow *(The Heartbreak Kid):* a loss of heritage, personal identity, and Jewish traditions. Her commitment is not only to political causes, but also to herself as a worthwhile human being and as a Jew, dramatically represented by the fact that she doesn't force her irregular curls into a straightness currently demanded by a homogenized society. To fit in, to become "respectable," Katie temporarily forsakes the parts of her personality that make her so compelling a character. Ultimately, she refuses to do this. Being accepted as a woman is part of her triumph. Being accepted as a Jew is equally important. Because it rejects the stifling "melting pot" mentality that characterizes the vast majority of Jewish-American films, *The Way We Were* becomes an anti-assimilationist picture that proclaims the virtues of the one over those of the many.

As the seventies witnessed the emergence of the strong woman protagonist, so too the decade saw a forgotten figure in Jewish-American films appear: the elderly Jew. The American cinema, in general, has never been particularly receptive to presenting older characters in leading roles. Filmmakers feared it would fail to interest the young moviegoers who were their steadiest customers in a culture that is almost totally youth-oriented. In the seventies, however, increasing attention was paid to the plight of the elderly, and the result is a series of pictures that examine old age from the perspective of sexuality, poverty, love, and death.

Two films featuring older Jews, *The Angel Levine* (1970) and *Lies My Father Told Me* (1975), were directed by Jan Kadar, the Czechoslovakian-born

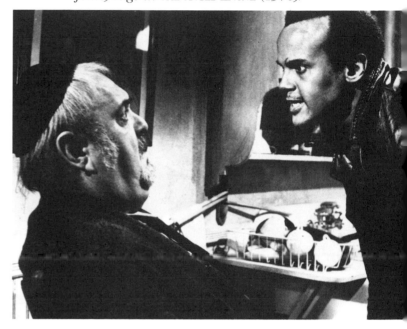

Morris Mishkin (Zero Mostel) retreats in the face of his black angel's (Harry Belafonte) rage in THE ANGEL LEVINE (1970).

David (Jeffrey Lynas) helps his grandfather (Yossi Yadim) collect junk in LIES MY FATHER TOLD ME (1975).

David Rosen (Lee Strasberg) confronts some black toughs in BOARDWALK *(1979).*

Becky (Ruth Gordon) amd David (Lee Strasberg) Rosen share a dance on their fiftieth wedding anniversary in BOARDWALK *(1979).*

director who had previously made *The Shop on Main Street* (1965) in his native land. Based on a short story in Bernard Malamud's outstanding *The Magic Barrel* (1958), the earlier film partakes of the old Jewish mystical tradition critic Irving Malin says occurs when "the supernatural and the trivial jostle each other." Certainly Morris Mishkin (Zero Mostel) needs a miracle. His only daughter has run off with a "nogoodnik," his beloved wife Fanny (Ida Kaminska) is dying day-by-day before his eyes, and his back is so sore it keeps him from working at his sewing machine to earn a living. The kindly neighborhood doctor (Milo O'Shea), who represents the limits of rational thought and scientific accomplishment in the face of death, can do little to help Fanny recover, though he assures the old man she will.

Mishkin's miracle arrives in the form of a Black man (Harry Belafonte) who claims to be not only a Jew but also an angel. Sent from heaven, he must get Mishkin to believe in him within twenty-four hours or lose his powers. Only when Mishkin believes can his miracle occur. Mishkin's early suspicions about this Black man's claims turn to complete disbelief when the angel's very earthy girl friend (Gloria Foster) shows up, insisting that he marry her in light of their four-year courtship. Eventually the white Jew who needs to believe in miracles and the black angel who needs someone to believe in him sit and argue over inconsequentials, as the clock ticks away. Only in the terrible twenty-fifth hour does Mishkin come to accept that the Black man is an angel, but by then it is too late to save Fanny.

In his later film, *Lies My Father Told Me,* Kadar sets his tale during the late twenties in Montreal. The Herman family are first-generation Russian Jews. David's (Jeffrey Lynas) parents—Harry (Len Birman) and Annie (Marilyn Lightstone)—were born in Canada, but his *zaida* (Yossi Yadim) emigrated from the old country in 1880. Conflicts between the old and the new dominate the Herman household. Harry, a modern man, dreams of designing "the inventions the world is waiting for," while Zaida, a junk dealer, is content to buy and sell old rags while he waits for the world of love that will come with the arrival of the Messiah. David gets caught between his father's dream of material success and his grandfather's vision of love. But neither Zaida's world of miracles nor Harry's world of money can spare six-year-old David the pains of growing up. His problems range from acceptance of a new baby brother who robs him of his mother's undivided attention, to conflicts with annoying neighbors who demand that Zaida remove his beloved horse, Ferdeleh, because the animal smells up the neighborhood. After Zaida dies, David climbs up to the loft in their small barn, desperately and vainly waiting for one more glimpse of the old man.

In both his films, Kadar treats older characters with dignity and respect. Both Morris Mishkin and Zaida come dangerously close to stereotypes at moments, but Kadar skillfully pulls back before they develop into cliches. When, for example, Fanny suffers a particularly acute attack, Morris does not dissolve into pathetic weeping. Instead, he begins sewing to relieve his pain, a much more moving gesture than crying would be. Similarly, Zaida's refusal to remove Ferdeleh becomes an eloquent "no" to a world that insists on enforcing arbitrary codes of behavior. When David rejects his father's logical explanations of the world, the "lies" of the film's title, he opts for Zaida's world of quiet love and miracles over Harry's vision of materialism and rational thought. In both these pictures, Kadar's elderly characters suggest a sense of life beyond our daily existence.

The most detailed presentation of Jewish old age in the seventies is director/writer Steven Verona's *Boardwalk* (1979), in which an aging Jewish couple face the crumbling realities of their Brooklyn neighborhood. From his opening montage of old people walking aimlessly around Coney Island, to his last image of David Rosen (Lee Strasberg) sitting alone, Verona fills his film with the joys and sorrows of aging. David is a vibrant, seventy-nine-year-old who still puts in a full day's work at his restaurant, ogles *Playboy* bunnies, and has a loving—and very physical—relationship with his wife Becky (Ruth Gordon). Married forty-nine years and living in the same house, David is a survivor. Unlike his neighbors the Friedmans, who commit suicide rather than "live in fear" of the world surrounding them, David is not intimidated by anyone. His wife is equally independent. Becky,

The Jew as gangster, vicious Marty Augustine (Mark Rydell) in THE LONG GOODBYE *(1973).*

who dies at home on the day of her fiftieth wedding anniversary, remains a spunky woman right up to the end. Though her beloved piano students have deserted her for younger teachers in newer neighborhoods, she keeps busy by collecting clothes for Israeli children. Together, David and Becky represent a caring Jewish couple for whom old age has added luster to love.

One of *Boardwalk's* notable attributes is Verona's attention to David's heritage. The old man faithfully attends near-empty synagogue services. At one point in the picture, he cleans the entire deteriorating temple as part of a bargain with God to save his wife's life. After Becky's death, the Rosen family sits *shiva* (seven days of mourning) and David responds philosophically to his loss: "God gives and God takes away. We must learn to live with it. Age is a series of losses and death a

The old-world father (Milton Berle) pleads with his new-world son (Tony Curtis) to change his criminal ways in LEPKE *(1975).*

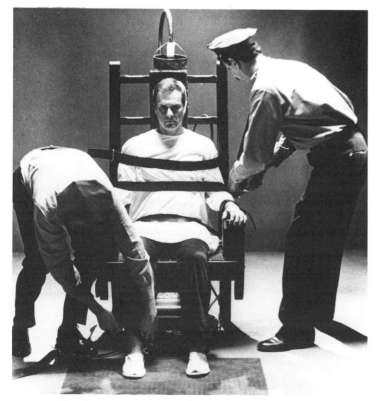

The final moments of Lepke Buchalter (Tony Curtis), president of Murder, Inc., in LEPKE *(1975).*

member of the family. Surviving, that's my career." His emphasis on Jewish traditions, in deeds as well as in words, makes David the moral center of the picture, a man who reaches out for others while not losing himself.

One aspect of David's reaching out for others is the strong ties of kinship which unite the Rosen family. David and his three children all work in the family restaurant. The entire family spends Sundays at David's house. In his role as family patriarch, David soothes the bruised egos of his daughter (Janet Leigh) and her son (Michael Ayr) after they engage in a number of bitter quarrels that threaten family unity. After a disastrous love affair, the boy chooses to come live with his grandfather—a decision that reflects his respect and affection for the old man. David's compassion reaches beyond his immediate family to a young Black child whom he bails out of jail after the boy is caught stealing food from David's restaurant.

Though *Boardwalk* succeeds in presenting the triumphs and tragedies of old age through a Jewish perspective, it lacks balance in its depiction of Blacks. Despite a scene in which David advises his prejudiced daughter to judge their new Black neighbors by their deeds alone, the film's portrait of Blacks stands as one of the most unpleasant instances of celluloid racism on record. Verona shows Blacks almost exclusively as mindless forces of violence intent on destroying anything that crosses their paths. The Black gang leader wears an Iron Cross. The gang needlessly desecrates David's temple and destroys David's home. Roaming bands of Black youths rape elderly women and rob defenseless old men. The inclusion of David's decent Black neighbors does little to mitigate the film's racism, for these minor characters appear in one short, ineffectual scene that adds little to the movie. Also, the movie's ending, though dramatically appropriate, is quite improbable: the frail David chokes the gang's Black leader to death. The point is, of course, that the Jew is no longer a victim, but his victory seems sadly hollow. One admires Verona's skill in handling the film's Jewish characters but wonders why he cannot create equally compelling, complex Black portraits instead of resorting to simplistic stereotypes.

Criminal mastermind Roth (Lee Strasberg) confers with Michael Corleone (Al Pacino) in THE GODFATHER, PART II *(1974).*

The seventies also saw the emergence of unattractive Jewish gangsters in a series of crime movies. Important Jewish gangsters appear in *The Long Goodbye* (1973), *Lepke* (1975), and *The Godfather, Part II* (1974). In the first film, director Robert Altman presents a Jewish hoodlum, Marty Augustine (Mark Rydell), who is a rich and powerful underworld boss. Early in the picture, Augustine seeks to frighten detective Philip Marlowe (Eliott Gould) with his capacity for cruelty. He points to his beautiful mistress, JoAnne (JoAnne Brady), and proclaims his love for her to Marlowe. The camera slowly tracks in on JoAnne's angelic face, allowing the viewer to admire her sensual beauty. Suddenly, and for no apparent reason, Augustine smashes a Coke bottle into the girl's serene face, its pieces ripping her skin in agonizing slow motion. Altman quickly cuts around the room, emphasizing the brutal insanity of the moment by capturing the looks of disgust and amazement on the faces of Augustine's own hoods. Even they shrink in the face of his cold sadism, one of the most horrifying pieces of cinema violence since Lee Marvin hurled scalding coffee into Gloria Grahame's face in *The Big Heat* (1951). "You see that?" Augustine asks the stunned Marlowe, "that's someone I love, and you I don't even like." Marlowe, though revolted by the incident, is powerless to counteract the evil and violence in the world surrounding him and symbolized by this Jewish thug.

Besides the obvious violence he represents, Marty Augustine becomes Altman's clearest symbol of corruption in *The Long Goodbye*. He tells Marlowe he lives next door to Richard Nixon, emphasizing how crime has become socially acceptable in the seventies. For Altman, Augustine embodies the sudden violence which permeates Marlowe's world. At times, the Jewish hood seems like an affable character: his obsession with physical fitness, his gang of ineffectual buffoons, and his amusing eccentricities are more a target of Altman's humor than of his rancor. Even as a sadistic murderer, the screen Jew acts like something of a clown. But he is more. By disfiguring someone he loves to make his point, Augustine shows the brutality that informs all the characters and situations in Marlowe's seedy world, as well as the suddenness with which violence can strike.

Another Jewish gangster who appears on the screen in the seventies is Louis (Lepke) Buchalter in Israeli director Menahem Golan's *Lepke* (1975), an attempt to create a Jewish godfather film. Hollywood dealt with Buchalter before in *Murder, Inc.* (1960) but never discussed his ethnic roots, nor those of his cohort, Mendy Weiss. The more recent film, however, contains various references to Buchalter's (Tony Curtis) Jewishness, including his Yiddish expressions, his wedding to an Orthodox girl (Anjanette Comer), and his electrocution-day visit from a rabbi. *Lepke* even features a bizarre performance by Milton Berle as Buchalter's old-world father-in-law. The film traces Lepke's career from his adolescent days in Brooklyn to his adult years as leader of the famous Murder, Inc. Throughout the film, Buchalter is clearly identified as a Jew, though the movie provides little insight into what turned him into a cold-hearted killer. Finally, Lepke is betrayed by his own people, is captured by the FBI, and gains the dubious distinction of becoming the only major Mafia mobster ever executed.

The most intriguing Jewish screen gangster of the decade is Hyman Roth (Lee Strasberg), the fatherly criminal so important in Francis Ford Coppola's *The Godfather, Part II* (1974). Roth, a fictitious character, is based on one of the most powerful Jewish criminals in American history— Meyer Lansky. Roth, like Lansky, rules his underworld empire more by brains than brute force. Since he is not the focus of the film, Roth's life beyond his criminal activities is not explored as fully as that of his Italian counterpart, Michael Corleone (Al Pacino). But what scraps there are prove interesting. At first, Roth is seen in his modest Miami house, munching on a sandwich and watching a baseball game on television. "I've loved baseball since Arnold Rothstein fixed the World Series in 1919," he tells Michael, the young don who has come to negotiate an alliance with the Jewish branch of the mob. In this initial meeting, Roth seems like a gentle old *zaida* (grandfather) who gives Michael advice and understanding. In fact, he resembles the most important person in the young man's life, his dead father (Marlon Brando), and at times during the film Roth consciously plays on Michael's need for a father figure.

But the innocuous-looking old man puttering around his Miami house is not to be taken lightly. Later in the film, Michael and Roth meet in the latter's plush Havana hotel to discuss a merger: Roth wants Corleone to invest in Cuban enterprises with him. As they sit on the hotel terrace, Hyman boasts of his power: "We're bigger than U.S. Steel," he tells the young gangster, repeating a claim once made by Meyer Lansky. Indeed, the mob controls the island. In one scene, Roth and ITT representatives join Cuba's corrupt dictator, Fulgencio Batista, for dinner to discuss how they will divide the spoils obtained at the expense of the Cuban people.

Once back in his hotel, Michael witnesses violence in the streets of Havana and becomes convinced that Batista's regime is doomed. He understands that Roth has made a bad decision by underestimating the people's desire to rid themselves of Batista. For this reason, he backs out of his deal with Roth. Michael looks over the course of the Cuban Revolution that follows and makes the following observation: "If history has taught us anything, it's that you can kill anyone." No one is safe in the world of Michael Corleone; no one can escape violence. Proving this point, Michael orders Roth assassinated when he seems most protected—surrounded by FBI agents. Roth's death leaves Michael the most powerful man in the underworld organization. His new-world business tactics, learned while a student at Harvard, triumph over the old-world manner of Roth. A new generation has taken over the underworld, and it has no room for Hyman Roth.

Lee Strasberg, the legendary head of the famous Actors Studio, endows Roth's character with a complexity far beyond the written words of the script. He emerges as an intriguing figure who looks like a cuddly grandfather but who has the instincts of a rattlesnake. Though he prefers to cajole rather than murder, Roth clearly understands the limits of persuasion. His soft-spoken manner is simply a cover-up for his murderous designs. Coppola makes at least two points in his portrait of the Jewish gangster within this predominately Italian environment. First, Roth has tremendous power, but he underestimates his own vulnerability. Eventually, the aging hoodlum falls prey to the newer business methods Michael employs with far superior skill. Second, the Jew, unlike his Italian counterpart, has no sense of personal honor. He violates the implicit code of Mafia loyalty and becomes an outcast even among this band of outsiders. The Jewish gangster is somehow different. As Carlos Clarens notes, atonement is such an inherent part of the Jewish ethos that the major Jewish gangsters to merit film treatments are all made into scapegoats of one form or another, something rarely seen in Italian gangster pictures.

During the seventies, several Jewish-American films featured contemporary problems like Black/Jewish relations and feminism. Other movies, however, sought to recreate the past. Among these was director Joan Micklin Silver's *Hester Street* (1974), an overly sentimental adaptation of Abraham Cahan's *Yekl, A Tale of the Ghetto* (1896). Cahan, editor of America's largest and most influential Yiddish newspaper, the *Jewish Daily Forward,* was himself an immigrant who harbored few illusions about the difficulty of life in the old country but was aware of the price that adjustment to American life extracted from his fellow immigrants. As a dedicated socialist and a perceptive observer of Lower East Side life, Cahan recognized the positive and negative effects of Americanization, the losses and gains this new land offered its incoming Jews. Silver, however, lacks Cahan's grasp of this complex situation. In place of his open-ended questions about life in America, she offers a series of either/or positions. In her world, one must either reject the past or the present, the new

Yankel Podkovnik (Steven Keats) goes from Greenhorn to Yankee in HESTER STREET *(1974).*

Gitl (Carol Kane) tries to become a "modern" girl to please her Americanized husband in HESTER STREET *(1974).*

Oskar Werner, a distinguished Jewish doctor who has been dismissed from his university post, and his aristocratic wife (Faye Dunaway) dress for dinner in VOYAGE OF THE DAMNED *(1976)*

Wendy Hiller and Luther Adler as an elderly Jewish couple who hope to find freedom outside Germany in VOYAGE OF THE DAMNED *(1976).*

or the old, the European or the American. Nowhere is there a recognition of the need to find a healthy blend between two alternatives, a middle ground that will provide the Jewish newcomer with some sense of traditional Jewish values and still allow him to adjust to the new realities of American life.

Hester Street follows Cahan's basic storyline. Yankel Podkovnik (Steven Keats), a Russian Jew, emigrates to America, changes his name to Jake, shaves off his beard, sheds his orthodox ways, and becomes involved with Mamie Fein (Dorrie Kavanaugh). Along the way to becoming an American, he forgets about his wife, Gitl (Carol Kane), and his son, Yossele, back home in the old country. Shaken by his father's death, Jake finally sends for his family. When Jake comes to Ellis Island to fetch them, he is repelled by his wife's traditional wig and his son's earlocks. He hurriedly hustles Gitl and Yossele back to a small flat on Hester Street, which they share with Mr. Bernstein (Mel Howard), a scholar in the old country but now an embittered sweatshop worker. Gitl's attempts at Americanization fail to satisfy Jake, and she turns to the gentle Bernstein for solace. When Mamie offers her a bribe if she will divorce Jake, Gitl, now thoroughly disgusted with her insensitive husband, accepts the money. She then prods Bernstein into marriage, telling him how she will use the funds to buy a grocery store, run it for them, and let him sit in the backroom and study. Jake and Mamie, now broke, must start over again.

The clear clash of values in *Hester Street* is personified in the characters of Jake and Bernstein. Jake plunges into American life, totally divorcing himself from his past. He strives to be a "Yenkee" right down to his ill-fitting new clothes, his name change, and his attempt to teach his son baseball. Bernstein, on the other hand, retreats to the past via his books. He hates his job and the satanic sweatshop owner who exploits him, he despises the customs of the new world, and he refuses to integrate more than is necessary for survival. "A Jew is a Jew," he lectures Jake, summing up his parochial attitudes. Neither Jake nor Bernstein seem able to unite past and present. The former rejects history and the latter rejects present reality. Using the differences between Jake and Bernstein,

Silver makes her point. All the characters who adopt American values and accede to the demands of modern life are negative. Bernstein, however, becomes the positive center of the film's value system; his past traditions are seen as more solid than the hollowness of present values.

It is in Silver's treatment of the past and the present, rather than in her evocation of the Lower East Side milieu, that *Hester Street* becomes the most sentimental Jewish-American film of the decade. It forces us to reject the present in favor of a dimly remembered past. Even Gitl, who possesses the intellectual and emotional potential to unite heritage with new-world demands, fails to accomplish much worthwhile. Her dream of operating a grocery store while Bernstein, symbol of the past, sits in the back room reading his books, merely continues the *shtetl* tradition of supporting the scholar. Bernstein's heritage and learning will not enhance the present. Gitl's running the store will have nothing to do with Bernstein, will have no meaning in his world of tradition, and will not alter his derisive attitude toward anything in the new world. Bernstein may as well be sitting in Kiev as in New York City. Thus, *Hester Street* fails to incoporate Cahan's complex vision of life in America, but offers only mutually exclusive alternatives that fail to satisfy.

The preoccupation with the past seen in Jewish-American genre films such as *Hester Street, The Frisco Kid, The Big Fix,* and *Fiddler on the Roof* is also evident in the decade's movies that deal with Nazis and Jews. Some like *Cabaret* (1972), *Voyage of the Damned* (1976), and *Julia* (1977), actually set their action in an historical context. Others, such as *The Man in the Glass Booth* (1975), *Marathon Man* (1976), and *The Boys From Brazil* (1979), transport Nazis into contemporary times and pit them against modern Jews. Almost all the pictures represent something of a response to the pro-German feelings prevalent during the seventies, both on and off the screen. Film critic John Mariani's discussion of this phenomenon in *Film Comment* (1979) concludes that "an understanding of man's inhumanity to man is one thing; hero worship is another.... Those who do not learn from the past generally make movies about it." Certainly, films like *The Eagle Has Landed* (1977) put the

Natalia Landauer (Marisa Berenson) and Fritz Wendel (Fritz Wepper) celebrate their wedding in CABARET *(1972).*

Bebe Levy (Dustin Hoffman) finally triumphs over Szell (Laurence Olivier), a sadistic Nazi dentist, in MARATHON MAN *(1976).*

Dr. Mengele (Gregory Peck) trapped by Nazi hunter Ezra Lieberman (Laurence Olivier) in THE BOYS FROM BRAZIL *(1979).*

The infamous Nazi geneticist Dr. Josef Mengele (Gregory Peck) displays no repentance for his horrible experiments in THE BOYS FROM BRAZIL *(1979).*

audience squarely on the side of the Nazis. For example, it encourages the audience to cheer a group of Nazi commandos sent to capture Winston Churchill, ostensibly to allow Hitler to negotiate a peace with the Allies. The Germans in this film, with the exception of Himmler (Donald Pleasance), are all well-behaved and courteous. One commando (Michael Caine) even spares a Jewish Polish woman from some unnecessary roughness.

The perverseness of *The Eagle Has Landed* is outdone by the self-righteous mawkishness of director Stuart Rosenberg's *Voyage of the Damned.* The historical events which inspired Steven Shagan and David Butler's script remain compelling today. In May 1939, the German liner *St. Louis* set sail for Havana carrying 937 Jews who had paid their government for the right to emigrate to Cuba. They proved to be pawns in an elaborate propaganda exercise. Hitler wanted to demonstrate that none of the countries—including the United States—protesting against his anti-Semitic policies would be willing to provide sanctuary for the refugees. He was right. Most of the Jews were forced to return home and many later died in concentration camps.

Rosenberg's star-studded spectacular jettisons any real examination of this event by creating a series of melodramatic vignettes that exploit the very real tragedies of the doomed Jews. Oskar Werner plays a distinguished doctor who has been dismissed from his university post, and Faye Dunaway his elegant wife. Sam Wanamaker depicts the mental collapse of a prominent German lawyer disbarred after Hitler comes to power. Nehemiah Persoff and Maria Schell portray a middle-class couple who have sold all their possessions to raise the fare for their trip to Cuba. Wendy Hiller and Luther Adler appear as a frail, elderly couple who hope to spend their final days together in freedom. Unfortunately, the plot is overloaded with stories treated in a fashion that robs them of any true dramatic impact. We never get to know these characters as real people; they remain merely types, as the actors and actresses deliver what, in effect, are a series of cameo roles.

German Jews also play a part in director Bob Fosse's *Cabaret,* a powerful evocation of Germany in the thirties that remains the cinema's most socially conscious musical. Though the protagonists, Brian Roberts (Michael York) and Sally Bowles (Liza Minnelli), become aware of the Nazi menace early in the film, they ignore the signals that spell danger, letting personal pleasure blind them to political realities. The brutality of the Nazi regime, evident in the beating of Sally's boss at the Kit Kat Klub where she sings, and the anti-Semitic slant of the musical number "Two Women," seem of little interest to the earnest British student and his kookie American neighbor at Schneider's Rooming House. In the film's most powerful scene, however, even the two hedonists are forced to face the world. Brian and Sally stop at a country beer garden when an angelic-faced young German begins to sing "Tomorrow Belongs to Me." The camera slowly pulls back to reveal more and more Germans rising to their feet and singing along with the boy. Slowly, but steadily, the music becomes stronger and more militant, almost everyone in the beer garden joining the youth.

Anti-Semitism strikes closer to home when Sally and Brian's friends, Fritz Wendel (Fritz Wepper) and Natalia Landauer (Marisa Berenson), become potential victims of the Nazis. Fritz and Natalia meet when Brian gives them both English lessons. After Fritz declares his love for her, Natalia shyly reciprocates. But with the Nazis becoming increasingly more of a dominant force in German life, she refuses to marry him because he is not Jewish. Apart, the two lovers remain miserable, until Brian prods Fritz into making a dramatic revelation to Natalia: he admits he is a Jew trying to pass as a Gentile in these troubled times. Together, Natalia and Fritz flee Berlin to escape the Nazi brutality.

In the films of the seventies, the Nazis' brutal treatment of Jews was not confined to the past. In several movies it surfaces in contemporary times and its victims are modern Jews. *Marathon Man,* for instance, features a sadistic ex-Nazi (Laurence Olivier) who tortures a Jewish graduate student (Dustin Hoffman) to obtain information the boy does not have. Eventually, the Jew turns the tables on his German tormentor, forcing him to feel some of the pain he caused others, and finally killing him. *The Boys From Brazil,* in which Olivier switches roles from Nazi to Jew, advances the science-fiction notion that rich ex-Nazis living in South America have placed clones of Hitler among ninety-four families throughout the world. They hope to recreate Hitler's childhood in the lives of these boys and thus bring into the world their ultimate product: another Adolf Hitler.

Heading this nefarious venture is the infamous Dr. Josef Mengele (Gregory Peck), who supervised the gruesome medical "experiments" at Auschwitz and was called "The Angel of Death" by the inmates there. A Holocaust survivor, Ezra Lieberman (Olivier)—a character based on the famous Nazi hunter Simon Wiesenthal—learns of the plot and sets out to foil the Nazis. He confronts Mengele at the home of one of the clones where the doctor has gone to murder the boy's father, thus duplicating the death of Hitler's father when he was fourteen. Ultimately, Mengele is ripped apart by a pack of killer Dobermans.

At the film's conclusion, director Franklin Schaffner has Lieberman burn the list showing where the clones have been placed, rather than allow a young, militant anti-Nazi to kill all the children. "We're not in the business of killing children," he tells the Jewish radical who demands the list, "any children." Lieberman also points out that it was not only genetics that accounted for a Hitler, but also a specific historical situation at a particular time in Germany's, and the world's, evolution. His instinctive morality, however, is far more important than his intellectual reasoning. Not blinded by the hatred that motivates the young Jewish radical, Lieberman understands that to kill the innocent children would put him in the same class as the Nazis: murderers who execute their atrocities by claiming a higher purpose. His refusal to allow the young anti-Nazi to kill the children breaks the chain of violence and shows the Jew as ethically superior to his fanatical oppressors.

The most thematically complex of the modern horror stories about Nazis and Jews is director Arthur Hiller's *The Man in the Glass Booth.* Its central figure, wealthy real-estate dealer Arthur Goldman (Maximilian Schell), is a strange and secretive tycoon obsessed with overwhelming feelings of guilt and paranoia. Much to the surprise of his loyal secretary, Charlie Cohn (Lawrence Pressman), Goldman is arrested by Israeli secret agents

Displaying no contrition, Goldman/Dorff (Maximilian Schell) tells an Israeli court-room how he delighted in torturing Jews in THE MAN IN THE GLASS BOOTH *(1975).*

Arthur Goldman (Maximilian Schell), who may be the sadistic SS Col. Karl Adolph Dorff, captured by Israeli secret agents in THE MAN IN THE GLASS BOOTH *(1975).*

Miriam Rossen (Lois Nettleton), the chief Israeli prosecutor, listens as Goldman/ Dorff graphically describes how he mur-dered thousands of Jews in THE MAN IN THE GLASS BOOTH *(1975).*

and accused of really being Karl Adolph Dorff—a former SS colonel, sadistic torturer, and brutal killer. Goldman, who never denies the charge, demands the right to wear a Nazi uniform at his trial and be addressed as colonel. Later, he tells an Israeli courtroom full of survivors how he de-lighted in torturing Jews and then delivers an impassioned hymn to Hitler. All through his trial, Goldman/Dorff spars condescendingly with the Israeli prosecutor, Miriam Rosen (Lois Nettleton). Suddenly, the case against Goldman/Dorff falls apart. The prosecution's key witness recants his testimony and asserts the man on trial is really a Jew who survived the camps. When he hears this, Goldman/Dorff locks himself inside his glass booth, sinks into a trance, and dies. The truth of his true identity is never revealed.

The Man in the Glass Booth shows how difficult it is to assign guilt and/or innocence in a world of complex realities. Throughout most of the film, only Charlie Cohn steadfastly maintains that his employer is not a Nazi, arguing he must be Jewish because he has a dark sense of humor, speaks Yiddish, and hates Jews. Others are equally sure that Goldman and Dorff are the same man. Is Goldman really the sadistic Dorff? Is he a pathetic victim driven insane by his treatment at the hands of the Nazis? Is Goldman a Jew so mortified by the failure of his people to rise up against "a fate beyond their imagination" that he assumes the burden of atonement himself? Unlike *Judgment at Nuremberg* (1961), which at least offered a qualified conclusion about guilt and innocence under the Third Reich, *The Man in the Glass Booth* leaves the viewer with more questions than answers.

Questions also rest at the heart of the seventies most important Jewish-American filmmaker. Woody Allen is a writer/director whose Jewish background and point of view are central to his art. In the seventies, Allen emerged as the Jewish filmmaker *par excellence,* and one of the finest director/writers ever to work in the American cinema. Laughter is Allen's shield, his protection against an oppressive world. In much the same way as other Jewish comics, Allen's wit functions as a defense mechanism, a form of self-aggression, and a cry of defiance. But at its best Allen's humor goes further. What critic/writer Isaac Rosenfeld observed in a 1962 essay about Sholem Aleichem holds equally true for Woody Allen: his comedy is built on "the incongruity between man's ambitions and his impotence to achieve them." Such a statement defines tragedy as well as comedy, and therein lies the essence of Allen's delicate mixture of the serious and the comic: he laughs at man's ineffectual attempts to obtain what he desires.

The Allen screen persona, therefore, is admired for his dreams while he is simultaneously mocked for his failures. Novelist Saul Bellow writes in his introduction to *Great Jewish Short Stories* (1963) that in much Jewish literature "laughter and trembling are so curiously mingled that it is not easy to determine the relations between the two. At times the laughter seems simply to restore the equilibrium of sanity; at times the figures of the story, or parable, appear to invite or encourage the trembling with the secret aim of overcoming it by means of laughter." Similarly, Allen's comedy blends laughter and trembling, pain and pleasure, into a unified, organic whole. To do so, he assumes the screen role of a modern day Menashe Skulnik, the greatest *schlemiel* (luckless creature) of the Yiddish stage, though with a sense of the absurd and a knowledge of contemporary philosphical thought Skulnik never demonstrated.

All of Allen's films contain Jewish humor and identifiably Jewish characters. In *What's Up, Tiger Lily?* (1966), he takes a routine Japanese spy picture *(Key of Keys,* 1964), re-edits it, and then dubs in his newly written, English dialogue. The resulting parody has Jewish detective Phil Moskowitz, played by an oriental actor (Tatsuya Mihashi), searching to recapture the recipe for the world's greatest egg salad, which has been stolen by the evil Wing Fat (Susumu Kurobe). Allen peppers the picture with various Jewish words and jokes. For example, Wing Fat tells Phil his egg salad is so delicious "you could *plotz* [split]," and the man who originally hires Phil is called the "high *macher* [big shot]." A dying character, Shepherd Wong (Tadao Nakamaru), informs his rabbi that, instead of being buried, he wants to be stuffed with crabmeat. Later, a shocked Wing Fat discovers his mother in a boatload of prostitutes, and her explanation would do any Jewish mother proud: "I decided to take an ocean

Miles Monroe (Woody Allen) wins the Miss Universe contest in a dream sequence from SLEEPER *(1973).*

voyage because you never write." *What's Up, Tiger Lily?* functions as an early film exercise for Allen, allowing him to test his wings before taking a full flight on his own. It also contains, albeit in embryonic form, the type of Jewish figures and humor that will characterize all his screen works.

In *Take the Money and Run* (1969) and *Bananas* (1971), Allen begins to develop as a filmmaker. The earlier picture parodies the documentary, cinema verité format so popular in the sixties and seventies. Allen uses this style to trace the crime career of Virgil Starkwell (Allen), a klutzy criminal who aspires to a career as a daring bank robber. Virgil represents Allen's first screen outsider, a figure who in most of his later movies will inevitably be Jewish. *Take the Money and Run,* like *What's Up, Tiger Lily?,* uses Jewish words as in-jokes. In one scene Starkwell assigns an ex-con, who was once a filmmaker, to "direct" the bank holdup. His plans for the *"shtick-*up," however, go awry when a rival gang decides to rob the bank at the same time.

In *Bananas,* Allen stars as Fielding Mellish, a lovable nebbish who falls for a student activist (Louise Lasser) he discovers demonstrating against the dictatorship in San Marcos. Eventually, after the girl dumps him, Fielding goes on a vacation to San Marcos, gets involved in that country's revolution, and winds up as the nation's new president. Returning to the United States to obtain foreign aid, Fielding is charged with treason (our government thinks the new country is Communist) and thrown into jail. Finally, Fielding is re-united with his student love, and their wedding night is detailed in a play-by-play manner by none other than sports announcer Howard Cosell.

Allen's Jewish wit makes some telling comments. At one moment in the film, San Marcos's ruthless dictator, General Vargas (Carlos Montalban), contacts the United Jewish Appeal for funds instead of the CIA. Politics and religion are mixed as Allen shows the UJA as a political organization as well as a religious one. But Jews are not the only target of Allen's satire; he also takes dead aim at Christian materialism. A television commercial for New Testament cigarettes pitches the cancer-producing product with the following logo: "You stick with New Testament and all is forgiven." With this one statement, Allen simultaneously pokes fun at revivalist rhetoric and lampoons the union of commercialism and religion that characterizes American life.

Allen concentrates even more heavily on Jewish jokes in his next film, *Everything You Always Wanted to Know About Sex* (But Were Afraid to Ask)* (1972) based—improbably enough—on Dr. David Reuben's very popular sex manual of the same name. The movie features seven comic vignettes, short stories really, in which the comedian satirizes modern America's obsession with sex. In one segment, "What are Sex Perverts?," Allen lampoons television game shows. *What's My Perversion?* features a panel of guest stars who try to guess their guests' sexual perversions. One contestant, old Rabbi Baumel (Baruch Lumet), actually gets to act out his perversion on the air: he is bound to a chair, a gorgeous girl whips him, and his wife sits beside him eating pork. For Baumel, watching his wife eat pork, a routine activity for most Americans, is a forbidden activity, a perversion.

In 1972 Allen scripted and starred in *Play It Again, Sam,* directed by Herbert Ross and based on Allen's own successful Broadway play (1969). He plays Allan Felix, a neurotic Jewish film reviewer trying to recuperate from a painful divorce. Unhappy with his own personality, the insecure Allan tries to adopt his idol Humphrey Bogart's sophisticated, tough-guy screen persona, an impossible feat for the balding, timid little Jew. His best friends, Dick (Tony Roberts) and Linda (Diane Keaton) Christie, also try to help the depressed Allan by arranging a series of blind dates for him; each new encounter proves a disaster, as Allan attempts to act like Bogart rather than himself. One night Dick is away on a business trip; Linda and Allan, who have grown closer together as the movie progresses, make love, and Allan is overcome with guilt and shame. Eventually, all is resolved when Linda decides to stay with Dick and Allan meets the girl of his dreams.

Throughout *Play It Again, Sam* there is a constant underlying tension between the successful young executive, Dick, and the unhappy film critic, Allan. Dick's last name, Christie, leads us to see this tension in Jewish/Gentile terms. Allan never quite fits into the world represented by Dick, symbolizing how the Jew never finds his place in Gentile society. Allan's desire for Linda Christie, who is part of Dick's world, shows the side of his personality that yearns for acceptance in that non-Jewish world. In spite of mutual attraction, however, Allan and Linda eventually return to their own worlds.

Allen returned to directing with *Sleeper* (1973), a parody of science-fiction movies. The central character in this picture, Miles Monroe (Allen), is the proprietor of The Happy Carrot Health Food Store. Put into suspended animation in 1973, he wakes up in 2173 to find himself thrust into an alien, totalitarian world. Ethnic jokes, many of them about Jews, abound in *Sleeper.* At one point, two robot tailors—Cohen and Ginsberg—try to make Miles a contemporary outfit. The machines argue constantly with each other, and their finished product is ridiculously large for their diminutive customer. But for all their incompetence, the two robots display a life and charm conspicuously absent in most of the inhabitants of this bland new world. After Miles is captured by government agents and programmed into a near comatose state, his girl friend, Luna (Diane Keaton), and her friends try to recreate his past to shake him out of his drugged condition. Some futuristic Gentiles fake horrible Yiddish accents to help create the moment Miles told his parents he was getting a divorce. Unfortunately, they confuse the meanings of the Yiddish words: the woman playing Miles's mother tells him "stop whining and eat your *shiksa.*" In another recreation from Miles's past, Allen lampoons Tennessee Williams's *A Streetcar Named Desire,* having the actors speak with heavy, Jewish accents. Nowhere in his work is Allen's vision of the Jew as outsider clearer than in *Sleeper.* Miles is an alien in the world of 2173, a man whose Jewish sensibilities are literally out of time and place. Allen envisions a futuristic society that forces its citizens into a uniform blandness, the ultimate extension of the "great melting pot" concept. Miles brings a few sparks of life to this dystopia in which people act like programmed robots.

Allen's art took a major leap forward in *Love and Death* (1975), a film which clearly displays his growing visual sophistication and thematic complexity. Basically, the movie is a visualization of a Russian novel through a comic, Jewish perspective. Allen plays Boris Dimitrovitch Semyonyovitch Grushenko, a cowardly Jewish peasant forced to fight in the Napoleonic Wars in order to save his family's good name and to win the heart of his lovely cousin, Sonia Petrovna Pavlovna Volkonska (Diane Keaton). Once again, Allen's passive Jewish intellectual is out of place, this time in a society dedicated to drinking, dancing, whoring, and fighting. Unsuccessful at all four of these activities, Boris turns philosophical, questioning the existence of God throughout the picture. Early, he dares God to reveal his presence by working some miracle, such as "making Uncle Sasha pick up the check." Sounding much like a put-upon Job, Boris asks Sonia, "If God is testing us, why doesn't he just give us a written?" Boris's obsession with God culminates during his imprisonment for trying to assassinate Napoleon. An angel visits his cell and tells Boris that Napoleon will not execute him. Of course, he is wrong, and Boris is shot in the morning. As the film ends, Boris's spirit tells us that "If it turns out there is a God, I don't think he's evil. The worst you can say about him is that basically he's an underachiever."

An unemployed actor (Zero Mostel) tells Howard Prince (Woody Allen) how the blacklist works in THE FRONT *(1976).*

Howard Prince (Woody Allen) chases a script he will sell for his blacklisted friend Alfred Miller (Michael Murphy) in THE FRONT *(1976).*

A romantic boatride in Central Park is interrupted for Isaac Davis (Woody Allen) and Mary Wilke (Diane Keaton) in MANHATTAN *(1979).*

Alvy Singer (Woody Allen) and Annie Hall (Diane Keaton) walk through the streets of New York City as friends and lovers in ANNIE HALL *(1977).*

In *The Front* (1976), which he neither wrote nor directed, Allen plays the straight dramatic role of Howard Prince, a small-time Jewish bookie who becomes a front for some television writers blacklisted during the fifties. Initially, Howard is a man without much of a conscience or a political consciousness, one who thinks the biggest sin is "to buy retail." As the film develops, however, Howard is forced to abandon his noninvolvement and take a political stand. His friend, blacklisted writer Alfred Miller (Michael Murphy), tells Howard: "You always think there's a middleground you can dance around in. I'm warning you, this time there is no middle." The film proves Miller correct. Harold is hauled before a committee investigating the role of Communists within the television industry and must either inform on his friends or give up his job. By refusing to inform, Howard becomes a *mensch*—a real person. He stands up for his newfound principles, supports his friends, and refuses to buckle under to the committee's intimidation. In Prince, director Martin Ritt shows a Jew to whom history has taught the value of circumspection. Ritt shows his conversion into a man ready to take a stand and fight for his ideals.

Allen's next film, *Annie Hall* (1977), is his most successful, winning four Academy Awards (Best Picture, Screenplay, Actress, and Director), as well as numerous other prizes. Like Paul Mazursky, who brought many of his thoughts about his own heritage together in *Next Stop, Greenwich Village,* so too Allen's *Annie Hall* ties up many of the loose strands about the comic's Jewishness into one artistically satisfying package. The film starts with Allen facing the camera, alone, and delivering a stand-up comedy routine to the audience in the movie theater. He begins with a joke about a Catskill Mountain hotel guest complaining to her friend about how terrible the food is at the resort. "Yes," replies her friend, "and such small portions." He ends the picture with a similar joke. A man complains to his psychiatrist that his brother thinks he's a chicken. "Why not have him committed?" asks the puzzled doctor. "Because we need the eggs," responds the man. Allen turns both jokes into parables, short tales which convey a sense of spiritual truth beyond their comedy. Like the friend in the first story, Allen understands that life is "full of loneliness and misery and suffering and unhappiness and it's all over too quickly." Like the patient in the second joke, he thinks that relationships are "totally irrational and crazy and absurd. But I guess we keep going through them because we need the eggs." Allen thus frames *Annie Hall's* story between two Jewish jokes, and in fact, the entire film presents an almost uninterrupted series of jokes that have meaning far beyond the obvious humor.

Allen's protagonist in *Annie Hall,* comedian Alvy Singer (Allen), is the most Jewish of all his screen characters, a man obsessed with paranoia, guilt, sexual hangups, death and childhood fantasies. He claims, for example, that the Federal government's refusal to support fiscally ailing New York, the city of "leftwing, Communist, Jewish, homosexual pornographers," is clearly an anti-Semitic act: he tells his friend Rob (Tony Roberts) such a refusal is "a matter of foreskin, not economics." Alvy's personal relationships are also dominated by his paranoia. He feels television executives have it in for him because he is Jewish. "Did Jew go to lunch yet?" he imagines them saying, when all they really ask is "Did you go to lunch yet?" Though he sums up life as a mixture of the "horrible and the miserable," Alvy, like the Catskill Mountain hotel guest, absurdly wants a larger portion.

Alvy's bittersweet love affair with the archetypal WASP dream girl, Annie Hall (Diane Keaton), is doomed to failure because of their cultural and emotional differences. She is a blond *shiksa* from Chippewa Falls, Wisconsin, whose favorite expression is "La De Da," who orders pastrami on white bread with mayo and lettuce, and who tells Alvy he's what her Grammy Hall would call a "real Jew." He is the cynical New York Jew, the morbid intellect who only reads books with death in the title. It is through Annie, this refugee from a "Norman Rockwell painting," that Alvy finally comes to accept his own alienation, his own separateness from Gentile America. Of course, Alvy has had trouble with women before. His first marriage ended in divorce when he refused to make love to his wife (Carol Kane) because he was too obsessed with the John F. Kennedy assassination theory. His second marriage disintegrated when his preten-

tious mate would no longer tolerate Alvy's boorish behavior at literary cocktail parties. Even the hippie *Rolling Stone* reporter (Shelley Duvall) describes sex with Singer as a "Kafkaesque experience."

Like many other Jewish screen characters, Alvy Singer displays an obsession with his past. The whole film, of course, is about a love affair now over, about how he won and ultimately lost Annie Hall. Alvy, however, plunges ever deeper into his own personal background. At one point, a frustrated Mrs. Singer (Joan Newman) drags her son to see the family physician, Dr. Flicker. Little Alvy has stopped doing his homework because he has read that the earth will explode millions of years from now. When Flicker tells Alvy, "We've got to enjoy ourselves while we're here, don't we?" the supposed rhetorical question hangs in the air unanswered. Allen also related several other incidents from Alvy's childhood, much of which was spent in a cramped apartment located directly beneath an amusement park roller coaster, but these journeys into the past are not simple flashbacks: the director mixes past moments with Alvy's adult consciousness. For example, at one point Alvy finds himself back in his grammar school classroom, where a teacher punishes him for kissing one of his schoolmates. A grown-up Alvy watches the scene, sitting comfortably at a small elementary school desk.

The scenes of Alvy's past give us some indication of how his Jewish childhood influenced his life. Alvy's Thanksgiving Day dinner at the Halls, however, becomes the film's ethnic highlight, and Allen locates it prominently at the picture's halfway point. There, in beautiful heartland America, amid baked ham and under Granny Hall's menacing stare, Alvy turns into a Hasidic Jew, Allen's visual representation of his character's sense of strangeness. Splitting the screen, the director shows the differences between the quiet, refined Halls at their ham dinner and the raucous, noisy Singers arguing over a brisket. Allen endows the scene with even greater impact by allowing Mrs. Hall (Colleen Dewhurst) to discuss the issue of guilt with Mrs. Singer, as we eavesdrop on their conversation:

Mrs. Hall: How do you plan to spend the

Tracy (Mariel Hemingway) and Isaac (Woody Allen) shop for groceries in MANHATTAN *(1979).*

	holidays, Mr. Singer?
Mr. Singer:	We fast.
Mrs. Hall:	Fast?
Mr. Singer:	No food. To atone for our sins.
Mrs. Hall:	What sins? I don't understand.
Mr. Singer:	To tell you the truth, neither do we.

As Alvy's visit to the Halls continues, however, Allen shows that quiet insanity can lurk under Midwestern calm. Annie's cleancut brother, Duane (Christopher Walken), brags at the dinner table about his wholesome 4H club activities, but later

he calmly tells Alvy that he often contemplates suicide by crashing his car. As a result, when Duane then drives Alvy and Annie to the airport, she rides calmly beside a totally petrified Alvy who knows more about her brother's secret thoughts than she does.

After the astounding critical and financial success of *Annie Hall,* Allen abandoned comedy in his next picture, *Interiors* (1978), which he wrote and directed but did not appear in. The film's only Jewish character, though never specifically identified as such, is Pearl (Maureen Stapleton), the second wife of Arthur (E. G. Marshall), a successful lawyer. Arthur's marriage so soon after the suicide of his coldly proper wife shocks his three, grown daughters—Renata (Diane Keaton), Flyn (Kristen

Griffith), Joey (Marybeth Hurt)—who barely hide their dislike for Pearl. To the girls, she represents an outside force. They fail to see the life she gives their father and the warmth she is capable of bestowing on this stuffy, New England family. Allen highlights Pearl's "otherness" in a number of different ways. Her bright red dresses, for example, clash with the rest of the film's frozen white interiors. Everything about Pearl and Arthur's first wife, Eve, is dissimilar: Pearl collects slightly erotic black ebony figures, Eve gray vases; Pearl enjoys dancing, Eve visiting old churches. Allen even has Pearl literally breathe life into the family. She gives Joey mouth-to-mouth resuscitation after the girl is dragged from the ocean. Indirectly, the film continues Allen's concern for Jewish vs. Gentile tensions and the role of the outsider in society.

Allen's final film of the decade is *Manhattan* (1979), a visually stunning, black-and-white tribute to New York City and the people who inhabit it. Allen plays a Jewish television writer, Isaac David, faced with a variety of problems. His ex-wife (Meryl Streep) has become a militant lesbian and written a book about their relationship that exposes Isaac as an insensitive boor. His best friend, Yale (Michael Murphy), has left his wife, Emily (Anne Byrne), to have an affair with Isaac's ex-girlfriend, Mary (Diane Keaton). Isaac, himself, is in love with a seventeen-year-old nymphet, Tracy (Mariel Hemingway). The film focuses on the shifting relationships between Yale, Emily, Mary, Tracy, and Isaac. At one point Isaac says, "People in Manhattan are constantly creating these really unnecessary, neurotic problems for themselves to keep them from dealing with more unsolvable, terrifying problems about the universe."

Maurice Yacowar's insightful book about Allen's career, *Loser Take All* (1979), shows how the comic's Jewishness shapes the often contradictory aspects of his movie personality: wise-cracking onlooker, persecuted victim, anxiety-ridden weakling, eternal outsider, guilty paranoid, stand-up comic, hopeless but unbowed lover, figure of moral rectitude. Like Chaplin's immortal tramp, Allen's put-upon little Jew usually finds himself locked into conflict with the alien world surrounding him. Only in his latest movies does Allen allow his Jewish personas some respite from their constant struggles against the alien environment they

Isaac Davis (Woody Allen) confronts his ex-wife (Meryl Streep) over a book she has written about their marriage in MANHATTAN *(1979).*

inhabit, perhaps a sign that the offscreen Woody Allen has grown more comfortable with himself.

For Woody Allen, the paranoia, sexual inadequacies, guilt, and fears of his Jewish characters are preferable to the truly scary instability and intolerance that one often sensed in other milieus. In a serious moment, Allen told interviewer Frank Rich that "life is like a concentration camp. You're stuck here and there's no way out. You can only rage impotently against your persecutors." For Allen, that rage takes the form of an unceasing stream of half-comic/half-serious jokes that speak to our fears and uncertainties while they poke fun at our inadequacies. Through his unique blend of laughter and trembling, of horror and of humor, Allen has become the comic conscience of the seventies, a master of sardonic humor that places him in a league with Jonathan Swift and Laurence Sterne.

With the explosion of Jewish gangsters on the screen during the seventies, it was inevitable that Jews would eventually appear on the side of law and order as well. A Jewish cop surfaced earlier in *No Way To Treat A Lady* (1968), and in 1978 Hollywood presented its first Jewish detective: Moses Wine (Richard Dreyfuss) in director Jeremy Paul Kagan's *The Big Fix*. Though I have usually

Private Investigator Moses Wine (Richard Dreyfuss) enjoys a light moment with Lila Shea (Susan Anspach), his former girlfriend in THE BIG FIX *(1978).*

refrained from delving into the backgrounds of the moviemakers who wrote, directed, produced and performed in Jewish-American pictures, it seems necessary to pay at least passing attention to this factor in relation to *The Big Fix*. Kagan, the film's director, is the son of a rabbi and was brought up in a religious household. During a recent visit to Syracuse University, Kagan told me:

> My interest in alienated figures, in outsiders like Moses Wine, comes from my background as a Jew and as the son of a rabbi. The Moses Wine character in *The Big Fix* represents the kind of commitment I associate with Jews. There's an admiration I have for Jews based on the fact that they've been in the forefront of social movements that have tried to equalize the civilizations they've been in. I guess if you get fifteen hundred years of being burned at the stake and being fried in ovens because you're not a Christian you begin to have tolerance for other people. We've been getting the stick for a long time, so I have an identification with those people who are getting the stick now.

Richard Dreyfuss has also commented on his own Jewishness, claiming:

> I am immensely proud of being Jewish, to the point of bigotry....I was raised in Bayside which is ninety percent Jewish. I went every week to Temple Emanuel from the time I was nine until I was sixteen....In a sense, everything I do has to do with my being Jewish.

With its director and its star so aware of their Jewish heritage and how it influences their art, it is no wonder that *The Big Fix* is permeated with a Jewish consciousness that accounts for its tone and feeling, as well as its thematic content.

Dreyfuss's Moses Wine is a kind of counterculture Philip Marlowe. A former sixties radical at Berkeley, Moses is now saddled with a complaining ex-wife, a pair of precocious kids, alimony payments, and a feisty socialist aunt who keeps trying to radicalize her senior citizens' center. He has, however, left his political past behind him. Disenchanted by the failure of sixties activist movements to alter American society, he is now totally apolitical. All this changes when a former lover, Lila Shea (Susan Anspach), re-enters Moses' life. Lila, a worker in the Hawthorne-for-Governor campaign, asks Moses to investigate some dirty political tricks that threaten her boss's election hopes: someone is distributing a flyer that shows Hawthorne with a notorious underground fugitive, thus suggesting an endorsement that could ruin Hawthorne's political future. Once drawn into the case, Moses finds himself on a bittersweet voyage into his political past, a journey that leads him deeper and deeper into a labyrinth of violence, murder, and betrayal. Finally, he unmasks the film's villain, a wealthy businessman (Fritz Weaver) who will go to any lengths, even murder, to keep the class he represents in power.

Like the Jewish characters from *Vengeance of the Oppressed* (1916) to *The Pawnbroker* (1965) to *The Frisco Kid* (1979), Moses Wine is obsessed with the past, in this case his college activist days. His attempt to repress the impulses set free in those times results in a mundane life of boredom. Mostly, his cases are routine. Early in the film, for example, Moses stands counting turkeys outside Poppy's

Poultry as part of an industrial investigation. His private life is no better. He sits waiting for something to happen or he drags his children with him on his silly assignments. But when Lila comes back into his life, Wine suddenly rejoins the living, like a somnambulist snapped out of his trance. Long-dormant romantic feelings spring to life, as the relationship between Lila and Moses blossoms. His political consciousness also returns. As Wine researches the case, he views some television file footage of the riots at the 1968 Democratic Convention. In one of *The Big Fix's* nicer moments, Kagan cuts to Dreyfuss's face as he watches these events, tears rolling down his cheeks in a painful, silent tribute to the idealism that once motivated a generation.

Clearly, Moses Wine is not the hardboiled Sam Spade or the cynical Philip Marlowe. He represents a new breed of private eye: the sentimental shamus. How appropriate that such a deviation from the traditional detective's approach to life comes in the form of a Jewish gumshoe. Usually, the screen detective has no past and no future; he exists only in relation to his present case. Here, however, Moses is haunted by his past and frightened by his future; he is a Jew in the sense that he recognizes his place within time. As Rabbi Abraham Joshua Herschel, the leading philosopher of conservative Judaism, once wrote, "Judaism is a religion of history, a religion of time. The God of Israel was not found primarily in the facts of nature. He spoke through events in history." The political case Moses undertakes unites the past with the present and provides hope for the future.

Through the character of Moses Wine, Kagan calls out to the disenchanted sixties activists, beckoning them back to life and castigating the ennui that has turned America's best and brightest into apolitical nebishes. Though they failed to reorder the world, the ideals of the sixties must be turned into a new kind of action in the seventies. If they are not, warns Kagan, then the sixties were simply an aberration and the people who gave the decade its life merely children unable to sustain their faith in the midst of adversity. In a sense, then, Kagan calls to the children of the sixties who became Jewish marginal men when their inner ideals clashed with society's outward demands. Moses, as

Reuben Warshovsky (Ron Leibman) and Norma Rae (Sally Field) go over union strategy in NORMA RAE *(1979).*

his name implies, functions as a kind of exemplar for these disaffected persons, one who leads himself out of the bondage of inaction, through the desert of confusion, to the promised land of activity, a place defined by each individual through his role in bettering society.

Though some screen Jews of the seventies, such as Duddy Kravitz and Len Cantrow, abandon so much of their heritage that little of consequence remains, other Jewish figures like Reuben Warshovsky in director Martin Ritt's *Norma Rae* (1979) maintain their unique individuality. Reuben (Ron Leibman) enters a totally alien environment and changes it for the better. In the sleepy little Alabama town of Henleyville, a Southern Baptist community dominated by the local textile plant, Reuben finds Norma Rae (Sally Field), an intelligent and spunky woman oppressed by her life of drudgery in the plant. Reuben shows Norma Rae a better way. He inspires her with his zeal for unionizing, a natural extension of her basic sensitivity for others. In spite of the differences between them, Reuben and Norma Rae become friends, people who care about and respect each other. Together, they become the sparks which ignite the downtrodden textile workers into action, into doing something about their exploitation at the hands of the plant's owners.

Though Norma Rae is clearly the focus of this film, Reuben serves as its intellectual force, an outsider with an alternative vision of life. At times, he undergoes slanderous anti-Semitic attacks by the textile plant's managers—though Ritt downplays this overt form of bigotry—even Norma Rae finds his Jewishness curious. "Are you a Jew?" she asks him early in the film, adding: "I never met a Jew before. Heard you all had horns, but you don't look different from the rest of us." To this, Reuben responds, "We are. History makes us different." Indeed, Reuben is a man with a sense of history. His knowledge of the oppression suffered by his people makes him more sensitive to that experienced by all exploited people. But unlike Duddy, Reuben never abandons his basic morality in his quest for a goal. At the end of the film, Norma Rae and Reuben win their victory: the textile workers overcome their fears of the plant's managers and vote to join the union. Ritt, however, does not let *Norma Rae* drift into simple-minded romanticism. Norma Rae and Reuben part as friends, not as lovers. Each has learned something from the other. Neither will be the same again. Both remain individuals who have not subverted themselves to anyone, or anything, else.

The Western is a particularly good example of the way seventies filmmakers tried to infuse traditional genres with ethnic appeal, adding Jews to the typical cast of villains and heroes usually present in such movies. Historically, Jews and other minorities were among the early settlers of the West. San Francisco's Temple Emanuel was founded during the Gold Rush. Jim Harper, a rabbi, traveled throughout the New Mexico territory serving small towns and earning extra money as a rider in Wild West shows. Otto Meers, known as "The Pathfinder of San Juan," was a prospector, Indian fighter, railroad worker, horse trader, and mountain climber; he was also a Talmudic scholar and founder of a frontier synagogue. According to James Yaffe, Meers was the only western hero who spoke Indian languages with a Yiddish accent.

The most elaborate treatment of Jews in the Old West is director Robert Aldrich's *The Frisco Kid* (1979), which features Gene Wilder as a gullible Polish rabbi, Avram Belinski, and Harrison Ford as a soft-hearted, rough-talking outlaw who helps Belinski adjust to frontier life. The film traces the growing relationship between the two comrades as they journey from Pennsylvania to California, where Belinski is to assume the leadership of a San Francisco congregation. Their trek becomes paradigmatic of America's westward migration, and for the first time, the Jew shares the frontier adventures so important in molding America's national character. In *The Frisco Kid,* he contributes to the development of American values, dramatically conveyed via the mutual exchange of values and knowledge between Belinski, the foreigner, and Ford, the native Westerner. This Old West odd couple teach each other wisdom, ethics, and even figures of speech: Ford learns "Oy Veh" and Wilder "She-it."

The most interesting part of the film is Aldrich's handling of the put-upon Polish rabbi who graduated eighty-seventh out of his class of eighty-eight. Early in the movie, Belinski is simply the butt of humor. His naïveté results in his being robbed and stripped, symbolically entering this new land like the helpless babe he is. But Aldrich never robs Belinski of his morality. When, for example, Ford involves the unsuspecting Belinski in a bank robbery, the horrified rabbi promptly sends back his share of the loot, much to the annoyance of the outlaw. In addition, Belinski never forsakes his traditions. He refuses to ride on Saturday, even though he risks getting caught by a posse sent to capture them after the robbery. Finally, Belinski risks death at the hands of Indians by refusing to abandon the Torah he has carried from Poland to place in the San Francisco synagogue he is to lead. This demonstration of his courage and dignity impresses the Indians, and they welcome him as a brother. Belinski, acting like a Borscht Belt social director, seals their brotherhood by teaching the Indians to dance a hora. In the film's climactic showdown, Belinski stands up to a murderous villain, showing an ethical courage that equals Ford's skill with a sixgun.

For all its positive qualities, *The Frisco Kid* is no model of historical authenticity. There is, for example, the too perfect democracy of the Western frontier folk. In his journeys westward, Belinski never encounters anti-Semitism, even at the hands of the villain. His strangeness is by and large accepted, except for a few harmless jokes about his accent made by people who speak English less clearly than he does. In addition, Belinski's observance of religious customs is somewhat selective. He won't ride on Saturday, but he seems unconcerned about the lack of kosher food and eats everything put in front of him. But these are relatively unimportant points. What remains central in *The Frisco Kid* is the way America transforms the Jew and how the Jew, in turn, enhances American life. Helped by the engagingly sympathetic performance of Wilder, Aldrich successfully walks the thin line between amiable sentimentality and mawkishness. Belinski emerges as a person worthy of respect because he respects himself and his own traditions, not because he forsakes his beliefs for American customs. In this sense, the film finds a workable middle ground between heritage and necessity. Belinsky comes to understand and then accept the demands of his new world, while he manages to infuse it with his own sense of morality and tradition.

Seventies filmmaker's paid more attention to the heritage and religion of Jews than did their predecessors. With the emergence of Paul Mazursky and Woody Allen as major American directors whose films demonstrated a consistent Jewish sensibility, the Jewish-American cinema became far more complex and engaging than it had been previously. In addition, the films of the seventies presented a diverse series of Jewish portraits across a vast spectrum of Jewish experiences. Jewish characters now inhabited almost every film genre, possessed both positive and negative traits, and participated in most American occupations. The Jewish-American cinema validated Jews as an integral part of American life; indeed, America could not conceive of itself without its Jews.

Rabbi Avram Belinski (Gene Wilder) finds it difficult to maintain his innocence upon meeting his buxom seatmate in THE FRISCO KID (1979).

Rabbi Avram Belinski (Gene Wilder) frantically holds onto his hat as his horse rears out of control in THE FRISCO KID (1979).

As her proud parents (Barbara Barrie/Sam Wanamaker) look on, Judy Benjamin (Goldie Hawn) marries the man of her dreams, lawyer Yale Goodman (Albert Brooks), in PRIVATE BENJAMIN *(1980).*

Chapter 8

The Eighties

The American film industry entered the eighties with confidence. The year 1979 had been a record one for Hollywood profits, with overall film receipts hitting the eight-billion-dollar mark. Novelist and scriptwriter Budd Schulberg's April 27, 1980, article in *The New York Times* provides some glimpses into the filmmaking business at the start of the new decade. Schulberg found the studios "ready to call themselves major again," buoyed up by electronic marvels "that will revolutionize the very nature of entertainment in America." Even

venerable old MGM, which had essentially stopped making movies in the seventies, was setting up a separate production company to signal its return to the world of motion pictures. "The year 1980," concludes Schulberg, "is a watershed [for the film industry] not unlike 1930 when talking pictures were coming in."

Two films early in the eighties, *Private Benjamin* (1980) and *Ordinary People* (1980), show very different attitudes toward their Jewish characters. Judy Benjamin (Goldie Hawn) in Howard

Zieff's *Private Benjamin* initially appears as an emotionally immature adult. A spoiled Jewish-American Princess from a wealthy Philadelphia family, her life is chugging along according to plan. In fact, the film opens with the ceremonial breaking of the glass at Judy's lavish wedding to an up-and-coming young lawyer, Yale (Albert Brooks). Her proud parents (Sam Wanamaker and Barbara Barrie) give the newlyweds a large check to start their life together, warning Judy she's not to spend it all at Lord and Taylors. Yale, himself, is a neurotic, sex-starved Jewish adolescent. During the reception, while their guests are inside dancing a hora, he lures Judy into a car parked outside and cajoles her into performing oral sex. Later that night in their plush honeymoon suite, Yale degrades Judy, pushing her down to have intercourse with him on the bathroom floor. Though a bit taken aback by Yale's crudeness, Judy worries more about her hair than her pride. She soon discovers that she has more to fear than messy hair; Yale dies right after ejaculating. In the Jewish funeral that follows, Yale's grieving mother begs Judy to tell her what her son's last words were, and then faints when the bereaved Judy responds, "I'm coming."

So at twenty-eight, and having always "belonged to somebody," Judy Benjamin finds herself alone, untrained, and mourning for a lost life with her Jewish Prince. "If this were a movie," she wails, "I would have been Mrs. Alan Bates," a sly dig at the simplistic answer to loneliness Paul Mazursky provides in *An Unmarried Woman* (1978). Instead of finding Alan Bates, Judy runs into a dishonest Army recruiter (Henry Dean Stanton) who sells her on a life in the service by promising luxurious condominiums and assignments in exotic places. But once in basic training, the pampered princess finds no condominiums and nothing very exotic. At first Judy doesn't understand. She complains because fatigues come in only one color and runs afoul of a tough by-the-book sergeant (Eileen Brennan). Soon she learns to defend herself against the streetwise recruits in her multi-racial platoon and ultimately survives. Judy views her survival as a victory, but her distraught parents fail to see that basic training has finally forced Judy to stand on her own. Ashamed of her enlistment, they prefer to tell their friends she is in a mental hospital. "We

The Jewish-American Princess as warrior, Judy Benjamin (Goldie Hawn) in PRIVATE BENJAMIN *(1980).*

Yale Goodman (Albert Brooks) turns Judy Benjamin's (Goldie Hawn) wedding evening into a nightmare in PRIVATE BENJAMIN *(1980).*

*Conrad (Timothy Hutton) tries to commu-
nicate with his emotionally unresponsive
mother Beth (Mary Tyler Moore) in
ORDINARY PEOPLE (1980).*

*Conrad (Timothy Hutton) talks about his
suicide attempts with Dr. Berger (Judd
Hirsch) in ORDINARY PEOPLE (1980).*

gave you everything. Why are you punishing us?"
demands her uncomprehending father, begging
her to come home with him. Refusing, Judy returns
to her platoon, excels during the rest of her basic
training, and gains admittance to an elite fighting
unit—the Thorn Birds.

Later in the movie, Zieff provides Judy with one
more chance to grasp an acceptable version of the
Jewish-American Dream. She has completed basic
training and meets Henri (Armand Assante), a
handsome French gynecologist attending a convention in the United States. The two are immediately attracted to each other, but Judy at first
refuses to sleep with him. After Henri tells her he's
Jewish, however, she hops right into his bed. "Now
I know what I've been faking all these years," she
gushes after having intercourse with the suave
Frenchman. When Judy is stationed in France, she
resumes her relationship with Henri, and the two
eventually decide to marry. On the day of their
wedding, however, she discovers her dream lover
had already been unfaithful and has lied to her
about it. Punching Henri in the face, she stalks from
the wedding ceremony to begin a life of her own.

For all its attempts at modern-day feminism
with a light touch, *Private Benjamin's* vision of
Judaism comes right out of the silent films of
eighty years ago. Basically, Judy's Jewish background is simply used as the butt of the film's
humor, starting with her first wedding, through
her basic training, and ending with the aborted
wedding scene. All the Jewish characters are negative. Judy's father is an insensitive materialist who
prefers watching a baseball game to seeing his
daughter married; her mother is an ineffectual
crier who provides no emotional support. Together, the film implies, they have indulged their
narcissistic daughter to the point where her values
have been warped, her talents destroyed, and her
sensibilities deadened. Judy's Jewish suitors are not
better. Yale conducts business on the wedding day
and has the sexual attitudes of a hyperactive ape.
Henri proves to be a hypocritical philanderer. The
toughness Judy acquires in basic training allows
her to reject her Jewish parents, homelife, and
boyfriends. Zieff seems to be saying that Judaism is
somehow incompatible with maturity, growth, and
independence. To become an adult woman, Judy

must stop being a Jew. *Private Benjamin* virtually celebrates Judy's rejection of Judaism, which it sees as a stultifying and debilitating heritage that hinders her emotional progress.

But if Zieff rejects Judaism in *Private Benjamin,* director Robert Redford sees its worth in *Ordinary People* (1980), the film version of Judith Guest's best-selling novel. After his brother dies in a boating accident, Conrad (Tim Hutton) suffers a severe mental breakdown that culminates in a suicide attempt and his institutionalization. His father, Calvin (Donald Sutherland), reaches out to his surviving son, but his mother, Beth (Mary Tyler Moore), remains incapable of responding to his pain. After leaving the mental hospital, Conrad begins seeing a Jewish psychiatrist, Dr. Berger (Judd Hirsch), who struggles to get the boy to confront his feelings of loss, pain, and guilt over his brother's death. Eventually, Beth can no longer stand the emotional strain this situation puts on her life. She leaves Conrad and Calvin to fend for themselves, to reach some sort of accommodation with their grief, and to renew their relationship with each other.

Because Dr. Berger is a character explored in much less depth than either Calvin, Beth, or Conrad, it is dangerous to read too much into his symbolic role. Yet Redford clearly establishes the Jewish Berger as a positive alternative to the outwardly emotionless Beth, whose refusal to confront her suppressed feelings of rage and pain tear the family apart. She imposes a rigid code of behavior on the household, a disciplined coldness that demands family problems be kept private, eschews outside forces (such as Dr. Berger) to help handle personal matters, and responds to emotional stress by denying its existence. Berger, conversely, encourages Conrad and then Calvin to accept their distress, to talk freely about their feelings. Whereas Beth remains passive when embraced by Conrad, Berger warmly hugs the boy. Beth's spic-and-span, everything-in-its-proper place home conveys her concern for appearances and for a life which must look outwardly normal no matter what the internal struggles. Berger's office is a cluttered, comfortable space, a setting that befits a man who explores the inner rather than the outer concerns of life. It is the Jewish psychiatrist who

teaches this "ordinary" WASP family to express their feelings and emotions. For once, it is the Gentile mother who becomes the focus of the film's criticism, as she deserts her family because she cannot stand the emotional "mess" her son's death has caused.

Emotional "messes," of course, have always been the focus of Woody Allen's films, his Jewish characters bouncing from one trauma to the next with barely a moment to catch their breaths. The eighties present four Allen pictures. In *Stardust Memories* (1980), however, the problems of Allen's protagonist seems different from those shown in his earlier movies. As a successful film director, Sandy Bates (Woody Allen) no longer struggles through life as the put-upon schlemiel endlessly and vainly searching for love and respect. In fact, Bates can barely keep women and an adoring public away from him long enough to eat a meal. No longer are the problems investigated simply the result of a Jewish upbringing or Jewish paranoia. Like Guido, the hero in Fellini's classic *8½* (a film alluded to numerous times in *Stardust Memories),* Allen's Sandy Bates is beset with esthetic concerns (he rejects his producer's desire to lighten up his serious films), public problems (viewers wonder why he doesn't make comedies anymore), and romantic traumas (he is drawn to self-destructive women).

Stardust Memories, however, does contain several familiar elements from Allen's earlier films. For example, Allen includes touches of his old, self-deprecating persona: two of Bates's actresses sit in a screening room and discuss how difficult it was to kiss Sandy during his movie's romantic segments. Bates recalls an incident from his Jewish childhood when he was selected to be Abraham in a Hebrew School play, although he felt much more comfortable in the role of God. Technically and thematically, *Stardust Memories* has moments that also hearken back to previous Allen pictures. Allen's constant shifts between Bates's past and present, as well has his delicate interplay between film illusion and everyday reality, remind the viewer of *Annie Hall.* The film's stunning black-and-white cinematography resembles that of *Manhattan*—both films were shot by Gordon Willis. But more than any of his other pictures, Allen's

Leonard Zelig (Woody Allen) flanked by Presidents Calvin Coolidge and Herbert Hoover in ZELIG *(1983).*

Leonard Zelig (Woody Allen) clowning with heavyweight champion Jack Dempsey in ZELIG *(1983).*

Stardust Memories strives to transcend the specific. "You see reality too clearly," Sandy's psychiatrist tells him. It is precisely this clarity that elevates Allen's films above the specific into the realm of the universal, as the director continues to dissect our modern world with sensitive wit and compelling compassion.

Both these elements of wit and compassion are evident in Allen's next picture, *Zelig* (1983), where he plays Leonard Zelig, the son of a Yiddish actor best known for his role of Puck in the Orthodox version of *A Midsummer Night's Dream*. Leonard has the worst identity crisis in the history of psychiatry: he assumes the physical and mental characteristics of more dominant personalities. Thus, Allen/Zelig metamorphosizes into everything from a black trumpeter, to an opera singer, to a baseball player, to an American Indian, to a Nazi. More importantly, instead of turning into a sideshow freak á là the famous Elephant Man, Zelig emerges as a national celebrity nicknamed "The Human Chameleon." Zelig dolls become commonplace, and "The Chameleon" becomes the latest dance craze. Zelig bursts forth as a true cultural hero discussed by Irving Howe, analyzed by Susan Sontag, and characterized by Saul Bellow. Allen and cinematographer Gordon Willis shot *Zelig* in a pseudo-documentary style, a technical *tour de force* that places Allen into old film clips so superbly that we actually come to accept what never really happened.

In terms of its Jewish content, *Zelig* represents the most devastating film about Jewish assimilation ever produced. At long last, Allen not only talks endlessly about assimilation; he actually shows it within the very texture of the movie. When, for example, a psychiatrist asks Zelig why he wants to look like other people, his answer is painfully simple: "I want to be liked." What better reason for Jews to accept both the outer trappings and inner values of Christian-American society. The film's most disturbing moment occurs when we witness Allen/Zelig, decked out in full Nazi regalia, attending one of Hitler's speeches. Will the Jew go to this length? Will he metaphorically join with his oppressors, simply to become an accepted part of whatever society he currently inhabits? *Zelig* looks like no other Allen film, but its thematic center confronts issues that have obsessed Allen throughout his career. Woody Allen may not have an answer for these complex issues, but at least he refuses to ignore the questions.

Broadway Danny Rose (1984), another in a series of black-and-white films by Allen, depicts another Jewish loser, this time as a hapless theatrical agent. It should be no surprise to any Allen-watcher that his Danny Rose represents some of the worst talent ever assembled, including a one-legged tap dancer, a blind xylophone player, a one-armed juggler, and a stuttering ventriloquist. But for one flickering moment all his bad luck seems over. Danny's best act is Lou Canova (Nick Forte), a once-popular singer who appears ready to ride the crest of the nostalgia craze to renewed prominence. Rose has been supporting Nick for years. In essence, he has become his Jewish mother, soothing his ego, building his confidence, and even paying his debts. Of course, when Nick does finally start to become popular once again, when he actually lands some jobs at second rather than his normal fifth rate clubs, he immediately drops Danny and signs with a more prestigious agent.

Allen's latest movie, *Hannah and Her Sisters* (1986), starts at a family Thanksgiving dinner and ends at a similar meal two years later. In between these symbolic meetings, Allen introduces us to a cast of urban neurotics: Hannah (Mia Farrow), an ex-actress who gives up her career for her family; Elliot (Michael Caine), her husband, who is sexually obsessed with her sister Lee (Barbara Hershey), who lives with an overbearing mentor (Max von Sydow); Holly (Diane Wiest), a middle-class druggie who failed as an actress and now runs the Stanislavski Catering Company. For the first time in one of his movies, Allen casts himself in a supporting role as Mickey Sachs, a chronic worrier about everything from his health to profound philosphical questions. Sachs, Hannah's ex-husband, becomes another of Allen's death-obsessed characters who wander the streets claiming life has no meaning as they continue to search for it.

In one of the film's most hilarious segments, the very Jewish Mickey, who cannot believe in God, attempts to convert to Roman Catholicism. Of course, his parents go crazy, his mother (Helen

Danny Rose (Woody Allen) tries to reason with an irate Tina Vitale (Mia Farrow) in BROADWAY DANNY ROSE *(1984).*

Mickey Sachs (Woody Allen) tries to explain his problems to ex-wife Hannah (Mia Farrow) in HANNAH AND HER SISTERS *(1986).*

Mickey Sachs (Woody Allen) receives some disturbing news in a Park Avenue phone booth in HANNAH AND HER SISTERS *(1986).*

Willy (Michael Ontkean) and Jeannette (Margot Kidder) meet in New York's Washington Square in WILLY AND PHIL *(1980).*

Miller) locking herself in the bedroom and his father (Leo Postrel) not understanding his son's actions. "If there is a God, why does he allow evil? Why were there Nazis?" Mickey questions his father. "How should I know," responds the puzzled old man, "I can't even understand how the can opener works." Mickey cannot comprehend that his father is not worried about death and what happens afterwards. "Why should I worry? If I'm unconscious I won't know it and if I'm not I'll worry about it then," his down-to-earth father responds. Mickey even buys the outer symbols of Catholicism, a crucifix and some statutes, as well as a loaf of Wonder bread and some mayonnaise. By the end of the film, however, Mickey realizes he cannot be anything other than what he is, a skeptical Jewish intellectual. He finally rejects Catholicism, calling it a "die now, pay later" religion.

In a recent interview with Caryn James, Allen talked about *Hannah and Her Sisters* as "an ensemble story about the intersecting lives of groups of characters," a methodology that struck him after rereading *Anna Karenina.* Indeed, Allen once again demonstrates, his incredible ability to weave diverse characters into a stunning cinematic tapestry of intriguing complexity, this time following each of Hannah's sisters through an affair with one of Hannah's men. The movie, with its hopeful happy ending, shows Allen affirming life, though in a slightly reluctant manner. The key scene depicts Mickey watching a Marx Brothers movie. "He realizes," says Allen, "he'll never know whether life has meaning, but maybe it's worth living after all. Maybe life isn't meaningless, and that's the best you can do....Be part of the experience....Enjoy it while it lasts." For Allen, the thinking man must eventually give way to the feeling man, an attitude which marks a new phase and a significant change for Woody Allen.

Film critic Vincent Canby claims that "There is no one else in American films who comes anywhere near Woody Allen in originality and interest. One has to go back to Chaplin and Keaton...to find anybody comparable." Like those revered early masters of the medium, Allen totally controls his pictures, from story idea to shooting to advertising. He wouldn't have it any other way: "If I had to make films without complete control from start to finish, I definitely would not do it." Allen, like Chaplin and Keaton, continually treads the thin line between sentimentality and sweetness. In *Hannah and Her Sisters,* he fashions another stunning film about life and death, love and honesty, alienation and interaction.

The other pre-eminent Jewish-American director, Paul Mazursky, was as busy as Woody Allen during the eighties, completing four very different films: *Willy and Phil* (1980), *The Tempest* (1982), *Moscow on the Hudson* (1984), and *Down and Out in Beverly Hills* (1986). *Willy and Phil* (1980) explores contemporary Jewish/non-Jewish relations in a direct, straightforward, and serious manner. Willy (Michael Ontkean), a Jewish high school teacher, and Phil (Ray Sharkey), an Italian photographer, meet at a Bleecker Street Cinema screening of Francois Truffaut's *Jules and Jim* (1961) in 1970. "They hated the war in Vietnam and they loved Truffaut," says Mazursky on the film's soundtrack, enough reasons to become friends. Soon, both men fall in love with Jeanette (Margot Kidder), a Kentucky country girl come to seek her fortune in New York City. Jeanette moves in with Willy, but she still sleeps with Phil, which doesn't stop Willy from eventually marrying and having a daughter with her. Finally, all three, plus the child, end up in Phil's luxurious Malibu Beach house, an uncomfortable *ménage à trois* that satisfies none of their needs. Jeanette soon tires of the three-way affair, and she moves back to New York. Followed by Willy and Phil, she rejects both of them for Igor, a Russian immigrant. In the film's last scene, Willy and Phil go to see *Jules and Jim* once more.

Ontkean's Willy is a modern, wandering Jew. His vague search for "answers" leads him to a country farm in upstate New York, a Hawaiian beach commune, and an ashram in India. But, as Mazursky tells us, Willy is not even sure what questions he should be asking. He can find contentment of some sort only in various unions with the people he loves most in the world—Jeanette, Phil, and his daughter. For all his desire to engage in meaningful relationships, however, Willy remains unable to make any sort of lasting, personal commitment to an ideal or to a person. In him, Mazursky paints a portrait of the intellectual searching for significance everywhere but in his own heritage. At times,

Willy (Michael Ontkean), Jeannette (Margot Kidder), and Phil (Ray Sharkey) try to create an extended family in WILLY AND PHIL *(1980).*

Willy is not even sure how Jewish he is. When, for example, he finds a Volkswagon he likes, Willy hesitates to buy it because the car is made in Germany. "Are you Jewish?" the car dealer asks him. "Sort of," he responds, "I was bar mitzvahed and go to Passover seders." "Is your mother Jewish?" questions the saleswoman. "Yes," Willy answers. "Then you're Jewish," she concludes.

Willy's mother (Jan Miner) is indeed Jewish. When Willy brings Jeanette home to visit his parents in Brooklyn, his mother alternately brags about her son's high IQ and scolds him for not eating enough. Her major worry is that Willy and Jeanette are not married. Though she tries to be "modern" about this whole situation, she keeps pestering the couple about setting a wedding date. For all her familiar traits, however, Willy's mother is far more accepting than Phil's domineering Italian mama: she demands to be taken back to the airport on the day she arrives in California and discovers that Jeanette and Phil are living together. Willy, Phil, and Jeanette find that peace and contentment are unattainable ideals in the everyday

Dave (Richard Dreyfuss) and Barbara (Bette Midler) Whiteman, a Jewish couple who cannot find happiness despite their wealth, sit atop their Rolls-Royce in DOWN AND OUT IN BEVERLY HILLS (1986).

world of jobs, marriages, and misfortunes. Neither Phil's business successes nor Willy's wanderings make them very happy. The end of the picture finds the two men as they began it, watchers observing the actions of others. It is an American's God-given right to pursue happiness, not necessarily to find it.

The Tempest and *Moscow on the Hudson* are two of Mazursky's least Jewish pictures, though both contain minor characters who are Jews. Mazursky and his wife play Mr. and Mrs. Bloomfield, a wealthy Broadway producer in *The Tempest*. In addition, Henry Gondroff (Jerry Hardin) appears as a Jewish comic employed by an Italian millionaire. Of course, he specializes in jokes about Jews. *Moscow on the Hudson* features Robin Williams as a Russian musician who seeks political asylum in New York City. Mazursky fills the film with immigrants from many nations, including a Jewish refugee from the Soviet Union. Neither

picture, however, contains any lengthy or complicated portraits of screen Jews, but each centers on characters who search for happiness and the American Dream.

In Mazursky's newest film, *Down and Out in Beverly Hills,* The Whitemans seem not only to pursue happiness and the American Dream but to grasp them in a headlock and squeeze. Dave (Richard Dreyfuss) is a coat hanger king who lives in a mansion, drives a Rolls-Royce, and provides his family with everything they need. So why is his wife Barbara (Bette Midler) unable to relax? Why is his daughter (Tracy Nelson), who goes to posh Sarah Lawrence, unwilling to eat? Why is his son (Evan Richards) unsure of his sexual preferences? Why does his dog, Matisse, need a shrink for his pre-anorexic condition? The tentative answers are provided when Dave saves a down-and-out bum, Jerry Baskin (Nick Nolte), from drowning in his pool. (Mazursky based his film on Jean Renoir's classic, *Boudu Saved From Drowning*.) Jerry is a kind of emotional Santa Claus bringing each character what he/she needs, from manly bonding to sexual fulfillment to personal confidence to mature understanding.

The Whitemans are clearly Jewish. Dave sprinkles his conversations with Yiddish expressions like "putz," "nudge," and "schmuck." Jerry and Dave share a Brooklyn background, and they cement their friendship over bagel, cream cheese, and lox sandwiches. Yet Mazursky's portrait of the financially successful Jews remains quite disturbing. What is missing, he implies, is the family strength so evident in many earlier Jewish-American pictures. The wife and husband have an unsatisfying sexual relationship. The parents are so alienated from the son that, in order to communicate with them, the boy makes vitriolic videos that show his mother and father yelling at him. The daughter shares little of herself with her parents, refusing even to introduce them to her boyfriend. The Whitemans are less a family than a series of related neuroses. Each feeds off the other in a sick and sickening manner. Externally, this family is a picture of Jewish success; internally, they represent the destruction of the Jewish family structure.

One of the best comedies to appear so far in the eighties is director Richard Benjamin's loving recreation of television's early days, *My Favorite Year* (1982). Mark Linn-Baker stars as Benjy Stone (née Benjamin Steinberg), a fledgling gagwriter for a Sid Caesar-like comic (Joseph Bologna) in the year 1954. Into his young life drops all his dreams and illusions embodied in the form of his favorite film star, Alan Swann (Peter O'Toole). Unfortunately, Swann has deteriorated into a still charming but totally undependable alcoholic forced to appear on the television program to pay his income taxes. The suave matinee idol and the frenetic Jewish writer make the oddest couple since Felix and Oscar. Yet Benjamin manages to provide us with several delightful moments as we watch a now-older Benjy relive the memorable experience that made him a man.

Though Jewish humor permeates *My Favorite Year,* it becomes pivotal in the unforgettable scene where Benjy takes Swann to Brooklyn to meet his family. Of course, he is mortified by the behavior of his domineering mother (Lainie Kazan), humiliated by his prying uncle and gauche aunt, and embarrassed by the array of Jewish tenants who intrude upon the meal. The whole scene alternately praises and condemns Jewish homelife. In

Benjy Stone (Mark Linn-Baker) shares an intimate first-date dinner with the object of his unrequited affections (Jessica Harper) in MY FAVORITE YEAR *(1982).*

Torquemada (Mel Brooks), the Grand Inquisitor, leads a chorus of singing monks during the Spanish Inquisition sequence of HISTORY OF THE WORLD, PART ONE *(1981).*

one tender moment, for example, Mrs. Steinberg affectionately pats Swannie's cheek (ignoring Benjy's anguished cry that "He's a man not a river") and extols the virtues of a loving family homelife. The next, she screams at her Filipino husband to bring on the next course. Benjy writhes in agony as his Uncle Mortie asks Swann about a nasty paternity suit, concluding with, "Well, did you shtup her or not?" And the sight of his aunt costumed in her wedding dress because she "only wore it once before," reduces Benjy to a blithering fool. This dinner sequence allows one to understand an earlier conversation between mother and son. "What are you ashamed of?" asks Mrs. Steinberg, to which her long-suffering son can only reply, "Everything."

The most disappointing comedy of the decade has been Mel Brooks's *History of the World, Part One* (1981), an uneven romp through history from the dawn of man to the Roman Empire to the French Revolution. Brooks, himself, plays several roles in the movie: a klutzy Moses who drops one of God's tablets, leaving us with ten instead of fifteen commandments; a stand-up Roman philosopher, Comicus; a waiter at the Last Supper; a double for King Louis XVI who arrives just in time for the French Revolution. In his forward to the paperback spinoff from the picture, Brooks speaks seriously about his intentions: "My job as a comedy filmmaker is to point out and remind us of what we are—to humble us, in a way. I want to expose our foibles and to show that we are not such big shots, that we are merely animals with nodules of gray matter in our skulls." Brooks's comedy does, indeed, humble us. In this particular picture, it also humbles some of the great figures of history.

History of the World, Part One's most outrageous section, and the one that some Jews have found quite objectionable, is a lavish musical number about the Spanish Inquisition in which Brooks stars as Torquemada, the Grand Inquisitor. Throughout this Busby Berkeley parody, complete with nuns doing synchronized swimming in a sumptuous pool, Brooks shows shots of Jews undergoing various tortures at the hands of cruel priests. The lines of the song which Brooks (and Ronny Graham) wrote to accompany this sequence display the director's feelings about how religious zealots have persecuted the Jews. Torquemada revels in such torture and explains to the audience:

> We have a mission to convert the Jews.
> We're gonna teach them wrong from right.
> We're gonna help them see the light
> And make then an offer they can't refuse.

The Spanish Jews have done nothing to warrant their treatment. One is simply "flickin' chickens and suddenly dese goys break down my walls." Another is sitting in a temple, minding his own business, listening to some lovely Hebrew music when "these papist persons plunge in/and they threw me in a dungeon/and they shoved a red-hot poker up my ass." Within Brooks's broad, farcical humor, he depicts Jews as victims for simply being different from their Christian neighbors.

As in his earlier picture, *The Producers,* Brooks attacks anti-Semitism, as well as other forms of racism, through his blend of slapstick and scatological comedy. In both films, Brooks treats anti-Semitism with laughter, though his point is deadly serious:

> Nothing can burst the balloon of pomposity and dictatorial splendor better than comedy. Comedy brings religious persecutors, dictators, and tyrants to their knees faster than any other medium. In a sense, my comedy is serious, and I need a serious background to play against. That's why, for example, the Spanish Inquisition was so perfect for me. Poking fun at the Grand Inquisitor, Torquemada, is a wonderful counterpart to the horrors he committed.

"So come on, you Moslems and you Jews," sings Torquemada. "You'd better change your point of views." Point of view is precisely what Brooks's film is all about. By urging us to laugh at the prejudices of earlier generations and by making us understand how destructive these religious excesses were, Brooks points out the evils of racism.

Another Jewish character in search of the American dream, and one who finally captures it, is a familiar figure in the history of the Jewish-American cinema: the cantor's son forced to choose between the synagogue and show business in the latest remake of *The Jazz Singer* (1980). Like Al Jolson's Jakie Rabinowitz, Neil Diamond's Jess Robinovitch feels the pull of modern American music that draws him away from his father's (Laurence Olivier) Orthodox synagogue and toward the world of popular entertainment. "You can't change what has always been," the old man tells his son. "You have to know who you are and where you come from." Rejecting the pleas of his father and his traditional Jewish wife, Rifka (Catlin Adams), Jess journeys to California to find out if his songs are good enough to become hits. They are, of course, and Jess quickly becomes a rock star.

While in Hollywood, Jess becomes involved with the Gentile Molly Bell (Lucie Arnaz), an aggressive agent who opens doors for him in the music industry. At first the two ignore their attraction to each other. But when Rifka divorces Jess because he will not return home to resume their Orthodox life, the two give expression to their feelings of love. Director Richard Fleischer includes several scenes that depict Molly's attempts to understand something of Jess's heritage. At one point, she puts on a white headcover (white symbolizes traditional Judaism throughout the film) and Jess shows her how to perform the blessing over the Sabbath candles. Together, they sip the Kiddush wine, kiss, and make love. Molly's attempts at Judaism, however, fail to mollify Jess's father. When the old man journeys to California to visit his son, he quickly realizes that Jess and Molly are living together. He rips his clothes, a traditional Jewish symbol of mourning, tells Jess, "I have no son," and starts reciting the mourner's Kaddish (the Jewish prayer for the dead).

As in the original, this modern version culminates on Yom Kippur, the holiest day of the Jewish year, the day on which Jews atone for their sins. Unlike the 1927 film, however, the 1980 picture posits no choice between Judaism and American success: Jess can sing the Kol Nidre service and still get to the television studio in time to do his song. After the service, Jess tells his father, who still refuses to speak to him, that now he has "his own congregation that loves his music." He knows who he is and where he is going. Still, the old cantor refuses to speak. Only after seeing a Polaroid of his new grandson, Charles Parker Robinovitch, does

Jess Robinovitch (Neil Diamond) becomes involved with Molly Bell (Lucie Arnaz) in the JAZZ SINGER *(1980).*

Jess Robinovitch (Neil Diamond) presses a picture of his son into the hands of his disapproving father (Laurence Olivier) in THE JAZZ SINGER *(1980).*

Tony, the grandson of Russian Jewish immigrants, consoles his lover Frankie in AMERICAN POP *(1981).*

Joseph (Christopher Plummer), a suave Israeli diplomat, seduces Toni Sokoloff (Sigourney Weaver) in EYEWITNESS *(1981).*

he consent to accept Jess back as one of the living. The film's last scene shows Cantor Robinovitch and Molly in the television studio audience as the joyful Jess performs his songs to an enthusiastic crowd.

The message of the modern version, somewhat different from the original, is that American success and Judaism are not mutually exclusive, a theme underscored by the film's color scheme. Throughout the picture Fleischer uses blue to represent the world of rock and white that of Judaism. In the last two scenes, these two colors mix. When Jess sings the Kol Nidre service, he is dressed totally in white, the color traditionally associated with Yom Kippur. On his head, however, is a glittering, blue yarmulka, a symbol that he is still part of the rock music world. In the film's final sequence, Jess sings his songs dressed in a shiny blue shirt. Around his neck is a pure white scarf, *tallis*-like in its appearance and shape, that reminds us Jess has not forsaken his religion. In the world of *The Jazz Singer,* a Jew may hold onto his heritage.

Ralph Bakshi's animated characters in *American Pop* (1981) fail to find Jess Robins's happiness in contemporary America. But unlike Fliescher in *The Jazz Singer,* Bakshi blames the American dream for this failure, seeing it as an ideal that has lured generations of Americans to their spiritual deaths. "The American dream is realized in the freedom we have, not in the success we achieve," says Bakshi. "The struggle for success saps all our energies and when you get it, what do you have? You have the pressure of remaining there, and you have the crushed bodies of friends and families who were sacrificed along the way."

American Pop follows the fortunes of several generations of a Jewish immigrant family, from Russia at the turn of the century to Los Angeles in the eighties. After his father is murdered by Cossacks, ten-year-old Zalmie and his mother seek refuge in America. Once there, his mother, a sweatshop worker, is killed in a fire, and the orphaned Zalmie joins a vaudeville troupe to pursue his love of music. Eventually, he marries the company's stripper and they have a child, Bennie. But once again fate deals Zalmie a crippling emotional blow: his wife is killed by a bomb meant for a gangster who has befriended him. The stricken father arranges for Bennie to marry the mobster's

Daryll Deever (William Hurt) pursues Toni Sokoloff (Sigourney Weaver), an upper-class Jewish girl, in EYEWITNESS (1981).

daughter and pushes him toward a career in music. "If you won't live my dreams," he tells his son, "then live my life." Instead, Bennie enlists in the Army and is killed in World War II, leaving behind Tony, a son he has never seen.

Tony continues the family's obsession with music. As a young man, he leaves home to seek a musical career in California. Hitchhiking through rural Kansas, Tony has a brief affair with a beautiful blond waitress, and as we later find out, sires an illegitimate son, Pete. The two finally meet when Pete arrives in California looking for his father, who is now a down-and-out pusher. Pete soon joins him. Ironically, this leads to the boy's big break. A rock group he supplies with cocaine hears him singing one of his compositions and helps him record the song that catapults him into rock stardom.

So this great grandson of a poor Jewish immigrant finally realizes the elusive dream of success that his ancestors sought so compulsively. But the cost has been great. Pete has no notion of his roots or his heritage. By the time he has achieved stardom no trace of his Jewishness remains. In one short scene, Bakshi shows Pete passing some Orthodox Jews praying on a street corner. He stops for a moment, entranced by the music of their prayers. Something in him reaches out to these strange figures, a part of his being that he, himself, does not recognize. Then he quickly moves on. Nothing remains of his past, no sense of Jewish history or community. In this sense, then, *American Pop* implicitly attacks the assimilationist ethic so common in Hollywood films. "What has been gained after eighty years of this immigrant family's questing after the American Dream?" asks Bakshi: "They won a platinum record and lost their souls."

A development calculated to cause Jews alarm in the eighties is the growing economic and political power of Arab countries. Using the vast riches gained from selling their oil to an energy-hungry world, Arabs have bought into American life. Some have purchased farmland in Iowa; others have invested heavily in U.S. corporations. Col. Muammar Kaddafi, the oil-rich dictator of Libya, recently gave Georgetown University a large grant to establish a chair in Islamic Studies. A similar grant from Saudi Arabia was rejected by the University of Southern California because it stipulated that control over distribution of the money was to be left in Saudi hands, effectively creating an autonomous unit within the college. The April/May issue of *The Link,* a magazine published by an organization called "Americans for Middle East Understanding," is entirely devoted to attacking the media's negative portraits of Arabs, particularly in conjunction with positive images of Israelis. Editor Jack G. Shaheen, an American of Arab heritage, claims that "the creation of the state of Israel brought about a new Arab image in both motion pictures and on television" and goes on to "consider the possibility that stereotyping of Arabs is the result of a continuing campaign by pressure groups to discredit Arabs, thus preventing the development of American-Arab relations." *The Link* makes some valuable points about the gross caricatures of Arab figures in the mass media, but Shaheen's covert message that Jews are responsible for this distortion, perhaps even in an organized way as the tools of Israel, is a flight of fancy that is itself a stereotypical attack on the Jews for controlling the American media.

One film, director Peter Yates's *Eyewitness* (1981), illustrates that the American media is not totally controlled by Jews sympathetic to Israel by reversing the positive image of Israelis that Hollywood presented throughout the forties, fifties, and sixties. In fact, the movie totally alters the traditional silent stereotype: an upper-class Jewish girl, Toni Sokoloff (Sigourney Weaver), becomes romantically entangled with a lowerclass Irishman, Daryll Deever (William Hurt). Of even more interest, however, is the film's Israeli character, Joseph (Christopher Plummer), a suave diplomat who turns out to be a murderer. Early in the film, Toni and her parents admire Joseph for his eloquent and impassioned speech urging Jews to do everything in their power to obtain the release of their co-religionists suffering in Russia. His speech provides the first clue that associates Joseph with a murdered Vietnamese businessman, Mr. Long. The Israeli government has paid Long to arrange for the release of Jews held captive in the Soviet Union. But when he raises the price for his services and threatens to expose the entire operation if his outrageous demands are not met, Joseph kills him.

Later, when Joseph thinks Deever knows about the murder, he decides that Daryll, too, must be eliminated, even though he is an innocent bystander in this game of international terror and intrigue.

Joseph is not unlike Ari Ben Caanan of Otto Preminger's *Exodus* (1960), struggling heroically against overwhelming odds to protect the homeland for his persecuted people. Both men are dedicated to a cause above all personal, or even moral, considerations. But whereas Preminger saw this dedication as positive, Yates and screenwriter Steve Tesich emphasize its negative side. Joseph's total adherence to his goals allows him to justify murder. The filmmakers excuse his murder of Mr. Long by presenting the latter as an unethical go-between willing to sell his services to the highest bidder regardless of the consequences. But Joseph's willingness to kill Deever, the film's most positive figure, forces us to recognize his moral blindness and reject his overzealous dedication.

The character of Joseph is the first negative depiction of an Israeli in Hollywood's history, and as such, represents a significant event in the evolution of the Jewish-American cinema. Throughout the picture, Joseph's actions are sanctioned by the Israeli government. Thus, he represents more than an isolated lunatic fringe of dedicated fanatics; he embodies Israeli policy. In effect, Joseph's actions come to symbolize the corruptness of an entire nation that has lost its soul. Such a portrayal springs from a changing American perspective on the Middle-Eastern situation, one that encourages more negative portraits of Israeli and more positive images of Arabs. Implicit in this new view of Israel symbolized by Joseph is a terrible, unspoken irony: by sanctioning murder in defense of its national policies, Israel has become as blind and as cruel as Nazi Germany. Thus, the pristine dream of statehood based on historical and ethical imperative Preminger presented in *Exodus* becomes a corrupted vision of violence in *Eyewitness*.

Warring factions that refuse to co-exist in the Mid-East are also the subject of director George Roy Hill's controversial adaptation of novelist John le Carre's bestseller, *The Little Drummer Girl* (1984). This film sparked a great deal of Jewish ire because it showed Israelis sympathetically present-

An unsuspeacting pawn caught between Israeli and Palestinean factions, Charlie (Diane Keaton) must fight for survival in THE LITTLE DRUMMER GIRL *(1984).*

Super-terrorist Khalil (Sami Frey) confronts Charlie (Diane Keaton) when he suspects her loyalties in THE LITTLE DRUMMER GIRL *(1984).*

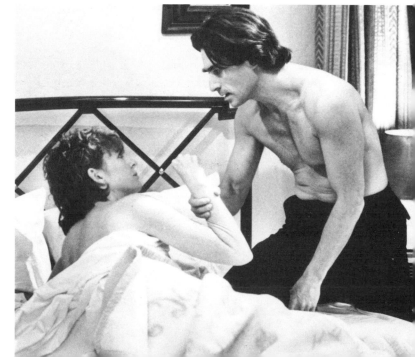

Heroes of the 1924 Olympics, Eric Liddell (Ian Charleson) and Harold Abrahams (Ben Cross) in CHARIOTS OF FIRE *(1982).*

depicted with such simplistic acceptance. In fact, one of the picture's ironies is that a war-weary Israeli agent (Yorgo Voyagis) presents this position so effectively. Once Charlie goes on her undercover mission to the Palestinian training camp, she constantly encounters "freedom fighters" who proclaim themselves to be anti-Zionist rather than anti-Semitic. The filmmakers seem to accept their distinction as being both sincere and correct. Second, Jewish-Americans denounced the movie's portrait of ruthless Israeli agents. They were particularly offended by the characterization of Kurtz (Klaus Kinski), a manipulating, almost psychotic, espionage chieftain. In one of the most emotionally brutal brainwashing sequences ever filmed, Kurtz breaks down Charlie's psychological and emotional defenses, eventually convincing her to seduce and finally to set up the murder of an elusive Arab leader, Khalil (Sami Frey). Ironically, this plot line harkens back to a popular silent film, *Judith of Bethulia* (1914), in which another maiden is called upon to seduce and then destroy Israel's enemies. Once she has played her part, however, Charlie is left to her own shaky devices, now unable to function in her theatrical world because of the role she has played so well in the real world of betrayal, terrorism, and brutality.

Chariots of Fire (1982), unlike *The Little Drummer Girl,* stirred up few controversies though perhaps it should have. The surprise winner of the 1982 Oscar for best picture; its stylish production, invigorating musical score (by Vangelis), stirring story, and uplifting ending caused many viewers to cherish this tale of two runners competing in the 1924 Olympics. Unfortunately, often missed or at least tactfully ignored, was the film's implicit anti-Jewish sentiments. An objective treatment is implied from the beginning of the film when the title, "A true story," appears. A closer look at this particular movie, however, shows how its creators subtly infuse it with a particularly Christian bias, one that makes Judaism far less acceptable than Christianity.

Director Hugh Hudson constructs the film via a series of cuts back and forth between the lives of the two athletes, an editing structure that invites comparisons between the two men. Eric Liddell

ing the Palestinian position. The convoluted tale follows the adventures of Charlie (Diane Keaton), a guillible actress, as she alternately takes sides with Palestinian terrorists and Israeli assassins. Much of the time both Charlie and the viewer are unsure who is on what side, as Israeli agents masquerade as Arab agents and Arab radicals pretend to be peaceloving diplomats. This is the "theater of the real," one Israeli tells Charlie, though separating the real from the unreal becomes one of the most difficult tasks in the film.

Two things about *The Little Drummer Girl* angered the Jewish community the most. First, they objected to the Palestinian point of view being

(Ian Charleson) is a Christian missionary and the national hero of Scotland. He runs to honor God; he even refuses to race on Sunday, though it may mean forfeiting his chance for an Olympic medal. In fact, in one scene after he wins a race in the rain, Eric talks about loving Christ as the best way to run a straight race. Miraculously, the downpour suddenly stops and it becomes sunny. Eric, the perfect Christian, sees running as a form of worship, of showing God he appreciates the gifts bestowed upon him.

Harold Abrahams' (Ben Cross) motives for running are quite different from Eric Liddell's. Harold seems to run in order to get back to a Christian world that has denied him access to its upper levels of power. "They lead me to water," he says early in the film, "but they won't let me drink." Yet, except for some snobby comments by the Master of Trinity College, Harold is never seen as the victim of anti-Semitism. His classmates respect and even envy him. He wins the most sought-after girl (Alice Krige) in the picture, a beautiful non-Jewish actress to whom his religion is a matter of indifference. He triumphs in the Olympics. So when Harold claims "I'm going to take them on one at a time and beat them," a viewer can only wonder who he is talking about and what experiences have made him so bitterly obsessed with winning. Finally, one must question why, given these feelings, Harold eventually converts to Christianity, since it is obviously a Christian funeral that frames the film. Does he, as Pat Erens suggests, place ambition and assimilation above personal and religious commitment?

A small scene clearly points up the emotional distinctions between these two men. Harold's trainer, Sam Mussabini (Ian Holm), shows him a slide of Eric running. He says that Liddell is not a sprinter, but a "true runner" because he has "heart." Sam then tells Harold that he is a sprinter and that sprinters run on "nerves." Mussabini's speech implies that running on heart is superior to running on nerves; one is natural and the other neurotic. In fact, Sam's very presence goes to the center of the matter. To win the Jew must hire a professional coach, while the Christian can simply train with his friends. Eric can switch events at a

Contemporary Jews as strangers, Danny Saunders (Robby Benson) and Reuven Malter (Barry Miller) in THE CHOSEN *(1982).*

moments notice and still triumph. Harold chokes and loses a race he should have won. When Eric refuses to run on Sunday, another runner gives him a note which reads, "He that honors me, I will honor." Therefore, when he wins God seems to be behind the victory. Conversely, when Harold wins it is because he had the money to hire a professional coach. Throughout the picture, the Christian wins for God, while the Jew competes for nothing higher than personal glory.

The Chosen (1982) presents a far less harsh but equally complex portrait of Jewish life, this time in America. As such, it ranks as one of the most interesting pictures of Jews ever to emerge from Hollywood. The story recounts the growing friendship between two teenage boys: Danny Saunders (Robby Benson), the brilliant son of a charismatic Chassidic rabbi (Rod Steiger), and Reuven Malter (Barney Miller), the scholarly son of a secular, intellectual journalist (Maximilian Schell). Set in the Brooklyn of 1940, Kagan's movie becomes a fascinating and intricate study of Jews confronting each other as near strangers and moving toward true understanding. At first, Reuven has far more in

The beautiful and delicate Hadass (Amy Irving) serves a perfect meal to Avigdor (Mandy Patinkin) and his study partner (Barbra Streisand) in YENTL *(1983).*

common with American Gentiles than with the black-clad Danny, whom he sneeringly describes as "stepping out of another century." Soon, however, the two draw closer together out of a common love of learning. Danny helps Reuven understand his heritage, and Reuven aids Danny's secretive study of Freud. Though the two part when Reb Saunders forbids Danny to see Reuven in retaliation for Mr. Malter's passionate Zionism, the boys finally recapture their friendship at the film's conclusion.

The Chosen is probably the most Jewish commercial movie ever made, in that it delves deeply into Jewish customs and traditions. Kagan carefully explains each item he introduces, a tactic which slows down the film's pacing, but his insistent faithfulness to Potok's popular novel makes the picture reverberate with touching sincerity and poignant authenticity. The crucial issue here is

Kagan's refusal to apologize for the film's ethnicity, through which he develops the larger themes of youthful rebellion, painful adolescence, father/son conflicts, true friendship, and familial love. Even Danny's final refusal to become a rabbi, a decision which breaks a five-generation tradition, is not seen as a rejection of Judaism. Rather, it is an affirmation of Jewish freedom of choice: the battle of the son to become a man who honors his religion and his heritage by asserting his uniqueness and using his God-given intellect to better mankind.

Together, Reuven and Danny unite Jewish traditions of secular social involvement and spiritual torah scholarship. Each, for Kagan, enriches the other. Thus, Judaism adds to American life via the religious Danny's decision to study psychology at Columbia University, and American life alters traditional Judaism through the secular Reuven's choice to become a rabbi. In *The Chosen,* Judaism and Americanism are not mutually exclusive goals; in fact, one nurtures the other so that both grow and prosper. The characters in this film are American Jews seen equally clearly as Jewish Americans.

Without a doubt, the most lavish film ever to feature a Jewish female protagonist is director/star Barbra Streisand's $20 million production of *Yentl* (1983). Streisand had fought to do this film since 1968, when she first read and fell in love with I. B. Singer's wry tale ("Yentle, the Yeshiva Boy") of a Polish rabbi's daughter who disguises herself as a man to study at a Yeshiva. Initially, every studio turned the project down, even with the attraction of having the industry's most bankable female star in the lead. Studio head after studio head told Streisand the project was "not commercial," that it was "too ethnic." But Streisand persisted because the dream of directing this movie had become very important to her on a personal as well as professional level. Singer's story appealed to her as a woman forced to act like a man in the male-dominated hierarchy of Hollywood. It also allowed Streisand to reconstruct her own past, creating a statement for her father who died when she was just fifteen months old. "I suppose this film gave me a chance to have the father I could only imagine," she recently told an interviewer. Finally, *Yentl* came to symbolize Streisand's strong commitment to Judaism. Her preparation for the film, during which she immersed herself in Jewish studies, engendered her return to her own cultural roots, culminating with her endowing a medical chair in her father's name, supporting a Jewish elementary school, and funding a Center for Jewish Cultural Arts at UCLA. Unfortunately, *Yentl* was an artistic and commercial failure, as Streisand allowed its dramatic pacing to drag, included a mediocre musical score, and shot a visually uninteresting movie.

As his earlier novel, *The Confessions of Nat Turner,* divided the American Black community, so William Styron's *Sophie's Choice* angered many in the American Jewish community. Jewish critics like Alvin Rosenfeld and Jewish writers like Cynthia Ozick attack it. Rosenfeld castigates Styron for taking the Holocaust out of "Jewish and Christian history" and placing it within "a generalized history of evil; for which no one in particular need be held accountable." Ozick claims Styron has taken the easy slide from "the particular to the abstract," and feels sadness to see such a "compassionate

Alan J Pakula, screenwriter and director of SOPHIE'S CHOICE *(1983).*

perceiver go down that cold road." Others, like historian Richard Rubenstein, feel "enriched because this son of the South and heir of the slave tradition has found his own unique way of exploring this unique historical tragedy."

Director Alan Pakula's film found as many supporters and detractors within the Jewish-American community as did Styron's novel. His picture faithfully follows the heartbreaking tale of Sophie Zawistowka (Meryl Streep), a Gentile survivor of Auschwitz; Nathan Landau (Kevin Kline), her tormented Jewish lover; and Stingo (Peter MacNicol), an aspiring Southern writer. An important point too often overlooked is that neither the film nor the novel is really about the Holocaust; rather, both relate how the relationship with a Holocaust survivor fires the imagination of an impressionable young author. In fact, Pakula chooses to separate the death camp scenes from the rest of the picture

Nathan (Kevin Kline), Sophie (Meryl Streep), and Stingo (Peter MacNicol) ride the Magic Carpet Slide at Coney Island in SOPHIE'S CHOICE *(1983).*

by shooting them in a sepia tone and by having his characters speak Polish or German with subtitles running underneath the images. Such an aesthetic choice places these sequences into some nightmare realm removed from the more natural reality which dominates the remainder of the movie. Even the horrible moment when Sophie's "choice" is revealed seems somehow less powerful, less real, than the other parts of the film because Pakula has so relentlessly distanced us from its full emotional impact.

More than the entire Holocaust issue which has preoccupied so many critics, the significant Jewish element in *Sophie's Choice* (1983) is the demonic portrait of the insane Jew, Nathan Landau. Styron and Pakula present him as just one more brutal man who vents his rage on the long-suffering Sophie. The Germans tortured her body, and Nathan abuses her mind. In fact, he even succeeds where the Nazis have failed: he induces Sophie to her death. The tortured Jew is equally cruel to the vulnerable Stingo, alternately encouraging his literary efforts and ridiculing his writings. Kline's Nathan emerges as a larger than life figure who boldly swings from bridges and elegantly costumes himself for outlandish parties. Unfortunately, his deeply disturbed personality makes the brilliance and charm pall beside his vicious behavior and sadistic personal attacks on people who care about him.

The Big Chill (1983) demonstrates that negative Jewish stereotypes remain alive and well in the Hollywood consciousness. The film presents a reunion of sixties archetypes for the funeral of their former leader, a brilliant student who has committed suicide. Among them is Michael (Jeff Goldblum), once a radical journalist then a ghetto schoolteacher and now a writer for *People* magazine. The plot consists of a series of gatherings over the ensuing weekend, as the group relives old times, resets new priorities, and rearranges their relationships for middle age. Throughout this process, Michael—the Jewish intellectual who gave up serious writing for gossip reporting—fares the worst. For example, one old friend (Mary Kay Place) is a single lawyer so desperate for a child that she propositions all the men in the group—

Dutch Schultz (James Remar), the savage crime king, pours champagne for his girl (Diane Ladd) and their friends in THE COTTON CLUB *(1984).*

except Michael. Even when he volunteers to father the baby, she turns him down. In fact, everyone at one point or another makes love to someone else during the weekend to reaffirm their continued intimacy—except Michael. He sleeps in his childish airplane bed, an apt symbol of his emotional immaturity, bereft of both sexual passion and emotional fulfillment.

Another repugnant aspect of Michael's personality is his use of the funeral for business purposes. Obsessed with opening a chic New York City nightclub, Michael comes to the funeral looking to convince his now wealthy ex-roommates to back his dubious enterprise. Finally, in his most callous gesture, Michael even attempts to seduce his dead

Michael (Jeff Goldblum, seated) tries to console the young girlfriend (Meg Tilly) of an old college roommate who committed suicide in THE BIG CHILL *(1983).*

buddy's young girlfriend with a series of distasteful overtures. Though director/writer Lawrence Kasden gives Michael some of the movie's funniest lines, the audience quickly realizes that his cynical humor merely masks his basically superficial, and selfish, view of life. As a writer for *People* magazine, Michael sums up the existence of others in six short paragraphs, or as he puts it, in as much time as it takes for one toilet sitting. His artistic-radical aspirations have degenerated into excremental musing.

Though *The Big Chill* does not explore Michael's Jewishness or use it as an excuse for his obnoxious activities, he clearly remains the least likable character in the picture. At the conclusion of the film, when the other figures seem to have sorted out their lives at least a little bit, Michael remains essentially as shallow as when the weekend started. "I'm going to write a novel about this weekend," he proudly declares at their last meal together. "What were you going to write your last book about?" asks one of his friends. "Last weekend," he replies, barely recognizing the sad irony of his response.

Horror and humor inform director Francis Ford Coppola's extravagant (estimates of its cost run from forty-five to sixty million dollars) story of crime and music in the legendary Harlem of the twenties and thirties, *The Cotton Club* (1984). As such, the movie displays a virtual compendium of ethnic groups battling for supremacy over New York City's crime world. Jews, Irishmen, Blacks, and Italians vie for power in the city's grimy backstreets and bustling nightclubs. But even here, in a world of sudden violence and deadly mayhem, the Jew remains an outsider. The most vicious portrait in the picture is of Dutch Schultz (James Remar), whose real name was Arthur Flegenheimer. For example, the most brutal moment in a picture dripping with violence is when Dutch almost literally cuts out the heart of his major rival. The motivation for his brutality is when the man declares, "A Jew is nothing but a nigger turned inside out!"

Dutch's main hitman is Sol Weinstein, played by the leader of the experimental Living Theater, Julian Beck. Characterized by one of the other figures as "the golem," Sol is a chilling portrait of violence depicted with frigid understatement. Both Dutch and Sol remain alienated outsiders even in

Boyhood friends (Robert De Niro/James Woods) from the lower East Side become adult criminal partners in ONCE UPON A TIME IN AMERICA *(1984).*

Rose (Herta Ware) and Bernie (Jack Gilford) Lefkowitz as the obstinate Jewish couple who reject immortality in COCOON *(1985).*

David (Richard Gere) is so struck with the beauty of Bathsheba (Alice Krige) that he contrives her husband's death in KING DAVID *(1985).*

this realm of archetypial outsiders. The suave and savvy Italians who finally take over the territory view Dutch's violent outbursts as brutal and animalistic. Even more importantly, the Jewish gangsters don't operate under the same code of honor as do their Italian counterparts. They are not to be trusted. They cannot be counted upon to behave as "gentlemen" or abide by the rules that make it possible for these warring factions to co-exist, no matter how uneasily.

Another world of betrayal, terrorism, and brutality is that created by director Sergio Leone in *Once Upon a Time in America* (1984), a sprawling film which traces the lives of some Lower East Side Jews from 1923 through 1933 up till 1968. Central are the criminal careers of David "Noodles" Aaronson (Robert De Niro), a composite character based on Jewish gangsters Bugsy Siegel and Meyer Lansky, and Maximillian Bercovitz (James Woods), the brilliant and ruthless leader of "the Company." What is perhaps most frustrating about this film is Leone's failure to investigate his Jewish characters in any depth. In fact, except for a couple of expressions, mannerisms, and moments, the characters seem to have no connection to any discernible form of Judaism, either religiously or culturally. It's as if Leone realized that one too many gangster films had been made about Italians, so he arbitrarily decided to shift the ethnic terrain to Jews, a culture about which he knew little and communicated even less. In addition, the presence of Robert De Niro, so well-known for his *Godfather II* role as the young mobster Don Corleone, simply adds to one's feeling that these are very Italian Jews. *Once Upon a Time in America* remains a sadly misguided effort from a talented director, a film with snatches of visual beauty that mask a basically superficial viewpoint.

Four films from the summer of 1985 demonstrate that Jewish stereotypes continue to thrive in contemporary Hollywood: *King David, Goonies, Cocoon,* and *St. Elmo's Fire.* Another misguided effort from a talented director is an apt description for *King David,* Bruce Beresford's bewildering Biblical potboiler. Actually, the first hour of the picture depicts a rather interesting portrait of King Saul (Edward Woodward), as his attitude toward David (Richard Gere) evolves from admiration to affection to jealousy to fear to madness. But, once David becomes King of Israel, the movie meanders aimlessly from one incident to the next with little dramatic tension, character development, or even plot coherence. For example, director Beresford (along with writers Andrew Birkin and James Costigan) present only superficial interactions between David and his second-born, Absalom (Jean-Marc Barr), so when the King rolls in the dirt and cries aloud to mourn his son's death his grief becomes absurdly histrionic. Other characters, such as David's eldest son Amnon (James Coombes) and his daughter Tamar (Gina Bellman), appear so fleetingly as to be almost non-existent. Even the lovely Bathsheba (Alice Krige) has little to do except stand around, look beautiful, and mumble some forgettable dialogue every so often. Never is the adultery between two of the Bible's lustiest sinners ever explored, analyzed, or even presented very erotically.

The saddest part of *King David* is that Beresford obviously strives to create a different kind of Biblical film, one unlike the silly costume epics so popular a generation ago. "I wanted to do the film in as realistic a way as possible," Beresford told an interviewer. For a while it almost works. The world of King Saul is a brutal, primitive environment where religion and politics dominate daily life. When, for instance, the prophet Samuel (Denis Quilley) tells Saul to obliterate the Amalekite king, the infidel's head is immediately severed from his body. Later, Beresford shoots the famous battle between David and Goliath without special effects and in a very believable manner. Cinematographer Don McAlpine fills this section with dark and dismal scenes, and one can almost feel the oppressive atmosphere created by Saul's Lear-like descent into madness.

While Beresford captures the starkness of ancient Israel, as well as the political intrigue between Saul and David, he fails to incorporate a religious consciousness into the film. "This is not a film about religion," claims producer Martin Elfand. "It's about a large group of people trying to work things out and live their lives." Of course, Judaism was the center of their lives, so to ignore it is to misrepresent the very crux of their existence. Equally strange about Elfand's statement is the fact

Chunk (Jeff Cohen), the George Sidney of the eighties in GOONIES *(1985).*

that the filmmakers employed two renowned religious experts as technical advisors. Dr. Jonathan Magonet, head of the Bible department at Leo Baeck College (London), worked with Gere, Woodward, and Krige, instructing them on the historical personages they portrayed in the movie. Rabbi Hillel Avidan was a constant observer of the actual filming both in England and in Italy. At one point, he noted that a scroll used in one of the scenes was printed in the incorrect Hebrew script and spent several intensive days rewriting the artwork that would be seen on camera. Yet even with the expertise of Magonet and Avidan, *King David* remains devoid of a vibrant religious sensibility. The filmmakers may have captured the outer shell

The new women of the eighties, Mare Winningham, Demi Moore, and Ally Sheedy of ST. ELMO'S FIRE *(1985).*

of Judaism, but they never present it as a vital tradition which informs the characters and events in the picture.

Goonies includes Chunk (Jeff Cohen) as the Jewish representative in an ethnically mixed bunch of kids known as the Goonies. Chunk does several things which typify him and, in fact, paint a portrait of Jews common since the early days of silent pictures. His language is sprinkled with references to Jewish elements in his culture. While exploring his friend's attic, where they find a treasure map, Chunk exclaims that all he has in his house are "left-over Hanukkah decorations." Later, he describes bullet holes as "the size of matzah balls." When confronted with the film's villain, the cow-ardly Chunk is reduced to mumbling some Hebrew prayers, which provide him with scant protection.

Chunk's most typical actions revolve around his relationship with Sloth (John Matuszuk), a mis-shapen and ill-treated creature who ultimately saves the Goonies from the clutches of some hoods. For a good part of the film, Chunk is tied up with Sloth; in fact, he misses much of the action segments. Finally, he takes pity on the monster kept chained and locked up by members of his own family. It is his act of compassion which convinces Sloth to turn against his family and help the Goonies. At the end of the movie, Chunk declares he will take Sloth home to live with him and his own family, an appropriately fat and constantly eating crew. So, once again, the Jewish outsider shows compassion for other outsiders, this time a hideous-looking but tender-hearted monster.

Chunk is both a physically and emotionally familiar figure. In fact, he represents an uncomfortable reincarnation of an earlier age's archetypal Jew, George Sidney. Like Sidney's Nathan Cohen, Chunk is fat, emotional, funny, volatile, compassionate, and very Jewish. For much of the story, Chunk functions as the butt of the film's humor, though he is given an incongruous heroism at its climax when he becomes "Captain Chunk." Yet no small amount of bravery can counteract the portrait of the scarred, obese figure who screams and eats his way through most of the film. Director Richard Donner and Executive Producer Steven Spielberg, however, do endow Chunk with a sense of personal kindness and private compassion, traits which allow him to rise at least a bit above the ethnic stereotypes which threaten to overwhelm him.

If Chunk is a throwback to male stereotypes, Wendy Beamish (Mare Winningham) and her parents (Martin Balsam/Joyce Van Patten) in *St. Elmo's Fire* represent a return to the Jewish family struggles depicted in the films of the sixties. First of all, Wendy is an almost totally assimilated Jewish woman, even to the point of attending Catholic Georgetown University. Wendy's wealthy parents cannot understand why she wastes her life working in the Department of Human Services, worrying about her weight, and loaning money to a married Christian musician (Rob Lowe). Mainly, they want her to settle down with a nice Jewish boy like Howie Krantz (Jon Culter) and give them a few grandchildren.

The most overtly Jewish scene occurs when Wendy goes home for dinner with Billy the musician. Her father, a wealthy greeting card manufacturer, constantly brings up news of their Jewish friends. Her mother whispers certain words like "cancer," "drugs," and "money," words that should not be said too loudly in public. To Mr. and Mrs. Beamish, "family business is important," whereas for Wendy her college friends have become more important than her mother and father. In fact, she is part of an extended family where ethnicity, relatives, and religion are simply of passing interest. Finally, Wendy must leave the stifling environment of her parents' house, though she expresses a strong love for them. Like so many Jewish men and women of the past, Wendy finds freedom away from her childhood home, her given religion, and her cultural identity.

Finally, there is *Cocoon*. Director Ron Howard and screenwriter Tom Benedek turned a story by David Saperstein into the surprise summer hit of 1985. The story of a group of retired Florida residents who meet some altruistic aliens who offer them immortality struck a responsive cord in a gradually aging American population. Viewed from one perspective, therefore, *Cocoon* is the baby boomer generation's first confrontation with their own mortality. The reaction from a generation accustomed to getting its own way is, as one might expect, rather optimistic: Death won't get us. At the last moment some supernatural happening will save us from the fate of others who went before us. Yet one dissenting vote is cast in this film, the Jewish Bernie Lefkowitz (Jack Gilford).

The film opens with Bernie cast as the grouch. Unhappy with his life, unwilling to be flexible, he complains about most everything. Eventually, these traits result in tragedy. When his friends tell Bernie about the life-restoring powers of the aliens' pool, he refuses to believe them or to use the miraculous water to help his wife. Finally it is too late for the gentle Rose (Herta Ware). In one of the film's most emotional moments, Bernie brings Rose's lifeless body to the pool and begs the extraterrestrial to give her back to him. His inability to believe anything beyond his five senses has doomed the person most precious to Bernie.

Yet perhaps even more crucial is Bernie's refusal to accompany his friends to the aliens' home planet. This is not done out of fear. Instead, Bernie articulates a philosophical position: "I'll play out the hand I was dealt." Though the film never explores his ethnic identity, Bernie's plain response echoes many Jews over the centuries. He accepts what God has given him. He knows you cannot really cheat death by leaving on a spaceship, even if that is what an audience wishes to believe. Bernie does not ignore the possibility of supernatural intervention; in fact, he has witnessed it first hand. But he plants himself firmly on the side of those who do not seek it. By rejecting this possibility of immortality, Bernie simply accepts the human condition, a state characterized by our movement toward death from the moment we are born. For Bernie, surviving is a matter of living life not avoiding death.

As they survived in the "real" world that at times threatened their very existence, so Jews have survived in the "reel" world of the cinema. The Jewish-American films discussed here have recorded the triumphs and the defeats of a people adjusting to an alien environment. They have measured what Jews were when they landed here, what they went through in the next eighty or so years, how they changed, and what they became. As such, these images frozen in time contribute to our concept of America as a nation of immigrants, of outsiders. They vividly depict the power of the American Dream to weave its spell over the hearts and minds of immigrants throughout the decades. Some found the Dream a shell of empty phrases and unfulfilled promises. Others found what they were looking for, captured it, and made it theirs. But one thing remains certain. Like an endless Saturday matinee serial, the celluloid history of the American Jew always has at least one more chapter.

Bibliography

Allen, Robert C. "Motion Picture Exhibition in Manhattan: Beyond the Nickelodeon." *Cinema Journal*, Vol. 61, No. 2 (Spring, 1979), pp. 1–15.

Alpern, David M. "Again, Anti-Semitism." *Newsweek* (February 16, 1918), p. 38.

Altman, Sig. *The Comic Image of the Jew.* Rutherford: Fairleigh Dickinson Press, 1971.

Bellow, Saul (ed.). *Great Jewish Short Stories.* New York: Dell, 1963.

Belton, John. *The Hollywood Professionals, Vol. 3.* New York: A. S. Barnes, 1974.

Bergman, Andrew. *We're In the Money.* New York: New York University Press, 1971

Berman, David. "Movies: Viewing TV as a Threat." *Syracuse New Times* (February 18, 1981), pp. 1–3.

Bohn, Thomas and Richard Stromgren. *Light and Shadows.* Sherman, Conn.: Alfred Publishing Company, 1978

Bowles, Stephen E. *Sidney Lumet.* Boston: G. K. Hall, 1979.

Brooks, Mel. *History of the World, Part One.* New York: Warner Books, 1981

Brownlow, Kevin. *The Parade's Gone By.* New York: Ballantine Books, 1968.

Campbell, Russell. "The Ideology of the Social Consciousness Movie: Three Films of Daryl F. Zanuck." *Quarterly Review of Film Studies*, Vol. 3, No. 1 (Winter, 1978), pp. 51–54.

Canham, Kingsley, *The Hollywood Professionals, Vol. 5.* New York: A. S. Barnes, 1976.

Carringer, Robert (ed.). *The Jazz Singer.* Madison: The University of Wisconsin Press, 1979.

Ceplair, Larry and Steven Englund. *The Inquisition for Hollywood.* New York: Anchor Press, 1980.

Chapman, Abraham (ed.) *Jewish-American Literature.* New York: New American Library, 1974.

Clarens, Carlos. *Movies.* New York: W. W. Norton, 1980.

Corliss, Richard. "Paul Mazursky: A Poet for People Like Us," *New Times* (April 3, 1978), pp. 53–58.

Cowie, Peter (Ed.). *Hollywood 1920–1970.* New York: A. S. Barnes, 1977.

Cripps, Thomas. "The Movie Jew as an Image of Assimilation, 1903–1927." *Journal of Popular Film,* Vol. 4 (1975), pp. 190–207.

Dawidowicz, Lucy. *The Jewish Presence.* New York: Holt, Rinehart and Winston, 1977.

Deming, Barbara. *Running Away From Myself.* New York: Grossman Publishers, 1969.

Dmytryk, Edward. *It's a Hell of a Life But Not a Bad Living.* New York: Times Books, 1978.

Eisenberg, Azriel. *The Golden Land: A Literary Portrait of American Jewry, 1654 to the Present.* New York: Thomas Yoseloff, 1864.

Erens, Patricia. "Gangster, Vampires, and J.A.P.'s: The Jew Surfaces in American Movies." *Journal of Popular Film,* Vol. 4 (1975), pp. 308–223.

————. "Mentshlekhkayt Conquers All." *Film Comment* January/February, 1976), pp. 48–51.

Fox, Stuart, *Jewish Films in the United States: A Comprehensive Survey and Descriptive Filmography.* Boston: G. K. Hall & Co., 1976.

Gans, Herbert. *The Levittowners.* New York: Pantheon Books, 1967.

Gay, Ruth. *Jews in America.* New York: Basic Books, 1965.

Glazer, Nathan. *American Judaism.* Chicago: The University of Chicago Press, 1972.

Greco, Mike. "Bakshi's American Dream." *Film Comment* (January/February, 1981), pp. 18–20.

Greenfield, Meg. "Pluralism Gone Mad." *Newsweek* (August 27, 1979), p. 76.

Gross, Barry. "No Victim She: Barbra Streisand and the Movie Jew." *The Journal of Ethnic Studies,* Vol. 3, No. 1 (Spring, 1975), pp. 28–40.

Gross, Theodore L. (ed.) *The Literature of American Jews.* New York: The Free Press, 1973.

Hardy, Phil. *Raoul Walsh.* London: Vineyard Press, 1974.

Herschel, Abraham. *God In Search of Man.* New York: Meridian Books, 1959.

Hirt-Manheimer, Aron. "From Jews to *Jaws.*" *Davka* (Fall, 1975), pp. 32–40.

Howe, Irving, *World of Our Fathers.* New York: Simon and Schuster, 1976.

Insdorf, Annette. "Take Two: *To Be or Not to Be.*" *American Film* (November, 1979), pp. 80–81.

Isaacs, Harold R. "The One and the Many." *American Educator* (Spring, 1978), pp. 4–14.

Isaksson, Folke and Leif Furhammar. *Politics and Film.* London: November Books Limited, 1971.

Jamison, A. Leland. *Tradition and Change in Jewish Experience.* Syracuse: Syracuse University Press, 1978.

Jarvie, I. C. *Movies as Social Criticism.* Metuchen: The Scarecrow Press, 1978.

Jowett, Garth. *Film, The Democratic Art.* Boston: Little, Brown and Company, 1976.

Kaplan, Mordecai. *Judaism as Civilization.* New York: The Macmillan Company, 1934.

Kertzer, Morris N. *Today's American Jew.* New York: McGraw-Hill Book Company, 1967.

Kramer, Judith R. and Seymour Leventman. *Children of the Gilded Ghetto.* New Haven: Yale University Press, 1961.

Landis, Joseph C. "Fiddling with Sholom Aleichem." *Arts and Sciences,* Vol. LXV, No. 24 (June 14, 1965), pp. 29–33.

Litvin, Baruch. *Jewish Identity.* New York: Feldheim Publishers, 1970.

Litvinoff, Barnet. *A Peculiar People.* New York: Weybright and Talley, 1969.

Madsen, Axel. *William Wyler.* New York: Thomas Y. Crowell, 1973.

Malin, Irving. *Jews and Americans.* Carbondale: Southern Illinois University Press, 1965.

Mariani, John. "Let's Not Be Beastly to the Nazis." *Film Comment* (January/February, 1979), pp. 49–53.

Mayer, John E. *Jewish-Gentile Courtships.* New York: The Free Press, 1961.

Miller, Randall (ed.). *Ethnic Images in American Films and Television.* Philadelphia: The Balche Institute, 1978.

Monaco, James. *American Film Now.* New York: Oxford University Press, 1979.

Morris, Chris. "Roger Corman: The Schlemiel as Outlaw." In Todd McCarthy and Charles Flynn (eds.), *The Kings of Bs.* New York: E. P. Dutton and Company, 1975.

Navasky, Victor. *Naming Names.* New York: The Viking Press, 1980.

Nye, Gerald P. "Our Madness Increases as Our Emergency Shrinks." *Vital Speeches,* Vo. 7 (September 5, 1941), p. 721.

Phillips, Gene D. *The Movie Makers.* Chicago: Nelson-Hall Company, 1973.

Porter, Jack Nusan. "John Henry and Mr. Goldberg: The Relationship Between Blacks andd Jews." *The Journal of Ethnic Studies,* Vol. 7, No. 3 (Fall, 1979), pp. 73–85.

Potamkin, Harry A. *The Compound Cinema.* New York: Teacher's College Press, 1977.

Pratley, Gerald. *The Cinema of John Frankenheimer.* New York: A. S. Barnes, 1969.

Quinley, Harold E. and Charles Y. Glock. *Anti-Semitism in America.* New York: The Free Press, 1979.

Rose, Peter. *The Ghetto and Beyond.* New York: Random House, 1969.

Rosen, Gladys. *Jewish Life in America: Historical Perspectives.* New York: KTAV Publishing House, Inc., 1978.

Rosenthal, Erich. "Studies in Jewish Intermarriage in the United States." *American Jewish Yearbook,* Vol. 64 (1963), pp. 3–53.

Roth, Philip. *Reading Myself and Others.* New York: Farrar, Straus, and Giroux, 1975.

Schickel, Richard. *The Disney Version.* New York: Simon and Schuster, 1966.

Schulberg, Budd. "What Makes Hollywood Run Now?" New York *Times* (April 27, 1950), pp. 52–86.

Schulz, Max F. *Radical Sophistication: Studies in Contemporary Jewish-American Novelists.* Athens: Ohio University Press, 1969.

Shaheen, Jack G. (ed.). *The Link,* Vol. 13, No. 2 (April/May 1980).

Shain, Russell. *An Analysis of Motion Pictures About War Released by the American Film Industry 1930–1970.* New York: Arno Press, 1976.

Shevelson, Melville. *How to Make a Jewish Movie.* Englewood Cliffs: Prentice-Hall, 1971.

Shindler, Colin. *Hollywood Goes to War: Film and American Society 1939–1952.* Boston: Routledge and Kegan Paul, 1979.

Sklar, Robert. *Movie-Made America.* New York: Vintage Books, 1976.

Sklare, Marshall (ed.). *The Jew in American Society.* New York: Behrman House, Inc., 1974.

Sklare, Marshall and Joseph Greenblum. *Jewish Identity on the Suburban Frontier.* New York: Basic Books, 1967.

Spoto, Donald. *Stanley Kramer Film Maker.* New York: G. P. Putnam's Sons, 1978.

Suber, Howard. "Gays, Gals, and Goys." *Variety* (January 7, 1979), p. 22.

————. "Politics and Popular Culture: Hollywood at Bay, 1933–1953." *American Jewish History,* Vol. LXVII, No. 4 (June, 1979), pp. 517–533.

Suid, Lawrence H. *Guts and Glory: Great American War Movies.* Reading: Addison-Wesley Publishing Company, 1978.

Teller, Judd L. *Strangers and Natives.* New York: Delacorte Press, 1968.

Toeplitz, Jerzy. *Hollywood and After.* Chicago: Henry Regnery Company, 1974.

Tugend, Tom. "The Hollywood Jews." *Davka Magazine* (Fall, 1975), pp. 4–8.

Tuska, Jon (ed.). *Close-up: The Contract Director.* Metuchen: The Scarecrow Press, 1976.

Vidor, King. *On Film Making.* New York: David McKay, 1972.

Walden, Daniel. "The Socially Acceptable Immigrant Minority Group: The Image of the Jew in American Popular Films." *North Dakota Quarterly,* Vol. 40 (Autumn, 1972), pp. 60–68.

Williams, Dennis A. "And Now, The 'Israeli Mafia'." *Newsweek (January 5, 1981),* p. 40.

Wilson, Robert F. *"From Novel to Film: De-Sinistering The Boys From Brazil."* Film/Literature Quarterly, Vol. 7, No. 4 (1979), pp. 322–24.

Wolfenstein, Martha and Nathan Leites. *Movies: A Psychological Study.* New York, Atheneum, 1970.

Wong, Eugene. *On Visual Media Racism: Asians in American Motion Pictures.* New York: Arno Press, 1978.

Wood, Robin. "Democracy and Spontaneity." *Film Comment,* Vol. 12, No. 1 (January/February, 1976), pp. *615.*

Yacowar, Maurice. *Loser Take All: The Comic Art of Woody Allen.* New York: Frederick Ungar Publishing Company, 1979.

Yaffe, James. *The American Jews.* New York: Random House, 1968.

Zangwill, Israel. *The Melting Pot.* In *The Collected Works of Israel Zangwell.* New York: AMS Press, 1969.

Zierold, Norman, *The Moguls.* New York: Coward-Mc-Caan, 1969.

Zimmerman, Paul D. "The Mad Mad Mel Brooks." *Newsweek* (February 17, 1975), pp. 55–58.

INDEX